The Narrative of Liberation

The Narrative of Liberation

Perspectives on Afro-Caribbean Literature,

Popular Culture, and Politics

PATRICK TAYLOR

Cornell University Press

Ithaca and London

First published 1989 by Cornell University Press.

International Standard Book Number 0-8014-2193-4
Library of Congress Catalog Card Number 88-19005

Printed in the United States of America

*Librarians: Library of Congress cataloging information
appears on the last page of the book.*

*The paper in this book is acid-free and meets the guidelines for
permanence and durability of the Committee on Production Guidelines
for Book Longevity of the Council on Library Resouces.*

For Myrta, my mother's godmother
and
To the memory of my father and mother

If ever I give you freedom, Crim, then all your future is mine,
'cause whatever you do in freedom name is what I make happen.
Seein' that way is a blindness from the start.
—Powell, in George Lamming, *Season of Adventure*

Contents

Preface

IN Haiti, revelers dig up and destroy the coffin of "Papa Doc" Duvalier, former president-for-life and chief priest, under the watchful eye of the international media. In Barbados, a man sits in front of his television set with a mongoose trap, waiting to catch the sly trickster-politician who has just returned from overseas. In Jamaica, a country bus driving through the mountains at night, packed with complaining people, suddenly explodes into music as Bob Marley's "Redemption Song" comes over the radio.

What we know today as Caribbean popular culture has its roots in the seventeenth century, when slave plantations were established in the West Indian islands to grow sugar cane. From the very beginning, popular culture was political: African-based, European-influenced religious and aesthetic symbolism unified the community in opposition to slavery and oppression. The story of survival and struggle was handed down orally generation by generation and was later picked up in literary works.

Cultural traditions provide meaningful patterns through which members of a community can understand themselves and their world. Stories, legends, myths, history itself, all are narrative patterns by means of which people locate themselves in society. Narratives order the temporal processes and scattered events encountered in human experience and generated by human activity. But narrative is not merely a mental structure that can be imposed on reality: narrative is meaningful only to the extent that it captures the vitality and dynamic of social life. Narrative is transformed, its patterns are rearranged, its significance determined anew as the processes of history erupt into human experience.

Narrative is a call to order. In its grandest form, narrative is the story of the gods, the myths about their deeds, reenacted in ritual, making possible the regeneration of the natural and social world. Similar in social significance to myth proper are the tales and legends, the poems and songs, through which communities unify themselves and consolidate their world. Thus mythical narrative includes not only myth and ritual but other narrative forms as well. In situations of oppression, in the colonial situation, for example, these narrative forms are the vehicles through which the colonized lay out the terrain of social conflict, point to practices of resistance, call for rebellion, and provide hope for an alternative future. Mythical narrative reaches its limit, however, in the tragedy of endless repetition: everything is in flux, but nothing is very different; the weak defeat the strong, the strong defeat the weak; the weak become the strong. Lacking is the vision of a qualitatively new world free of human oppression.

For an alternative outlook on the world we must look to another fundamental narrative type, to the liberating narrative that takes myth beyond its threshold to the historical reality of human actors engaged in the struggle for a just world, for social equality, for shared political power regardless of class, race, gender, ethnicity, or any other dehumanizing differentiation. From the slave period to the present, some forms of Caribbean narrative have shown how mythical patterns can be transformed with liberating significance. Thus the story of reaction, of tragic suffering, resistance, and rebellion, has been told anew from the point of view of the imperative of liberation. The narrative of liberation reveals the limits of the struggle for a hallowed ancient past, the endurance of a wretched present, or the leap toward a utopian future; it engages the processes of historical transformation with a view to the possibility of creating a society based on human mutuality.

The work of Martinican psychiatrist and political activist Frantz Fanon provides a useful point of reference for understanding both mythical and liberating narrative in the Caribbean, whether in the form of *vaudou* ritual, the trickster tale, *négritude* poetry, the novel, theatre, or any other symbolic form. Fanon provides an analysis of the colonial situation and the reactions of the colonized to their oppression. Influenced by European social and political theory, yet addressing the specificity of the colonial situation, Fanon's works deal with the lived reality of racial oppression and colonial exploitation and provide the basis for the analysis of Caribbean narrative in relation to the struggle for liberation.

In this book, I focus on the experience of the Afro-Caribbean community, particularly where dominated by French, British, and more recently American colonialism. The Spanish-speaking Caribbean has had a long history of revolution and reaction culminating in the world-shaking Cuban Revolution. I do not deal with this area directly but emphasize instead the less well known story of liberation in the rest of the Caribbean, a story that has itself influenced and been influenced by the Spanish-speaking Caribbean. There exist parallel experiences and points of intersection in the experiences of Amerindian, East Indian, and other colonized communities in the Caribbean, but they are not my immediate focus.

This book is a response to the experience that Barbadian novelist Austin Clarke has called "Growing up Stupid under the Union Jack." I grew up in the Caribbean, ignorant of the Caribbean. I began to learn about the Caribbean first from artists, then from historians and political theorists. But in order to learn, I had to be distant from the source. The European tradition of critical social and political thought, which I studied at York University in Toronto, provided that distance.

I am deeply indebted to all who have made this work possible. I especially thank those teachers and colleagues who most influenced me: Frank Birbalsingh, Frederick Case, Russel Chace, Juan Maiguashca, Brayton Polka, Paul Ricoeur, Ato Sekyi-Otu, and David Trotman. Mildred Bakan, Melvyn Hill, Stephen Levine, and Bernard Zelechow provided encouragement in the early stages of my research. Many other people discussed ideas, recommended readings, or simply inspired me. My students from Canada and the Caribbean shared their experiences with me and made me constantly clarify my assumptions.

I am grateful to the Ontario Government for support in the form of a Queen Elizabeth II Scholarship and an Ontario Graduate Scholarship, and to the Canadian Government for support in the form of two Social Sciences and Humanities Research Council Fellowships that included funding for a research trip to France and Algeria.

Without the support and assistance of friends and family, I would not have completed this book. Rob Lawrence braved the crosstown rush-hour traffic to return early drafts that he had proofread. Lynne Davis and Cameron Brown, Arun and Alok Mukherjee, Joan O'Laney and Reg McQuaid, and others provided friendship and support. The staff of two excellent daycare centers, Regal Road and Hawthorne, gave me the time to concentrate on my work in the knowledge that my children were in good hands.

To my wife, Beverley Davis, I owe my deep appreciation for her constant support, encouragement, and care from the very beginning. Beverley read drafts and criticized them, typed manuscripts, proofread printouts, and more, despite her own vigorous schedule. When my convictions began to wane, she was always someone to whom I could turn. To my children, Shira and David, I am particularly grateful for their ever-present reminder that not everything can be contained within the world of the text.

PATRICK TAYLOR

North York, Ontario

Abbreviations Used for Titles
by Frantz Fanon

AR   *Toward the African Revolution: Political Essays.* Trans. Haakon Chevalier. New York: Grove Press, 1969. Translation of *RA*.

BS   *Black Skin, White Masks.* Trans. Charles Lam Markmann. New York: Grove Press, 1967. Translation of *PN*.

DC   *A Dying Colonialism.* Trans. Haakon Chevalier. New York: Grove Press, 1967. Translation of *SR*.

DT   *Les Damnés de la terre.* Paris: François Maspero, 1961.

PN   *Peau noire, masques blancs.* Paris: Points–Editions du Seuil, 1971.

RA   *Pour la révolution africaine: Ecrits politiques.* Paris: François Maspero, 1964.

SR   *Sociologie d'une révolution.* Paris: François Maspero, 1978.

WE   *The Wretched of the Earth.* Trans. Constance Farrington. New York: Grove Press, 1968. Translation of *DT*.

Note: Where indicated, I have amended the English translations. The French words *colon, colonisé,* and *colonial* have been translated "colonizer," "colonized," and "colonial," respectively.

The Narrative of Liberation

Prologue

There is a point at which methods devour themselves.
FRANTZ FANON, *Black Skin, White Masks*

IN one Caribbean trickster tale, Anancy, the spider-hero, is defeated by another cunning trickster, Puss. To provide food for his family, Anancy lures his two comrades, Peafowl and Ratta, into a trap. Puss catches Anancy in the same trap and walks off with all three creatures in his bag.[1] In one short tale we are vividly presented with the harshness and brutality of the Caribbean world since the sixteenth century. Anancy, the trickster-slave, struggles to survive in the wretched system created by his master. Anancy fights for his family's survival, but he turns against his friends. Anancy outwits Peafowl and Ratta, but Puss, the trickster-master, defeats Anancy. In one vision are combined the will of the weak to survive, the will of the strong to maintain their own power, and the irrationality of human existence under such conditions.

This stark vision of reality is in sharp contrast to an alternative Caribbean vision of human freedom and dignity. In Derek Walcott's *Pantomime*, the trickster's deceit and cunning are turned inside out.[2] The master and slave (servant), the white expatriate guesthouse owner and his black ex-calypsonian factotum, rehearse a Crusoe-Friday pantomime. The white man is Crusoe; the black man, too, is Crusoe. They play each other's roles, confront the slave's subjection to the

---

1. "Wheeler," *Jamaican Song and Story: Annancy Stories, Digging Sings, Ring Tunes, and Dancing Tunes,* ed. Walter Jekyll (London, 1907; rpt. New York: Dover, 1966), pp. 152–56.

2. Derek Walcott, *Pantomime,* in *Remembrance and Pantomime: Two Plays* (New York: Farrar, Straus & Giroux, 1980).

master, and acknowledge the master's dependence on the slave. The story is about bad faith, play acting, and, ultimately, recognition: the mutual recognition of two actors who realize that they have been living a humanly unacceptable, unreal drama.

Both the Anancy tale and Walcott's play are creole in form: they are cultural expressions of the particular situation created by European enslavement of Africans. Various African and European patterns and meanings were syncretized in response to a new sociopolitical situation. Caribbean creole culture is specific to Caribbean plantation society, yet it parallels in many respects creole forms in other areas of the Americas as well as the culture of the colonized in the Third World in general.

Although they are both forms of Caribbean creole culture, the two narratives can be distinguished from each other and taken as basic narrative paradigms. The Anancy tale is an attempt to order the contradictions of a Manichaean social situation; Walcott's play is an attempt to transform that situation. Both are narratives in the sense that they tell a story about humanly significant, temporal events. The trickster tale structures and unifies irrational, violent human activity; it tries to make sense of the world by portraying it as it appears to be organized. A view of the world is invented that must be called mythical because it depicts human beings as minor actors in a world that remains essentially the same in spite of its apparent flux. The clever slave may overthrow an oppressive master; the cunning master may defeat a rebellious slave. The slave may elevate him or herself or be elevated to the level of master; but then the former slave finds him or herself in conflict with other slaves. There is no narrative imperative demanding the fundamental transformation of the master-slave relation itself.

The Anancy tale is an example of mythical narrative. The core of mythical narrative is the basic plot or generic unity of the work, its *mythos*, or mythical center. Such core myths draw on the archetypal patterns of a cultural tradition in order to render meaningful new, contradictory, lived experiences. Myth provides a cultural order to reality and informs human activity. At the same time, this cultural order is transformed as human activity opens up new realms of experience that its mythical structure must encompass.

In the colonial and neocolonial situations, mythical narrative enhances the self-image both of the community and of the individual and unifies the colonized in opposition to the colonizer. However,

manity. The myth of Crusoe rom the very beginning.
Crusoe. Men and women beco human dignity and free-
mythical, inhuman situations. particular history, trans-
Mythical and liberating na surrender of the vaudou
cultural expressions in the Car ransformation, the social
system, vaudou is a total myth on against oppression be-
reality according to certain prir of liberation. The narra-
tale is one way of ordering (an mythical closure.
oppression and conflict, vaudo informs the revolution-
Samedi make sense of revoluti and terror rule of coloni-
The Haitian Revolution was i an beings to a reactive,
man at a vaudou ceremony. the other his or her hu-
restraining the community un violence with violence,
Some biblically oriented religi recreate traditional cul-
rooted in the quest for liberatic er, and culture is trans-
preached the equality of races reaction to colonialism.
slave uprising in Jamaica, whil and destroy the colonial
damental dignity and humanit onized. A revolutionary
Caribbean.⁵ f its guises: "it is neces-
There is a very thin line bet n, "to make explicit, to
tive structures and the restora d that exists in oneself."
The black quest for liberation r the necessity to totalize
the negritude theme: Africa settle everything, to be
redeemed; the black race is a s; *DT,* p. 224).
history is a story of heroic str ry in Western thought
mantic longing for a one-dim uated, despite its own
encounter with the tragedy of d, and Nietzsche, from
aspect of Anancy's character, t has been asked: if there
reaction to white oppression, y how is it possible to
ideology. it and communicate its
The work of Aimé Césaire e against its very pos-
the realm of the universal. r in which the drama of
ion of liberating narra-
this drama is radically

4. Michel S. Laguerre, "Voodoo as leap through which a
the Spirit, 3, no. 1 (1974), 25–26; R and to humanity is
Haiti," in *The African Diaspora: Interp*
Rotberg (Cambridge: Harvard Unive
5. Mary Turner deals insightfully political processes in-
Missionaries: The Disintegration of Jama is works are narratives
sity of Chicago Press, 1982). A ver
Joseph Owens, *Dread: The Rastafaria* consciousness of their

creative involvement in history. As symbolic acts and communicative statements, Fanon's texts function in a way similar to more obviously cultural narratives. They order into a meaningful whole the contradictory experiences of the Caribbean and of the Third World in general. As in Walcott's plays, myths are turned inside out as the story of human freedom and liberation is told. A pervasive, creative, and critical intertextuality binds Fanon's work to Afro-Caribbean narrative forms and makes his work essential to the study of Caribbean culture.

Chapter 1

Frantz Fanon and
the Narrative of Liberation

The History of the world is none other than the progress
of the consciousness of Freedom.
G. W. F. HEGEL, *The Philosophy of History*

It is a question of the Third World starting a new history
of Man, a history which will have regard to the
sometimes prodigious theses which Europe has put
forward, but which will also not forget Europe's crimes.
FRANTZ FANON, *The Wretched of the Earth*

FANON's political writings are part of a critical tradition of social thought. They order the events of lived experience into a dynamic whole and project possibilities for the transformation of this whole in the name of a common humanity. They relate a story of peoples, formerly trapped under colonialism, remaking themselves and their world in a process of decolonization. Addressing the colonial situation in general and born out of the Caribbean situation in particular, they form a basis for the critical understanding of the cultural structures that arose out of the colonial Caribbean.

Chester Fontenot has written that Fanon's works are based on a liberating myth of revolution. Fontenot misunderstands the critical basis of Fanon's analysis of the colonial situation and its cultural forms. However, his interpretation provides a useful starting point for an analysis of the narrative structure of Fanon's work and its relevance to the interpretation of Caribbean culture. Essentially, Fontenot argues that a politico-narrative fiction underlies Fanon's work. Fontenot distinguishes between an "open culture," or traditional society that has been allowed to develop organically, and a "closed culture," which has been forcefully altered.[1] Precolonial society was open until Prospero entered, subdued Caliban, treated him as racially inferior, and exploited him. According to Fontenot, Fanon confronts the colonial situation with a visionary plot that traces the overthrow of Caliban and his Manichaean order and culminates with the restoration of an indigenous, liberated culture.

Fontenot states that the purpose of Fanon's visionary apprehension of reality is to compel the reader to change his or her own perspective on the world and then the world itself. Fanon "creates a system, a myth, which he feels has the power to move the reader . . . into a mode which will allow the reader to participate in the insurrectionary activity described in *The Wretched of the Earth*."[2] Through mastery and manipulation of the European's language, Fanon demystifies colonialism and communicates the necessity of overthrowing the colonizer. The peasants of the Third World must respond to the power of Fanon's word, violently overthrow colonialism, and reestablish an open organic community. Thus, for Fontenot, a Manichaean fiction is reasserted, even if reversed: the last shall be first and the first last. Caliban will use Prospero's language in order to destroy his political hold; then he can withdraw into his own African community.

This normative, political perspective is fictional, argues Fontenot, not because Fanon is distorting the truth, but because he is creating a myth: he is an artist rather than a political scientist. He wants to involve us in a fictional revolution so that we will understand the path toward real revolution. Through myth, Fontenot states, the poet reveals dormant mores in a culture to the consciousness of the members of that culture so that these mores can be recognized and enacted.[3] What distinguishes the poet from the propagandist is the use of an "open" mythical system (one that is creatively open to a variety of interpretations) to demystify the language of oppression and plot the process of revolutionary recovery. The politico–normative structure is grounded in a framework of passionate symbolism and paradox that ensures that the meaning of the myth remains open to finding its completion in the reader's practical activity.

1. Chester J. Fontenot, *Frantz Fanon: Language as the God Gone Astray in the Flesh*, University of Nebraska Studies, n.s. no. 60 (Lincoln: University of Nebraska Press, 1979), p. 9.
2. Fontenot, p. 4.
3. Fontenot, pp. 6–7.

Though Fontenot is not the first to argue that there is a mythical quality to Fanon's works, Fanon's critics have usually understood the term "myth" in a negative sense, as something to be demystified, rather than in a positive, generative sense. To Aristide Zolberg, Fanon is another messianic utopian of the New Left and, moreover, a follower of Georges Sorel. Like Sorel's proletariat, Zolberg argues, Fanon believes the black masses need a rallying myth that will provoke the revolutionary moment. Zolberg's Fanon is a surrealist poet or, rather, a magician pathetically invoking the new world: "the damned are the rat pack, the *lumpenproletariat*, the prostitutes and pimps, the brutal peasants, who invade the city through the sewers. The city goes up in flames. The damned are purified in its fire; they are beautiful and holy." Rather than enlighten us about Fanon's work, this parody exposes Zolberg's own prejudice against the people of the Third World. Lewis Coser's language is no less revealing: Fanon ranks "among the very few great mythopoeists of our age," but his is an "evil" and "destructive" myth written in a "paranoid" and "reactive" style. In a related response, Edmund Burke has characterized *The Wretched of the Earth* as an "enormous and terrifying prose poem," a "utopian" form of "folk Marxism" aimed at conversion, just like a "sermon in a Southern Baptist Church." Marie Perinbam takes these arguments to another plane when she makes Fanon into a "war-time propagandist" who appealed to the myth of a holy war because only the irrational could arouse tribal chiefs and peasants. "[H]oly violence," Perinbam states, is the "sacred whore who kidnapped Fanon's mind and held it ransom unto death."[4]

Fontenot's interpretation of Fanon is important because, more than the other critics, he recognizes the symbolic power and creative role of narrative in society. With a mere twist in point of view, one can construe as revolutionary some of the characteristics of Fanon's works identified by the other critics. Fontenot would essentially agree to, and praise, what Burke thought was a deep criticism of Fanon: "It

4. Aristide Zolberg, "Frantz Fanon," in *The New Left: Six Critical Essays*, ed. Maurice Cranston (London: Bodley Head, 1970), p. 128; Lewis Coser, *Continuities in the Study of Social Conflict* (New York: Free Press; London: Collier-Macmillan, 1967), pp. 211, 213, 221–22; Edmund Burke, "Frantz Fanon's *The Wretched of the Earth*," *Daedalus*, 105 (Winter 1976), 129–31; Marie Perinbam, "Fanon and the Revolutionary Peasantry: The Algerian Case," *Journal of Modern African Studies*, 11, no. 3 (1973), 440–42, and *Holy Violence: The Revolutionary Thought of Frantz Fanon* (Washington, D.C.: Three Continents Press, 1982), pp. 14, 97.

is characteristic of Fanon's thought that in the end he should opt for culture rather than material conditions as the crucial factor in bringing about the revolution."[5]

The problem is that Fontenot is unable to make his way out of mythical narrative. With the mythicization of the political, the normative argument rebounds with the vengeance of the gods. Caliban, thinking that he could free himself by using Prospero's language to master him, finds himself paradoxically trapped by it. The new nation degenerates under the dictatorial rule of the national bourgeoisie in the context of neocolonialism. Fontenot concludes that, in Fanon's vision, the nation is like the Phoenix and "must be shaped by the eternal cycle of death and rebirth."[6] The implication of Fontenot's argument is that Fanon's myth of liberation will constantly renew itself as it appropriates the content of its social impossibility. Like Northrop Frye's archetypal identity, it remains ever renewed, but never fulfilled.[7]

If we take seriously Fanon's notions of consciousness and freedom, then we cannot treat them merely as the unattainable ideals of a Sisyphean revolutionary hero. National liberation from colonialism and neocolonialism cannot be identified with a mythical precolonial African golden age. Furthermore, Fanon explicitly distinguishes the humanistic national consciousness brought about by the revolutionary movement from the nationalism that is the degenerate consciousness of a dependent bourgeoisie.[8] The purpose of national consciousness is to prevent precisely this type of degeneration: it is possible to break out of the eternal cycle of damnation. Similarly, freedom for Fanon is not an ideal ever on the horizon: "No attempt must be made to encase [*fixer*] man, for it is his destiny to be set free [*lâché*]" (*BS*, p. 230; *PN*, p. 187). The inevitable transformation of a Manichaean dualism of Prospero and Caliban into a paradoxical reversal of Caliban become Prospero (the national bourgeoisie) is Fontenot's own mythical misinterpretation of Fanon.

5. Burke, p. 134. See Rex Nettleford, *Cultural Action and Social Change: The Case of Jamaica: An Essay in Caribbean Cultural Identity* (Ottawa: International Development Research Centre, 1979; Kingston: Institute of Jamaica, 1978), pp. 64–65.

6. Fontenot, p. 44.

7. Northrop Frye, *Fables of Identity: Studies in Poetic Mythology* (New York: Harvest–Harcourt Brace Jovanovich, 1963), p. 15.

8. *WE*, p. 204; *DT*, p. 138. See Ato Sekyi-Otu, "Form and Metaphor in Fanon's Critique of Racial and Colonial Domination," in *Domination*, ed. Alkis Kontos (Toronto: University of Toronto Press, 1975), p. 157.

Consciousness comes with the critique of mythology. Only by going beyond the mythologies of colonialism and neocolonialism can we adequately understand Fanon's contribution. Fanon's texts are totalizations that bring order to the circumstances and events of colonialism so as to present a historical process in which human actors can find themselves. At the same time, they provide tools for critically analyzing cultural forms and narrative structures that render the colonial situation meaningful. Traditional narrative patterns remain essential aspects of a culture in which a discourse of freedom is formulated. However, these patterns must be brought into relation with a historical narrative of liberation based on the assumption of universal human freedom and dignity.

Fontenot's understanding of narrative rests on the assumption that narrative is a form of mythical recreation. He shares this understanding with the hermeneutical tradition of interpretation. According to Paul Ricoeur, narrative combines the episodic, or chronological, dimension of experience with the configurational, or nonchronological, dimension. The plot of a narrative brings these two dimensions together by construing "significant wholes out of scattered events."[9] This symbolic act is characterized by the *mimesis* of human action in *mythos*. Aristotle does not mean by mimesis the reduplication of an object in an image, argues Ricoeur. Mimesis is a fictional or creative imitation of human reality. It takes human action as its referent, but simultaneously renders action its significance. As such, the mimesis of action is indissolubly bound to the configurational activity of the mythos of the textual work. Mythos underscores that the work is a fable or fantasy that makes social activity intelligible in terms of a traditional plot. Narrative brings discrete events into a configuration and is itself transformed and renewed as it orders these events.[10]

Victor Turner analyzes narrative in religious ritual using a notion of narrative that is close to Ricoeur's but that takes as its starting point social crisis rather than lived events. Narrative, Turner argues, attempts "to rearticulate opposing values and goals in a meaningful structure, the plot of which makes cultural sense."[11] Turner calls

---

9. Paul Ricoeur, "Narrative Time," in *On Narrative,* ed. W. J. T. Mitchell (Chicago: University of Chicago Press, 1981), p. 174.

10. Paul Ricoeur, "The Narrative Function," *Semeia,* 13: *The Poetics of Faith* (Society of Biblical Literature, 1981), pp. 183–84, 191–92.

11. Victor Turner, "Social Dramas and Stories about Them," in Mitchell, *On Narrative,* p. 164.

social crisis and its resolution "social drama." When a breach of a social norm occurs in a particular community, a crisis arises and the underlying contradictions in the group emerge. The community attempts to reintegrate itself through redressive mechanisms. Narrative is a vehicle for the reconciliation of a crisis because it orders the events of the social drama in terms of a mutually acceptable, meaningful whole. Narrative brings about social reflexivity and mutual recognition to the extent that particular values and ends are converted into a system of shared meaning. Turner thus defines narrative as "knowledge . . . emerging from action, that is, experiential knowledge."[12] The experience of a social drama enters discourse as a narrative order. This order becomes a figure of how a crisis is generated and resolved.

In contrast to the notion of narrative as the archetypal and generative unity of action over time is the structuralist notion of narrative as the distortion of the deep structure of meaning. Claude Lévi-Strauss argues that the "purpose of myth is to provide a logical model capable of overcoming a contradiction." For Lévi-Strauss, myth and other narrative forms such as the folktale are structured in terms of the resolution of a binary opposition.[13] A. J. Greimas and F. Rastier take Lévi-Strauss's insight and systematically apply it to narrative in general. The deep structure of any narrative, they argue, consists of a logical model, the semiotic rectangle. The essential binary opposition, the relation between two contradictory terms, can be meaningfully resolved when it is replaced by an equivalent or implied relation consisting of the opposition of two contraries.[14] (For example, the contradictory terms "white" and "nonwhite" can be replaced by the implied contraries "black" and "white" to allow for a meaningful resolution in terms of white and black.)

As Fredric Jameson has argued, Lévi-Strauss ties the logical notion of binary opposition to the concept of social contradiction.[15] Lévi-

12. Victor Turner, p. 163.

13. Claude Lévi-Strauss, *Structural Anthropology*, [1], trans. Claire Jacobson and Brooke Grundfest Schoepf (New York: Basic Books, 1963), p. 229; see also *Structural Anthropology*, 2, trans. Monique Layton (New York: Basic Books, 1976), pp. 129–30.

14. A. J. Greimas and F. Rastier, "The Interaction of Semiotic Constraints," *Yale French Studies*, no. 41 (1968), especially pp. 86–91.

15. Fredric Jameson, *The Political Unconscious: Narrative as a Socially Symbolic Act* (Ithaca: Cornell University Press, 1981), pp. 77–80; *Marxism and Form: Twentieth-Century Dialectical Theories of Literature* (Princeton: Princeton University Press, 1971), pp. 383–84; *The Prison House of Language: A Critical Account of Structuralism and Russian Formalism* (Princeton: Princeton University Press, 1972), pp. 161–62.

Strauss argues, for example, that the Caduveo Indians of Brazil were unable to resolve the real contradictions of their caste system. They therefore sought to overcome them in the imaginary realm. "The mysterious charm and (as it seems at first) the gratuitous complication of Caduveo art may well be a phantasm," says Lévi-Strauss, "created by a society whose object was to give symbolical form to the institutions which it might have had in reality, had interest and superstition not stood in the way."[16] Jameson develops this insight into a theory of ideology using Greimas's semiotic rectangle. Underlying a given text is a "political unconscious" or ideological fantasy the purpose of which is to resolve a particular social contradiction. The relation of contraries becomes for Jameson a real contradiction, while the resolution (or complex term) is the political fantasy resolving it.

Using what is essentially a Marxist metanarrative to unveil the hidden meaning or political unconscious of a particular literary text, Jameson distinguishes between three levels of interpretation. The first level is the political. The interpreter identifies the social contradiction and particular political fantasy or ideology in the text that resolves it. In Balzac's *La Vieille Fille*, for example, the Comte de Troisville is the ideal resolution of the conflict between a powerless ancien régime and a rising bourgeoisie. The second level is the social. The interpreter grasps the text as a strategic act in the ideological struggle between classes. The individual text is bound into a system of class discourse consisting of ideologemes. The ideologeme is the collective fantasy of a particular class the purpose of which is to resolve the social contradiction in which that class finds itself. The nineteenth-century resentment of the masses that is expressed in certain bourgeois novels is an example of the ideologeme. Resentment resolves class struggle in terms of a group fantasy upholding the justice of social distinction. The third level is the economic. Jameson argues that the text must be placed in terms of the sequence of modes of production. The form of the text, that is, the mode of cultural production, has an ideological significance. It resolves the contradiction between overlapping modes of production. The romance form, for example, may be understood as a utopian resolution of the contradiction between feudal and industrial capitalist modes of production.[17]

16. Claude Lévi-Strauss, *Tristes Tropiques*, trans. John Russell (New York: Atheneum, 1971), pp. 179–80. See also Lévi-Strauss, *Structural Anthropology*, [1], pp. 252–64.

17. Jameson, *The Political Unconscious*, pp. 75–76.

Both Turner's generative notion of narrative and the structuralist's critical notion rest on the assumption that narrative is an imaginary resolution of a real contradiction. In Turner's case, however, myth is based on a cultural tradition and is the precondition for action. Structuralist Marxism, in contrast, concentrates on the critique of illusion (ideology) in tradition. Jameson himself avoids the structuralist reduction by reintroducing history to the interpretative process. He is critical of the homological interpretations typical of some forms of Marxism that reduce a given text to an a priori metatext.[18]

Homological interpretation begins with contingent cultural events or illusions and arrives at an already assumed historical plot. Hermeneutical interpretation, in contrast, begins with the identity of myth but assumes that myth is always in a process of change and renewal as real crises arise and are resolved. Both approaches must be called mythical because they order experience in terms of enduring codes, even though for hermeneutics the code is open, while for homological interpretation it is closed. If the narrative code is the ultimate reference, then the agent is reduced to being a bearer of the code and the uniqueness of the historical actor and totalizer of social experience is lost. Mythical narrative fails to introduce decisively a notion of humanity as freedom in the world, bound to act in accordance with this freedom.

Jameson avoids homological reduction by combining the hermeneutic approach with the Marxist critique of illusion. The three levels of Marxist interpretation (ideology, ideologeme, ideology of form) are not methodological tools for reducing fantasy to its "real" determinants. Following Hans-Georg Gadamer, Jameson calls the three levels of interpretation three "horizons." For Gadamer, a horizon is a form of understanding that is bound to a particular situation and tradition, but that is nevertheless constantly open and changing.[19] Jameson uses the term "horizon" to capture the meaning of the text as a symbolic act that expresses a particular social situation. By invoking the idea of a horizon, rather than of a determinate situation, Jameson emphasizes that history consists of possibilities. Thus the symbolic act takes place in the three historical horizons, but it is only in symbolic activity that the horizons become meaningful. The text is

18. Jameson, *The Political Unconscious*, pp. 43–44.
19. Hans-Georg Gadamer, *Truth and Method*, trans. Garrett Barden and John Cumming (New York: Continuum-Seabury, 1975), pp. 269–74.

understood as an opening into history rather than as a reflection of history. The critic approaching the text does so from the point of view of an open-ended totalization of history in view of which the three horizons are constituted; the text, however, retains its specificity in relation to this subtext.

The deep implication of Jameson's work is that any text must be understood from the point of view of a narrative of liberation. One avoids the mythical rewriting of the text by bringing it into relation with history as the story of human liberation. Jameson does not use the term "liberating narrative." He does, however, make a distinction between romantic and historical writing. Romance is an ideal form of mythical narrative. It is a closed structure that conforms to Greimas's semiotic rectangle. From the point of view of history, it is ideologically bound and can be interpreted using the three historical horizons. The historical text—and such a text has nothing to do with the chronicling of events—reveals its own historical horizons and the process of history through which ideology is dissolved. Jameson argues that the romance structure in Conrad's *Lord Jim* dissolves in Jim's experience of anguish. Jim is the modern person transcending space and time and yet committed to ordering the discontinuity of events and absurdity of nature. Jim's discovery of Sartrean freedom has a demoralizing effect on the ideological myths that have allowed "the heroic bureaucracy of imperial capitalism" to assert its unity and legitimacy. Likewise, argues Jameson, Conrad's *Nostromo* reveals history as an absence that cannot be narrated in the closed ideological form of the romance. Out of the nonnarratable collective process in which individual acts are alienated and appropriated, history arrives: "So this great historical novel finally achieves its end by unraveling its own means of expression, 'rendering' History by its thoroughgoing demonstration of the impossibility of narrating this unthinkable dimension of collective reality, systematically undermining the individual categories of storytelling in order to project, beyond the stories it must continue to tell, the concept of a process beyond storytelling."[20]

Precisely because it is ahistorical, hermeneutical or myth criticism can be directly applied to Caribbean narrative. The identity of underlying mythical structures can be traced over time in the folktales, rituals, and literature of the area in a way that they might be traced in any other society. Historical criticism, however, cannot be satisfied

20. Jameson, *The Political Unconscious*, pp. 265, 279.

with the lack both of social grounding and ideological demystification found in such criticism. It is, therefore, tempting to take a totalizing and critical interpretative code such as Jameson's and directly apply it to the Caribbean. The problem is that the historical horizons of a Eurocentric metacode cannot be applied to a culture with a very different history. The problems of domination, enslavement, and dehumanization are not the same as those of bourgeois exploitation. At the same time, an interpretative approach grounded in historical, liberating narrative paradoxically engages one with its universal call for the realization of human dignity. This is where the "openness" of Jameson's narrative, the indeterminateness of its horizons, and the infinity of its totalizing claims entertain the possibility of dialogue with a specifically Third World or Caribbean interpretative metacode such as Frantz Fanon's. The historical horizons must be different, but at a deep level the structure of liberating (historical) narrative is the same.

To understand the historical intelligibility of Third World narrative, the analysis of class relations must be subordinated to the analysis of racial domination in a Manichaean colonial world. Ato Sekyi-Otu argues that Fanon's significance lies in his inversion of the Marxian paradigm in the colonial situation. Fanon focuses on the contingent event of racial dehumanization and violence. One group of nations conquered another and established a form of domination based on race. Endogenous political systems, class relations, and modes of production were subordinated to a specifically colonial mode of domination. Sekyi-Otu makes the following observation: "What Marxian ontology and theory of capitalist society identify as the determinative foundations of social being and social conduct, namely productive activity and, by derivation, class relations of production, emerge in Fanon's theory as contingent consequences of the political coercion of colonized man based upon a race structure of power."[21] Class structure and mode of production are derivatives of the primary political contradiction: the colonizer-colonized relation.

In the Caribbean situation, colonial society takes the form of plantation society. Europeans conquered the Caribbean islands in their search for precious metals. Settler colonies were established only to be transformed into plantation colonies when it was discovered that a

21. Ato Sekyi-Otu, "Frantz Fanon's Critique of the Colonial Experience" (Ph.D. diss., University of Toronto, 1977), p. 212.

substantial profit could be made through the centralized, organized production for export of staples such as sugar. This profit could be assured only through the supply of cheap labor. Africa provided a source for such labor. Black people were deprived of their human rights, brought to the plantation as slaves, and forced to work. The slaves were emancipated in the nineteenth century. The majority of blacks, however, continued to be oppressed. Indentured workers, mainly East Indian but some also Chinese, African, or European, were imported in some areas and forced to work in slavelike conditions. By importing these workers, the master was able to keep wages low; by exploiting racial disunity, he could enhance his own control. With the exception of Haiti, the colonies did not formally attain independence or departmental status until the twentieth century. Then a neocolonial mode of dependent production took the place of colonialism. The economy was controlled by the former European colonizer or, increasingly in the twentieth century, by North Americans. A mulatto or black bourgeoisie assumed political power but remained dependent on the metropolitan bourgeoisie and ensured the continued exploitation of the people in the new nations.[22]

Jameson's theory of interpretation cannot be directly applied to the Third World text because the historical horizons through which the Third World text is approached must be based on the specificity of the Third World situation. It is a political relation of domination rather than a social relation of production that is of primary importance. Accordingly, Jameson's political horizon must be taken as a resolution of the political contradiction between colonizer and colonized. A particular text can be understood in terms of its unique way of resolving this contradiction. Jameson's second horizon, that of class struggle, must be transformed in terms of the caste struggle between colonizer and colonized, and the derivative class formations under colonialism and neocolonialism. At this level, the text is understood in terms of its relation to the myths of the colonizer and of the colonized. Thus the white myth and the black myth play the role of ideologemes in Fanon's work. Manichaeism, as Abdul JanMohamed argues, is central to understanding the Third World text.[23] The con-

22. For a general history of the Caribbean, see Franklin W. Knight, *The Caribbean: The Genesis of a Fragmented Nationalism* (New York: Oxford University Press, 1978).
23. Abdul R. JanMohamed, *Manichean Aesthetics: The Politics of Literature in Colonial Africa* (Amherst: University of Massachusetts Press, 1983), pp. 3–4, 277, and "The Economy of Manichean Allegory: The Function of Racial Difference in Colonialist

tradiction between colonizer and colonized is resolved in terms of romantic unities. These myths have the ideological function of legitimating colonialism on the one hand and resisting it on the other. Jameson's final horizon, that of overlapping modes of production, may be retained provided that it is divorced from any notion of economic determinism and immanent development. The romance form can again be seen as a resolution of conflicting modes of production, particularly precolonial and colonial. However, Jameson's overemphasis on romance should not mislead us into ignoring other modes of cultural production. In the colonial and neocolonial periods, tragedy becomes particularly important as romance comes into conflict with lived reality. Tragedy becomes a form of unhappy and even resisting *acceptance* of the myths of colonialism and neocolonialism. Thus, it too has the ideological function of legitimating the system of oppression.

Fanon, like Jameson, identifies the form of narrative that goes beyond myth to render itself historical. (This is what I have called liberating narrative.) For Jameson, Conrad's works ultimately unravel their romantic core and bring the reader back to the indeterminacy that is history. JanMohamed argues that some texts reflect on the colonial mentality in such a way as to free themselves from the Manichaean allegory.[24] Fanon uses examples comparable to Jameson's to capture the way a particular cultural work can bring one into the realm of history as possibility. The poetry of the Guinean Keita Fodeba, he writes, marks the historic field in an invitation to thought, demystification, and battle. Cultural works such as Fodeba's "African Dawn" are symbolic acts through which the artist joins his or her people concretely at a national level in the depths of their indeterminacy; he or she joins them "in that fluctuating movement which they are just giving a shape to, and which, as soon as it has started, will be the signal for everything to be called in question" (*WE*, p. 227; *DT*, p. 157).

Whether we use Jameson's conception of social contradiction or

Literature," in *"Race," Writing, and Difference,* ed. Henry Louis Gates, Jr. (Chicago: University of Chicago Press, 1986), pp. 82–83. Much of the writing on literature, race, and colonialism, including some of the articles in Gates's volume, is itself ideologically bound and falls victim to what Houston A. Baker calls "the whitemale confessional" counterbalanced only by the "confessional *manqué*" of the former colonial subject ("Caliban's Triple Play," in Gates, pp. 388–89).

24. JanMohamed, "The Economy of Manichean Allegory," pp. 84–85.

Fanon's political contradiction, the conception of liberating narrative remains essentially the same. For Jameson, the ultimate interpretative task is the understanding of symbolic works in relation to a demystifying, open-ended narrative of liberation that is grounded in the imperative of human freedom. Fanon's narrative likewise seeks to render the myths of colonialism intelligible so that they can be transcended in free creative activity. For both writers the task of narrative is neither to erect an ideal that can only be longed for nor to entrap human beings in an impossible situation. The task is to tell the story of human freedom totalizing its situation in such a way that freedom is communicated and the oppressive situation transformed. It is the overthrow of the myths of finitude by the power of the infinite that makes such transformation possible.

The approaches of Jameson and Fanon are firmly rooted in a European tradition of liberating narrative. Sartre is their most immediate link to this tradition, but the tradition goes back especially to Kierkegaard, Marx, and Hegel. History, according to the tradition, is an incomplete narrative construction or totalization through which actors endeavor to make sense of their changing reality. How is it possible, the tradition asks in its different moments, to represent the quest for freedom in history? It is possible to do so only on the basis of an open-ended narrative that offers a critique of myths imposing finite closure on human possibility.

According to Jameson, Sartre makes the very basic distinction between the *récit* and the "genuine novel." The récit is told by an omniscient, wise narrator who relates the adventure of a brief disorder, its repeal, and the subsequent triumph of order. The teller (or author) and listeners (or readers) are, in Sartre's words, "absorbed by the task of *preserving* their culture, their customs, and of exchanging ritual *recognition* with each other according to the forms."[25] In contrast, Sartre's vision of the novel in its genuine form is, in Jameson's words, a vision of men and women "for whom the future, for whom destiny, has not yet taken shape, who grope and invent their own destinies, living blindly within the entanglement of one another's

25. Jameson's rendering of "sont occupés à *conserver* leur culture et leurs manières et à se *reconnaître* par les rites de la politesse" ("Three Methods in Sartre's Literary Criticism," in *Modern French Criticism: From Proust and Valéry to Structuralism,* ed. John K. Simon [Chicago: University of Chicago Press, 1972], p. 201). See Jean-Paul Sartre, *Situations,* 2 (Paris: Gallimard, 1948), pp. 180–81, and *What Is Literature,* trans. Bernard Frechtman (New York: Harper & Row, 1965), pp. 134–35.

unforeseeable actions and under the menace of history's unforeseeable development."[26]

What is at issue is the distinction between the principle of destiny and the principle of freedom, not the difference between these particular genres. The hero of the novel is the center of indeterminacy; like the Christian who is free to sin, the hero is free to err. François Mauriac, Sartre writes, fails as a novelist because he transforms human freedom into tragic destiny. With divine lucidity, Mauriac as omniscient narrator decides the fate of Thérèse, "just as the ancient Gods decreed Oedipus' parricide and incest," even lending his creation "some of Tiresias' power of divination."[27] This is a form of narrative closure. Closure appears not only in romance but in tragedy as well; it is characteristic of any form of nonhistorical narrative. In all cases history as possibility is lost in a pre-given narrative order, that is, in mythical narrative.

In *Search for a Method*, Sartre defines comprehension as "the totalizing movement which gathers together my neighbour, myself and the environment in the synthetic unity of an objectification in process."[28] What makes comprehension difficult is the existence of a multiplicity of human centers out of which history is constituted. One person's creation (objectification) becomes an object for other persons who surpass it toward their own ends. The individual in his group relation is a "quasi-sovereign" mutually responsible with others for historical totalization. "History," Sartre states, "which is the proper work of *all* activity and *all* men, appears to men as a foreign force exactly insofar as they do not *recognize* the meaning of their enterprise (even when locally successful) in the total, objective result."[29]

Sartre argues that history would have to be given as a completely knowable totality for all human activity to be comprehended with certainty (transparency) and rendered communicable as a shared narrative. The ternary relation on which understanding is based would have to be constituted by a Third Person (Sovereign) outside of histo-

---

26. Jameson, "Three Methods," p. 200.

27. Jean-Paul Sartre, "François Mauriac and Freedom," in *Literary and Philosophical Essays,* trans. Annette Michelson (New York: Collier, 1962), pp. 8, 14.

28. Jean-Paul Sartre, *Search for a Method,* trans. Hazel E. Barnes (New York: Vintage-Random House, 1968), p. 155.

29. Sartre, *Search,* p. 89.

ry, an omniscient narrator capable of totalizing all history.[30] Bound by finitude, the human subject cannot be an Absolute Third in this sense. The attempt to impose a closed totalization on history is the mythical prerogative of the ancient gods. However, the human agent as quasi-sovereign can become conscious of his or her practical activity as a totalizer of history. As my life becomes "History," writes Sartre, it must reveal itself "as the strict necessity of the historical process so as to rediscover itself at an even deeper level, as the freedom of this necessity and, finally, as the necessity of freedom."[31] The person, as freedom realizing itself in the world, is bound to act out of a consciousness of the totality of history toward the recognition of the quasi-sovereignty of others.

History is accessible only through an always incomplete process of comprehension, that is, through infinite totalization. As Jameson implies, the ideological strategy of narrative closure can be radically distinguished from the critical imperative to totalize infinitely.[32] Inasmuch as the human being is the center of indeterminacy, the absence in history, there is a Kantian sense to this imperative: all must be recognized in their freedom. History is accessible only in narrative form, that is, as an ordered totality. To reduce history to a determinate totality, however, is to reduce the person to a thing, to a fated creature. Thus, narrative must present history as absent cause, not as presence. It can do this only in the form of an open-ended but essentially liberating totality, that is, in the form of an infinite totality.

No one has more convincingly addressed the issue of communicating this open-ended imperative than Søren Kierkegaard in *Concluding Unscientific Postscript*. Johannes Climacus, Kierkegaard's pseudonymous author, distinguishes between direct and indirect communication. Whereas direct communication aims at total transparency, indirect communication conveys history as absence, lived truth, freedom. History as infinite totalization must be presented in a particular way: if the content, or "what," of communication is freedom, then the

30. Sartre, *Search*, p. 90; see also Jean-Paul Sartre, *Being and Nothingness: A Phenomenological Essay on Ontology*, trans. Hazel E. Barnes (New York: Washington Square Press, 1966), p. 547.

31. Jean-Paul Sartre, *Critique of Dialectical Reason*, trans. Alan Sheridan-Smith (London: New Left Books, 1976), p. 70.

32. Jameson, *The Political Unconscious*, p. 53.

form, or "how," of communication must manifest this freedom. Indirect communication is the process whereby freedom in time is so presented that the recipient is challenged to exist in this freedom. A direct communication of freedom is a contradiction, since one would be instructing persons in freedom without giving them the room to appropriate freedom freely.

Indirect communication takes the form of a double reflection. The first reflection is the movement from individual thought to universal word. The second reflection is the preservation in the word of this very relationship of creation and recreation through which the individual is bound to the universal. The communication is brought into relation with its author as an existing individual. The historical point of departure for the communication becomes a part of the communication itself. The existing thinker communicates his or her own freedom and makes possible the emancipation of others through this double reflection. If direct communication hides the person's spiritual being and prevents "the self-activity of personal appropriation," indirect communication recognizes that the recipient is him or herself "the inwardness of truth."[33] An indirect communication is a concrete totalization of history. Kierkegaard's categories of direct and indirect communication are analogous to mythical narrative (the principle of destiny) on the one hand and liberating narrative (the principle of history as absence) on the other.

The notion of narrative as infinite totalization goes back to Hegel, despite the fact that nineteenth-century thinkers turned Hegel on himself and criticized his mystification of knowledge (the philosopher as omniscient narrator with divine lucidity). What person, asks Kierkegaard, is capable of being the I-am-I (Being-in-and-for-itself, the external Third, God) that can be both outside and yet include all existence within itself? Who is the human being who constructs the system? "Is he a human being or is he speculative philosophy in the abstract?" Marx finds Hegel's totality to be likewise comical in its abstractness: "Hegel makes man the *man of self-consciousness* instead of making self-consciousness the *self-consciousness of man*, of real man,

---

33. Søren Kierkegaard, *Concluding Unscientific Postscript,* trans. David F. Swenson and Walter Lowrie (Princeton: Princeton University Press, 1968), p. 217; see also pp. 69–71.

i.e., of man living also in a real, objective world and determined by that world. He stands the world *on its head.*"[34]

There is an underside to Hegel's notion of totality, however, that renders totality in terms of absence as detotalized totality, and in terms of presence as totalization. Hegel distinguishes between the genuine or true infinite and the false infinite. Mind, states Hegel, is "the true infinite, that is, the infinite which does not one-sidedly stand over against the finite but contains the finite within itself as a moment." The true infinite is given only in a relationship with the finite; the false infinite is presented as existing outside of the finite (Sartre's omniscient narrator). There is no infinite (mind) existing outside of a relationship to the finite (body).[35] Knowledge of finite being presupposes spirit (mind, freedom, the infinite), but spirit finds itself in the world as finite opposition to itself (that is, as human) and must recognize itself in this opposition. From the point of view of the finite world of ever-changing data, totality is endless regress, endless search, endless failure. The true idea, however, steps out of the infinite regress to recognize itself, not only as already accomplished in the world, but also as eternally accomplishing itself.[36] Infinitely speaking, the person recognizes as his or her own the freedom that extends beyond the limits of the physical and social world but that must enter into, participate in, and change that world.

Hegel's notion of totality is firmly linked to the idea of narrative order. The "absolute idea is the universal, but the universal not merely as an abstract form to which the particular content is a stranger, but as the absolute form, into which all the categories, the whole fullness of the content it has given being to, have retired."[37] Content is the finite everyday experience of the world. Content takes on meaning only through the ordering of form; form finds its existence only in content. The unity of form and content in the movement to totality is

34. Kierkegaard, *Postscript,* pp. 108–109; Karl Marx and Frederick Engels, *The Holy Family, or Critique of Critical Criticism: Against Bruno Bauer and Company,* trans. Richard Dixon and Clemens Dutt (Moscow: Progress Publishers, 1975), pp. 225–26.

35. G. W. F. Hegel, *Philosophy of Mind,* trans. A. V. Miller and William Wallace, part 3 of *Encyclopaedia of the Philosophical Sciences* (Oxford: Oxford University Press, 1971), pp. 23–24; see also Hegel, *Logic,* trans. William Wallace, part 1 of *Encyclopaedia of the Philosophical Sciences* (Oxford: Oxford University Press, 1975), p. 139.

36. Hegel, *Logic,* pp. 274, 291.

37. Hegel, *Logic,* p. 293.

necessity. In literary terms, this unifying process or necessity is the plot. The plot of a narrative is the necessity that unifies form and content into a meaningful totality. Hegel states that form is "the innate development of the concrete content itself."[38]

This "innate development" should not be understood in terms of the immanence of an external dialectic (the omniscient narrator). The illusion of spirit is that the plot of history can be determined in the same way as the genesis of a natural organism. The absolute idea may better be compared with Hegel's old man "who utters the same creed as the child, but for whom it is pregnant with the significance of a life time."[39] The key to absolute spirit is the old man's recognition that starting with his creed (the idea), he has freely chosen from the infinity of his life experiences the content rendering that creed significant to him and transforming it. He realizes that he has created his own life and given it a particular necessity or unity. "The truth of necessity," Hegel says, "is freedom."[40] The old man, that is to say, spirit, encounters himself, recognizing his life experiences and their totalization (necessity) as his own being and creation. The idea (form) returns into itself when it recognizes itself in its other (content).

In his commentary on *Phenomenology of Spirit*, Alexandre Kojève emphasizes that the becoming of spirit (its necessity) is *not* preordained; it can be comprehended only a posteriori. History is "a free (*frei*) series of contingent (*züfallig*) events," states Kojève: "To say that the Spirit's becoming is 'contingent and free' is to say that, starting with Spirit which is the end or result of becoming, one can reconstruct the path of becoming, but one can neither foresee its path from its beginning, nor deduce the Spirit from it."[41] Even the reconstruction of the path is necessarily tentative, based as it is on the ongoing process of spirit. On the other hand, though the future is not preordained, there follows the imperative that it be ordered in terms of the necessity of freedom.

Hegel uses the term "liberation" (*Befreiung*) for the recognition of necessity as self-creation. "For thinking means that, in the other, one

---

38. G. W. F. Hegel, *Phenomenology of Spirit,* trans. A. V. Miller (Oxford: Oxford University Press, 1977), p. 35.

39. Hegel, *Logic,* p. 293.

40. Hegel, *Logic,* p. 220.

41. Alexandre Kojève, *Introduction to the Reading of Hegel: Lectures on the "Phenomenology of Spirit,"* ed. Allan Bloom, trans. James H. Nichols, Jr. (Ithaca: Cornell University Press, 1969), p. 154.

meets with one's self. It means a liberation, which is not the flight of abstraction, but consists in that which is actual having itself not as something else, but as its own being and creation, in the other actuality with which it is bound up by the force of necessity. As existing in an individual form, this liberation is called I; as developed to its totality it is free spirit; as feeling, it is Love; and as enjoyment it is Blessedness."[42] The recognition of freedom in necessity is liberating narrative. Plot as illusory necessity, as the totality of form and content independent of human creative activity, is mythical narrative.

Fanon took this tradition of liberating narrative and used it to understand the history of the Third World. By arguing that Fanon's works are mythical, Fontenot completely loses this crucial dimension. Fanon's works are practical and concrete totalizations of the anticolonial struggle. They reveal the interactions of individuals and groups in terms of the necessity of freedom. Their existential task is both to comprehend and to communicate the categorical imperative in a particular social situation. Fanon is like those urban party militants in *The Wretched of the Earth* who reject their class and join the peasantry to learn from them, teach, and organize them (*WE*, pp. 68, 125–27; *DT*, pp. 31, 77–78). The tragedy of colonialism is that it may succeed in retaining direct control over a subject people or maintain indirect control through co-opting the national bourgeoisie. Fanon encodes the structure of colonialism and traces the genesis of the national group and its possible degeneration. He takes this plot and insists on the necessity of freedom as conscious, active, and responsible totalization. The task is to enter history, history as infinite possibility. This is his wager: *either* accept the challenge of creating a liberated society *or* tragically and fatalistically legitimate the repetition of oppression.

Philippe Lucas argues that Fanon's work suffers from a dualism between a tragic vision of history founded on the subjectivism of the "I" and a liberating vision of historical necessity that the historical subject must realize. This attempt to force Fanon's work into an objectivist mold is the consequence of Lucas' elitist notion of an all-knowing vanguard (the Absolute Third). What Lucas's Goldmannian conception of history misses is the open-ended aspect of Fanon's wager. For Fanon, the process of totalization is an infinitely open process that cannot be reduced to a translucent historical movement,

42. Hegel, *Logic*, p. 222.

that is, to the false necessity of an external dialectic (the false infinite).[43]

The revolutionary potential of the peasantry, lumpen proletariat, and proletariat becomes actuality by virtue of the decisive change in consciousness that comes with liberating narrative. Ultimately, the colonized as a whole must be educated and must educate themselves. Manichaean consciousness and race consciousness (the false infinite) are transformed into a political and social consciousness grounded in a concrete, experiential, national consciousness (the true infinite). To totalize history in the colonial or neocolonial context is "to open out into the truth of the nation and of the world" (*WE*, p. 200; *DT*, p. 135).

Fanon's stress on the imperative to totalize infinitely as a communicative act helps to explain why he places so much emphasis on symbolic forms in the anticolonial struggle. As a practicing psychiatrist, he saw his task as the restoration of broken communication. As a political theorist and activist, he dealt with the problem of the restoration of meaning in a divided social order. A narrative of liberation, as a concrete totalization demanding the recognition and actualization of quasi-sovereignty, was the basis for reestablishing human meaning. Yet a narrative of liberation could be truly concrete only if it expressed the lived experience of the individual in the community in a form that was both appropriate and indigenous to the community.

Fanon is concerned throughout his work with the lived culture of the colonized and its recreation in the struggle for liberation. In some of his psychiatric works especially, however, the use of the culture of the community in the therapeutic process legitimates a form of cultural relativism that disregards the reality of the struggle for liberation. The political thrust of liberating narrative in the colonial situation gives way to the reintegrationist thrust of mythical narrative.

In his medical thesis, Fanon uses the term "drama" to describe the state of individual mental disorder. It is the same term that he uses in his political writings to describe the Manichaean colonial situation.[44]

43. Philippe Lucas, *Sociologie de Frantz Fanon: Contribution à une anthropologie de la libération* (Algiers: Société nationale d'édition et de diffusion, 1971), pp. 19–21, 138–40, 147, 158–61.

44. Frantz Fanon, "Altérations mentales, modifications charactérielles, troubles psychiques et déficit intellectuel dans l'hérédo-dégénération spino-cérébelleuse: A propos d'un cas de maladie de Friedreich avec délire de possession" (Thèse de médecine, Lyons, 1951) p. 15 (all translations from the thesis are mine); *WE*, p. 141; *DT*, p. 89.

Chiding "political zealots" as well as conservative psychiatrists for their ignorance of Fanon's psychiatric work, J. Postel and C. Razanjao have noted that "revolutionary action and psychiatric action are constants in an identical commitment."[45] The neurotic or psychotic must make a new entry into the social unit just as the colonized must enter into a new history. (The colonized, however, are part of a functioning social unit, whereas the mentally alienated person is not.)

Fanon's medical thesis is premised on a fundamental assumption of human liberty. Referring to Lacan, he argues that a mental disorder is possible only through "a consent of liberty" even if the disorder involves an organic complication. The person must be taken as a whole and cannot be mechanically reduced to his or her biological being.[46] Liberty makes possible the rupture of intersubjective relations by giving one the freedom to lose oneself. Delirium, hysteria, and neurotic behavior, even where associated with organic disease, must be considered as the reactional behavior "of a self ruptured from intersocial relations." The mentally disabled person has agreed "to inventory all the abysses which liberty opens up." Treatment must respect the liberty of the individual.[47]

In psychiatric hospitals of the period (1950s), mental illness was treated through chemical or surgical intervention and through physical restraint (straitjackets, confinement to bed, cells, closed wards, isolation). According to Fanon's postgraduate supervisor and colleague, François Tosquelles, treatment consisted of nothing more, nothing less than "*INTERNEMENT*."[48] The hospital was a prison and the psychiatrist the jailer. In a joint paper, Fanon and Tosquelles argue that instead of restoring meaning, hospitals subject patients to

45. J. Postel and C. Razanjao, "La Vie et l'oeuvre psychiatrique de Frantz Fanon," *L'Information Psychiatrique*, 51 (December 1975), 1071. (All translations from this article are mine.) See also J. Postel, "Frantz Fanon à cinquante ans," *L'Information Psychiatrique*, 51 (December 1975), 1049–50.

46. Fanon, "Altérations mentales," pp. 11–15, 69 (*L'Information Psychiatrique*, p. 1090). The thesis was written after *Black Skin, White Masks* had been deemed unacceptable as a medical thesis at the biologically oriented Lyons Faculty of Medicine. *Black Skin* was published in 1952, whereas the medical thesis remained unpublished until 1975, when a section appeared in *L'Information Psychiatrique*, 51 (December 1975), 1079–90. Fanon continued to take an interest in the physiological dimension of psychic existence until as late as 1959. See Postel and Razanajao, pp. 1053–54, for a discussion of the intellectual climate at the Lyons Faculty of Medecine.

47. Fanon, "Altérations mentales," pp. 73, 68 (*L'Information Psychiatrique*, p. 1089).

48. François Tosquelles, "Frantz Fanon à Saint-Alban," *L'Information Psychiatrique*, 51 (December 1975), 1074.

"the free play of sado-masochistic myths."[49] Writing with C. Geronimi, Fanon compares the conflict between the doctor and the patient to that between master and slave. The patient would revolt but is forced to submit in an unequal struggle. In the process of turning the person into a fixed thing (*chosification*), a personal history of struggle is ignored. The drama of alienation, in which the neurotic was situated prior to entering the hospital, is reinforced and deepened in the hospital environment; neurosis becomes psychosis.[50] In an article coauthored with S. Asselah, Fanon writes that hospitals force patients into states of hallucinogenic flight and "amputate" or "castrate" the person.[51]

Fanon strongly objected to this model of treatment and believed that a different therapeutic approach was possible. The hospital, he and Asselah write, is the last chance for the person trying to refind "*his* lost meaning [sa *signification perdue*]."[52] One anecdote tells of how Fanon disturbed hospital routines by allowing patients the freedom to go to the market, and another relates how he furiously released sixty-nine straitjacketed patients who had been chained to beds.[53]

The idea of liberty could be the basis of a new model of treatment. The subject who has experienced the abyss of liberty chooses to recognize his or her sin, is forgiven, and reenters the group. Is not analysis "confessional"? Fanon asks in his thesis. To confess is to accept the narrative order given by the community and, furthermore, to acknowledge one's place as defined by the community. The person recognizes the group as the limit to liberty and condition of participation in the social world. The primordial and alien self is sacrificed. By virtue of his or her liberty, however, the person is always in danger of again falling out of the group. The psychoanalytic perspective is trag-

49. Frantz Fanon and François Tosquelles, "Sur un essai de réadaptation chez une malade avec épilepsie morphéique et troubles de caractère grave," *Congrès des médecins aliénistes et neurologistes de France et des pays de langue française*, 51st session, Pau, July 20–26, 1953, p. 364. (All translations from this paper are mine.)

50. Frantz Fanon and C. Geronimi, "L'Hospitalisation de jour en psychiatrie," *La Tunisie Médicale*, 37 (December 1959), 717 (*L'Information Psychiatrique*, 51 [December 1975], 1122). (All translations from this article are mine.)

51. Frantz Fanon and S. Asselah, "Le Phénomène de l'agitation en milieu psychiatrique: Considérations générales—signification psychopathologique," *Maroc Médical*, 36 (January 1957), 22. (All translations from this article are mine.)

52. Fanon and Asselah, p. 24.

53. Postel and Razanajao, p. 1055; Peter Geismar, *Fanon* (New York: Dial Press, 1971), pp. 65–66.

ic to the extent that the confessional narrative is imposed from the outside, as sacrifice rather than concrete appropriation. Fanon hints at this when he states that psychoanalysis is "a pessimistic view of man."[54] Lacan overemphasizes the infinite abyss of liberty, thus creating a dualism between individual liberty and social existence. Fanon is not entirely happy with this conception of liberty, but he accepts it in his thesis. He wants to move away from the implications of the tragic conception in Lacan but sees the notion of confession and self-sacrifice as the only way of maintaining the premise of liberty. The consequence of this approach in Fanon's psychiatric writings is that the group becomes a mythical entity to which one sacrifices one's liberty, rather than a creative unity through which one realizes one's liberty.

This mythical conception of reintegration into the group is central to many of Fanon's strictly psychiatric writings. When he worked with Tosquelles at Saint-Alban Hospital, Fanon became closely acquainted with the technique of "institutional therapy" that Tosquelles was developing. Starting with the premise that the lost individual had to find him or herself again in the group, Tosquelles used the institutional milieu to create a community that would facilitate the process of social reintegration. According to Tosquelles, the Saint-Alban "hypothesis" was directed toward bringing human beings together in a situation in which they could "find others again." Therapeutic techniques included psychotherapy, social therapy (emphasizing small lifelike group interaction and work therapy), and medical intervention to facilitate the whole process (shock therapy, insulin therapy, medication). All the activities of the hospital were geared toward maximizing the patient's consciousness of his or her sickness. The hospital was to be a demystifying, disalienating institution. It was self-recognition, that is to say, recognition of oneself through the group, that was the key to therapy. The subject whose self-production had broken down was treated as a free subject, not as an object or thing to be manipulated.[55]

Fanon wrote several articles with Tosquelles on the theory and

54. Fanon, "Altérations mentales," p. 71 (*L'Information Psychiatrique,* p. 1090).

55. Tosquelles, "Frantz Fanon à Saint-Alban," p. 1074. For a concise summary, see Tosquelles's comments in the discussion following the presentation by Fanon and Tosquelles, "Indications de la thérapeutique de Bini dans le cadre des thérapeutiques institutionnelles," *Congrès des médecins aliénistes,* 51st session, Pau, July 20–26, 1953, p. 552. (All translations from this paper are mine.)

practice of institutional therapy. Despite their use of interventionist medical techniques, the authors emphasize the human dimension in their work, that is, "the *inter-human encounters* and *practical activities* in which the sick person engages during the process of rediscovering the self and the world."[56] The institutional milieu itself is a communicative network charged with meaning and has to be changed in order to facilitate the interhuman encounter. Mental dissolution is followed by mental reconstruction, culminating in a total consciousness (*prise de conscience*) of the situation.[57]

After he began to practice in Algeria, Fanon continued to stress the interhuman encounter and the ideal of reintegration into the group, the group being the ethical norm. In an article with François Sanchez, Fanon presents this position very clearly. The authors argue that whereas the Western attitude toward mental illness is based on the idea of punishing the victim for failing to accept responsibility, the Maghreb attitude is based on respect for the *person* who has fallen "prey to enemy power," but who remains "in spite of everything a human being."[58] The Maghreb community protects the mentally disabled person from the excesses of the foreign spirit and encourages him or her to visit a healer or go on a pilgrimage. The disability is a contingent event for which the person is not responsible. When cured, the subject reenters the group without meeting any mistrust or ambivalence on the part of the group. Traditional therapy respects the sick person and attempts to reintegrate him or her into the group, thus restoring a sense of self and world. Commenting on Fanon and Sanchez's article, Postel and Razanjao state that it is the group that must assume responsibility for the person's recovery for he or she "remains our fellow being [*semblable*]."[59]

Fanon and his colleagues realized that social therapy would be useful therapeutically for patients of different cultural backgrounds only if it allowed them to encounter the other within their own unique

56. Fanon and Tosquelles, "Indications de la thérapeutique de Bini," p. 548.

57. Frantz Fanon and François Tosquelles, "Sur quelques cas traités par la méthode de Bini," *Congrès des médecins aliénistes*, 51st session, Pau, July 20–26, 1953, p. 54 (*L'Information Psychiatrique*, 51 [December 1975], p. 1093). (All translations from this paper are mine.) See also Fanon and Tosquelles, "Sur un essai de rédaptation," p. 368.

58. Frantz Fanon and François Sanchez, "Attitude du musulman maghrébin devant la folie," *Revue Pratique de Psychologie de la Vie Sociale et d'Hygiène Mentale*, no. 1 (1956), 26–27. (All translations from this article are mine.)

59. Postel and Razanjao, p. 1070.

cultures. Social therapy would have to replace the assumption of the supremacy of Western culture with the assumption of cultural relativism. In the Thematic Apperception Test (the T.A.T.), a patient uses his or her imagination to structure and describe certain visual images with which he or she is presented. Fanon, working with Charles Geronimi, found that the test did not work for Muslim women because the scene presented was a Western one, which they could not appropriate.[60]

Techniques used to treat female European patients successfully completely failed to help male Muslim patients. Discussion groups and meetings to plan group activities awakened little participation. The men were uninterested in listening to records, watching movies, working on a newspaper, or even celebrating holidays. Even work therapy was of no therapeutic value. Patients fought, nurses punished them, and no common activity could be realized. French culture was being forced onto Algerians. Hospital doctors could speak neither Arabic nor Kabyle and relied on interpreters who seemed to patients to be representatives of the French colonial administration. The patients did not know what to say at meetings, they disliked singing in groups, they were not accustomed to nonreligious and non-Muslim celebrations, they found the games unfamiliar, and they could not identify with characters in foreign films. The journal reflected European social life, and besides, the majority of Algerians were illiterate. Much of the ergotherapy was considered female work.[61]

In order to precipitate the awakening of a Muslim community in the hospital, the doctors felt that it was necessary to integrate Muslim culture into hospital life. A Muslim café was introduced where patients, nurses, and doctors could mix. Fanon himself would frequently be seen chatting with patients in the café. Professional storytellers were brought in. Muslim holidays were celebrated in the

60. Frantz Fanon and C. Geronimi, "Le T.A.T. chez les femmes musulmanes: Sociologie de la perception et de l'imagination," *Congrès des médecins aliénistes,* 54th session, Bordeaux, August 30–September 4, 1956, p. 368. (All translations from this paper are mine.)

61. Frantz Fanon and J. Azoulay, "La Socialthérapie dans un service d'hommes musulmans: Difficultés méthodologiques," *L'Information Psychiatrique,* 30 (October–November 1954), 351–55 (51 [December 1975], 1097–99). Chapter 2 of Azoulay's medical thesis consists primarily of this article. See J. Azoulay "Contribution à l'étude de la socialthérapie dans un service d'aliénés musulmans" (Thèse de médecine, Algiers, 1954).

hospital mosque by religious leaders. Muslim men were given garden plots on which they could grow vegetables for sale to the hospital. Muslim women were allowed to wear veils and were provided with a café especially for them. Perhaps most important of all, by 1956 Fanon had learned Arabic.[62]

When his political commitment lead to his expulsion from Algeria in 1957, Fanon began to work in newly independent Tunisia, and there he took social-therapy techniques one step further: the patient was treated within the context of his own community, using the hospital only as an out-patient. In an article with C. Geronimi, Fanon argues that social therapy in the hospital created a fixed pseudosociety where there were no crises and there could be no creative invention. Day hospitalization, in contrast, allowed the patient to retain the freedom and richness of his or her own inner depths. The patient would come to the hospital during the day for therapy and treatment. The rest of the time he or she remained with family and friends, carried on cultural activities, and sometimes even maintained a professional life. The doctor studied the concrete personality as it lived its crises in a real environment. The patient learned to resolve a conflict through unifying action on the real. As with the earlier therapeutic approaches, therapy was oriented toward "the meeting of two liberties [*la rencontre de deux libertés*]."[63]

Geismar argues that these solutions, though obvious to those trained in social psychiatry, were impressive for Fanon's time, especially in Algeria. He also comments that cultural relativism should not be confused with the abandonment of modern medical technique. Fanon classified traditional healers (marabouts) as agents of Western colonialism, enslaving the country in ignorance and weakness. If requested, he would allow a healer to attempt to cure the patient. When the healer failed, Fanon would pay him and then use modern teachings to show how he could outdo traditional cultural techniques.[64] How this position is to be made consistent with cultural relativism,

62. Fanon and Azoulay, p. 361 (*L'Information Psychiatrique*, 51 [December 1975], 1106); Azoulay, pp. 47–48; Geismar, pp. 86–87; this information was confirmed by Monsieur Abdelkader Charef, a nurse who had worked with Fanon, when I visited the hospital at Blida (now the Frantz Fanon Psychiatric Hospital) in August 1982. Fanon's memory and influence live on in an impressive way in people like Monsieur Charef.

63. Fanon and Geronimi, "L'Hospitalisation de jour," p. 717 (*L'Information Psychiatrique*, 51 [December 1975], 1122).

64. Geismar, p. 87.

Geismar does not explain. Irene Gendzier argues that Fanon was beginning to appreciate that psychiatric innovations were useful only if "grounded in the particular human history to which they were to be applied."[65] She provides no evidence, however, to show that Fanon had resolved the tension between scientific medical techniques and the lived reality of Algerian culture. Does one show the ignorance of the marabout who uses folk medicine while at the same time proclaiming the artistry and originality of the marabout who tells a good story? Fanon and his medical colleagues did not work out the interrelationship between modern medical techniques and traditional beliefs at the level of lived meaning.

The problem with the social-therapy writings is that the notions of liberty and cultural relativism that are used in them imply a tragic conception of culture. As a *chef-de-service*, or department head, in the Blida-Joinville psychiatric hospital in Algeria, Fanon trained and worked with a medical student named Jack Azoulay. Azoulay's 1954 medical thesis—inspired by Fanon and dedicated to him—is useful for conceptually identifying this problem. Azoulay distinguishes the relation between patient and doctor from two types of encounter: unambiguous and ambiguous. He calls relations of domination (master-slave type relations) unambiguous encounters (*les rencontres non ambigues*). Relations of reciprocity (communal, husband and wife type relations) he calls ambiguous encounters (*les rencontres ambigues*). Ambiguous encounters are authentic encounters based on intersubjectivity; the other is revealed through me, and I am revealed through the other. The significant thing about ambiguous encounters is that the individual is recognized by the group as a member of the group in the fullness of his or her freedom and ambiguity. "The ambiguous encounter is not the dilution of the I in the abstract institution, but the enrichment of the I, the deepening of the ME, the concerted and edifying explosion of the WE."[66] Ambiguous encounters are the reciprocal third party relations of the Sartrean group (quasi-sovereignty). Presumably, the political imperative is to move from unambiguous encounters to ambiguous encounters.

Azoulay states that the relation between the doctor and the patient is neither an ambiguous nor an unambiguous encounter. It is not an

65. Irene L. Gendzier, *Frantz Fanon: A Critical Study* (London: Wildwood House, 1973), p. 84.
66. Azoulay, p. 14.

encounter at all. It is a shock or traumatism. Following Lacan, Azoulay argues that the subject identifies with the image of the other and the other captivates the subject. As the other, the doctor must use language (*la parole*) to bring about an encounter with the patient. He provokes emotional investments, identifications, transferences, dramatization, resistance, and repression. The psychiatrist's task is to make the subject encounter the We and thus enter into ambiguous and free relations with the other. Quoting Tosquelles, Azoulay states that the role of therapy is "to help the sick person recreate the YOU [*TU*], the WE, and the group within which the ME can disentangle itself."[67]

Two implications can be drawn from Azoulay's models of encounter. On the one hand the task of therapy is to make possible the reintegration of the individual into the group. To the extent that the group is taken as the cultural norm, cultural relativism must prevail. Azoulay explicitly emphasizes the importance of cultural relativism in therapy.[68] On the other hand, however, group relations, ambiguous encounters, are incompatible with relations of domination, unambiguous encounters. Cultural relativism opens the possibility of sustained domination, whereas the imperative of authentic group encounters demands that domination be challenged. Therefore, the critical issue is not reincorporation into a group loosely defined by finite social reality (cultural relativism). It is rather the reincorporation of the patient into an authentic, active, and historical group that is the therapist's ultimate task (liberation). Azoulay fails to draw out this implication and consequently reduces liberating narrative to mythical narrative.

The same problem applies to Fanon's social-therapy writings. The group is assumed to be the norm, the source of social meaning, with the consequence that the quasi-sovereignty of the individual in the group is sacrificed. Furthermore, the group itself does not come under scrutiny. In a situation of domination, such as the colonial situation, what is the norm of the group? In a paper with Azoulay, Fanon discusses the dissolution of traditional Muslim society in the postconquest period and the transformation of small holders into a landless proletariat or lumpen proletariat. Traditional Muslim society was based on strict moral codes, a rigid social framework, patriarchy and

67. Azoulay, p. 13.
68. Azoulay, chaps. 2, 4.

respect for the old, and a strong kinship and community network.[69] What, then, is the norm into which the patient must be reintegrated? To attempt to integrate the patient into colonial society would reinforce relations of domination. But to return the patient to a traditional Muslim world would be a failure to deal with the realities of the present. The patient learns to recognize him or herself in relation to a particular group but not in relation to the social totality or to the assumption of his or her dignity in relation to that totality. The implications for therapy of the critique of internment and colonial domination are not worked out. Liberating narrative collapses into mythical narrative.

Though social therapy ultimately fails to explicate its liberating thrust, it nevertheless has important political implications. It has as one of its fundamental premises the recognition of human freedom and dignity. Simply to treat the patient as a human being is to come into conflict with the colonial system. The cultural relativism that becomes therapeutically necessary in the colonial situation also has a political meaning: the claim that the Algerian belongs to a legitimate cultural entity directly challenges the colonizer's ideological system. Furthermore, to the extent that this cultural entity is already in opposition to the colonial order—and Fanon argues that it is—then to be reintegrated into colonized reality is to find oneself already in a situation of struggle with the oppressor.

However, there is nothing intrinsically liberating about cultural relativism or even Manichaean opposition. The community may or may not be a politically active group, and even if it is anticolonial in orientation, it need not be essentially liberating. The community may rest on a patriarchal order that is incompatible with the demand for freedom, or it may be in a state of degeneration. Cultural relativism restores dignity to the group, but it does not open the individual and the group to history. Nor does it take into account the psychiatrist's own ground in the modern scientific world (medicine). By taking the group as it manifests itself under colonialism as the normal group, social therapy accepts the colonial system and indirectly legitimates it. What is necessary is a notion of the group as a liberating entity and a clear conception of the relations between liberating psychiatry and liberating politics. The relationship between unambiguous encoun-

69. Fanon and Azoulay, pp. 356–57 (*L'Information Psychiatrique,* 51 [December 1975], 1102).

ters and ambiguous encounters must be clarified and the critical edge to ambiguous encounters grasped in its fullness.

Commenting in 1956 on the failure of Muslim women to make a story out of the European images presented to them, Fanon and Geronimi state: "The imagination, the imaginary, are only possible to the extent that the real [*le réel*] belongs to us."[70] This is more than a demand that perception tests be introduced that cater to the Muslim experience. It is an implicit demand that the Algerian people be given back their control over their own reality. Fanon was to submit his letter of resignation from his Blida post not long after writing this paper. For a year he had been helping the guerrillas operating in the mountains around Blida. He had harbored leaders in his house and in the hospital, had provided medical supplies, and had given lessons in caring for the wounded. He taught the *fidayines* (Muslim resistance fighters) how to control their reactions when engaged in military activities such as planting bombs, and how to withstand torture. After such lessons he might have to treat a police commissioner suffering from too many "interrogations."[71] He stated in his letter of resignation (1956): "If psychiatry is the medical technique that aims to enable man no longer to be a stranger to his environment, I owe it to myself to affirm that the Arab, permanently an alien in his own country, lives in a state of absolute depersonalization. . . . A society that drives its members to desperate solutions is a non-viable society, a society to be replaced." (*AR*, p. 53; *RA*, pp. 51–52).

Irene Gendzier comments: "It was not psychiatry that Fanon abandoned in Algeria. It was the commitment to help men and women adjust to colonial society."[72] Fanon had found a resolution in his own life to the tension in his psychiatric work between cultural relativism and the authentic recognition of oneself in relation to the other. Restoring to the Arab patient a sense of individual and cultural dignity was an implicit threat to colonial domination. However, cultural relativism also meant restoring to the worn-out French interrogator his sense of self so that he could continue to torture Algerians. Fanon had to resign because the institution for which he worked demanded that he support the colonizer. His resignation implies at an intellectual

70. Fanon and Geronimi, "Le T.A.T.," p. 368.
71. Simone de Beauvoir, *Force of Circumstance*, trans. Richard Howard (New York: Putnam's, 1965), p. 593; Geismar, p. 83. See also the case studies in *WE*, especially pp. 266–67; *DT*, pp. 189–92.
72. Gendzier, *Frantz Fanon: A Critical Study*, pp. 97–98.

level that it is necessary to explicate the liberating dimension in psychiatry. Normality would have to be understood as the explicit and lived recognition of oneself as a free being in relation to other free beings. Traditional psychiatry could be satisfied with the simple recognition involved in reinsertion into the community. A liberating psychiatry would have to transform this mythical position into a form of discourse truly informed by the recognition of the other. This would have the political implication of challenging the tyrant not only in his or her psychopathology but also in his or her politico-pathology. Fanon continued his psychiatric work in Tunisia until 1960, but his political commitment became his foremost activity.

Fanon's psychiatric writings indicate his endless concern for principles of human freedom and cultural dignity in very concrete and culturally specific circumstances. However, they are technical discussions, often coauthored by other psychiatrists and generally presented at medical congresses or in medical journals. Their tendency to espouse a mythical form of cultural relativism as a therapeutic technique contrasts with the commitment of Fanon's major works to liberating social transformation. In the latter, the psychiatric therapist becomes a social and political therapist whose concern is not to bring the individual into harmony with a mythical community but to facilitate the entry of the individual and the community into liberating history. Hence, the political causes of social and sociopsychological disorders and the understanding of these disorders are primary concerns. Culture is not an entity to be manipulated by the therapist but the structures of meaning through which these disorders are survived and transformed in a concrete history. It is the living and liberating basis of social action.

In *Black Skin, White Masks,* Fanon distinguishes ontogeny (the genesis of the individual) from sociogeny (the genesis of the group) (*BS,* p. 11; *PN,* p. 8). Each individual goes through a particular and personal version of "normal" psychological development. The analyst has the task of resolving the unconscious psychic conflicts that inhibit the normal functioning of that individual. Groups of individuals experience psychological processes peculiar to the genesis of the specific group. Fanon argues that racial domination, along with the ideology of racial superiority that accompanies it, creates group psychic conflict and cultural distortion. In the case of the bourgeoisie and intellectuals this conflict may take the form of a repressive, internalized collective unconscious that becomes the source of self-hatred. Among the peasantry, lumpen proletariat, and less privileged proletariat the problem may be different. Culture is transformed into a defensive and reactive formation through which the colonized resist as best they can. However, they are unable to take their destiny into their own hands.

Fanon's sociogenetic notion of the unconscious is close to Jameson's "political" unconscious. It refers, in general, to the collective unconscious (released from Jung's biological determinism) and, in particular, to the internalization of this unconscious by a colonized bourgeoisie. The individual unconscious and the collective unconscious resemble each other structurally, since both consist of the tension between desire (for parent, white person) and its restriction (other parent, white society). One frees oneself from the distortions created by these tensions by understanding the source of the conflict and learning to deal with it in the context of social reality. In individual analysis it is considered possible to deal with one's inner conflicts while at the same time accepting arbitrary domination in society. Fanon makes explicit, in contrast, the deep implication of psychoanalysis. The task is to refind my ego in relation to the other in such a way that I recognize the other as a person like myself. The person who recognizes his or her freedom through the resolution of his or her individual conflict can really become free only through the struggle for mutual recognition in its social dimension.[73]

Political leaders should be psychiatrists, Fanon once told Simone de Beauvoir.[74] From his work on psychiatry and politics we can infer that Fanon meant that the political activist had to initiate a communicative process through which his people could overcome their state of alienation. To do this he or she would have to be a political and social theorist who could provide a narrative opening the possibility of overcoming the social crisis and achieving liberation. However, a narrative of liberation could be meaningfully appropriated and enacted only if communicated in terms of the lived experi-

73. Fanon diagnoses black alienation in terms of both unconscious and conscious conflicts. These conflicts arise beause one is forced by the colonizer constantly to confront the fact that one is black, and yet one does not come to a full consciousness of the social totality of colonialism and the need for its transformation. Compare Sartre's notion of the unconscious as *le vécu* (lived experience), or comprehension, in "Itinerary of a Thought," in *Between Existentialism and Marxism*, trans. John Mathews (New York: Morrow, 1976), p. 41.

74. De Beauvoir, p. 596.

ence of the people addressed. The psychotherapist can encounter the neurotic and engage him or her in a process of self-recovery only if he or she begins by understanding individual myths and illusions as personally significant structures for ordering experience. Therapy must transform the drama of alienation into the critical reappropriation of history. If the patient's conflicts and even the patient are not to be turned into things, then the patient must be brought into a conscious relation with his or her own lived history. The political theorist must likewise begin by entering into the world of meaning constituted by the culture of his or her people if he or she is to arrive at liberating history. He or she must become a critical, cultural theorist.

Jürgen Habermas has drawn attention to the structural parallel between psychoanalysis and social theory. He considers psychoanalysis to be a form of "general interpretation." On the one hand, general interpretation offers fixed theoretical constructions that are applicable under different circumstances. On the other hand, a general interpretation is meaningless unless the patient is able to see how it fits his or her own case and is thus able to arrive at self-reflection. Habermas distinguishes the "dramatic model," through which meaning discloses itself, from the self-conscious appropriation of that meaning. In the course of people's interaction, meaning takes form as it would in theater: events are ordered in terms of a unifying structure or plot through which they can be understood. We are not, however, mere actors in a drama outside of our control: "in our own self-formative process we are at once both actor and critic. In the final instance, the meaning of the process itself must be capable of becoming part of our consciousness in a critical manner, entangled as we are in the drama of life history." If our ability as critics is blocked so that reflective self-understanding is distorted, we must rely on the help of general interpretation. A general interpretation such as that used in psychoanalysis provides a typical narrative that can aid the subject in reconstructing his or her own life history. It defines the relevant variables of a developmental history, including such things as typical roles, basic conflicts, and patterns of interaction. On the basis of this generalized history and the circumstances of the analytic dialogue, the analyst "makes interpretive suggestions for a story that the patient cannot tell." Such interpretations can be verified only if the patient is able to use them to understand him or herself, that is, to tell his or her own story. The patient reflects on his or her involvement in a personal drama with the help of a typical narrative.[75]

Habermas implies that the task of the social theorist is similar. He or she must understand his or her society's situation and communicate this understanding. The psychoanalyst is able to bring about communication through the transference. The patient is encouraged to transfer conflictual emotional bonds from their source onto the relationship with the doctor, who is then able to reveal them in a way that is appropriable by the patient. Likewise the theorist must bring to the fore the mythical understanding that social actors have of their experience so that they can critically reenter their own history. Entering into the story of the community, the social theorist provides openings for its critical appropriation. The typical narrative of liberation (or general interpretation) can be grasped only through the community's particular understanding of the world.

Fanon's theory of colonialism is a general interpretation in Habermas's sense. If we return to our distinction between mythical and liberating narrative, we can say that the story (history) of the colonized is mythical inasmuch as the colonized are entangled in a racially defined absurd drama from which they cannot release themselves. It becomes liberating when this mythical understanding is critically appropriated in terms of a general interpretation like Fanon's through which people are able to come to an understanding of themselves and their history.

Fanon analyzed the primary mythical patterns of colonial society. His analysis provides the basis for understanding and entering into Third World culture, especially in the Caribbean. The European racial myth, the white myth of superiority, is the basis of a Manichaean ideology that justifies and sustains military domination and economic exploitation. The colonizer portrays the colonized as a subhuman, animal-like creature, lacking the capacity for rational discourse and action; the colonized is "a sort of quintessence of evil." He or she is "the corrosive element, . . . the deforming element, . . . the depository of maleficent powers, the unconscious and irretrievable instrument of blind forces" (WE, p. 41; DT, p. 10). The colonized must be controlled by the intelligent European who can ensure that the colonial system is maintained for the benefit of all.

75. Jürgen Habermas, Knowledge and Human Interests, trans. Jeremy J. Shapiro (Boston: Beacon Press, 1971), pp. 259–63. Habermas's critique of ideology, however, assumes a Marxist theory of history.

Caliban may accept Prospero's myth and seek to regain his humanity; by denying his self and culture, he can attempt to assimilate Prospero's culture. He is "elevated above his jungle status [*échappé de sa brousse*]" in proportion to his adoption of the mother country's cultural standards (*BS*, p. 18; *PN*, p. 14). Fanon illustrates this process of internalization using characters such as the black Martinican protagonist of Mayotte Capécia's *Je suis Martiniquaise*. The narrator must turn white; she must marry a white man and live the social life of a white woman. Colonial society denies her this. Trapped by the white colonial mythology, she submits and accepts her suffering.[76] Caliban cannot give up his body. Confronted by a racist mythology, he is doomed to eternal failure. Even though he may have repudiated cultural darkness, the white person looks at him and imprisons him with that look. "A man was expected to behave like a man," states Fanon; "I was expected to behave like a black man—or at least like a nigger" (*BS*, p. 114; *PN*, p. 92).

Fanon's *Black Skin, White Masks* is an examination of the cultural tension experienced by the colonized bourgeoisie. It is a "sociodiagnosis" of a sociopsychological problem: the internalization of the stereotypes imposed by the colonizer. Its aim is to initiate the process by which that psychic alienation will be overcome (*BS*, pp. 11–12; *PN*, pp. 8–9). Fanon challenges the psychological analysis of the process of internalization that is offered by the Lacanian analyst O. Mannoni. In *Prospero and Caliban*, Mannoni argues that the colonized Malagasy personality, Caliban, must be understood in terms of an unconscious precolonial dependency complex by means of which the Malagasy avoids the feeling of inferiority. Accustomed to a relation of submission to the all-providing ancestors, the father, or the husband, Caliban relives this relationship when he comes into contact with the colonizer. According to Mannoni, the coming of the European was unconsciously expected by non-Europeans. In the face of this need for dependency the unresolved latent complexes in Prospero become manifest in the urge to dominate. Mannoni states that it is this unconscious structure that explains colonial racism rather than conquest and exploitation. When the relationship of dependency col-

76. *BS*, pp. 42–44; *PN*, pp. 34–36. Missing the irony in the work, Fanon takes Capécia's book as an autobiography and example of what he later calls the literature of assimilation, a form that imitates the styles and trends of the metropolis thus remaining essentially uncreative (*WE*, p. 222; *DT*, p. 153).

lapses, Caliban experiences an inferiority complex.[77] Though Mannoni's psychology of colonization claims to criticize domination in the name of freedom, it nevertheless legitimates colonial rule: psychology is used to blame the colonized for their situation.

In contrast to Mannoni, Fanon analyzes the way in which the collective unconscious of a colonizing people is imposed from the outside so that a colonized people is deprived of its human status. The black person is made into a phobogenic object. Representing the latent desires and impulses lying deep in the European psyche, black becomes the symbol of the biological, of everything that the European must reject as evil. By projecting the image of evil onto another group, the European is able to repudiate his or her inner desires as though they were not his or her own. Fanon argues that Jung was mistaken in attributing to the collective unconscious a primary biological component. The collective unconscious is "the sum of prejudices, myths, collective attitudes of a given group." In the Antillean situation, the collective unconscious is the result of the "unreflected imposition of a culture [*l'imposition culturelle irréfléchie*]" (BS, pp. 188, 191; PN, pp. 152, 154). It is this imposition that makes it normal for a black Antillean to be antiblack. He or she has internalized archetypes belonging to the European.

Unlike Mannoni, Fanon harbors no illusions about the ideological significance of these assumptions of European colonial culture. They form the mythical basis for the act of colonial domination and justify the violence of conquering, subjugating, and exploiting an alien group. To the extent that the colonizer's myth is internalized, the colonized can be controlled and shaped. If there is an inferiority complex, states Fanon, it is first of all the result of a socioeconomic process, the exploitation of one group by another, and then a psychological process in which members of an oppressed and exploited race interiorize the damning collective unconscious of the other (BS, p. 11; PN, p. 8). Whereas Mannoni puts the blame for an inferiority complex on a failed dependency complex, Fanon states that the inferiority complex is created and perpetuated by a racist society that seeks to eliminate the culture and personality of a particular group (BS, pp. 92–93; PN, pp. 74–75). Furthermore, as *The Wretched of the Earth* argues, it is mainly the colonized bourgeoisie and not, as Mannoni

77. O. Mannoni, *Prospero and Caliban: The Psychology of Colonization,* trans. Pamela Powesland (New York: Praeger, 1964), particularly pp. 63, 86, 108.

implies, the colonized peasantry and lower classes who suffer from an inferiority complex: the colonized person, Fanon recognizes, is treated as an inferior, "but he is not convinced of his inferiority."[78]

The colonized person may react to the white myth by cultivating a myth that legitimates his or her own group in opposition to the colonizer. This is a form of resistance to colonialism, but it has its limits. Such a person risks enclosing him or herself in a calcified cultural milieu consisting of "terrifying myths" and "instinctive patterns of behaviour" (*WE*, pp. 55, 236; *DT*, pp. 20, 166). The colonized person who has attempted to "pass" as white, but who has failed, may fall back on his or her traditional culture and romanticize the people. Paraphrasing the sentiments of some negritude writers, Fanon states: "I am black: I am the incarnation of a complete fusion with the world, an intuitive understanding of the earth, an abandonment of my ego in the heart of the cosmos, and no white man, no matter how intelligent he may be, can ever understand Louis Armstrong and the music of the Congo" (*BS*, p. 45; *PN*, p. 36; see also *WE*, pp. 221–22; *DT*, p. 153). In an ironic twist, the neocolonial bourgeoisie may immerse themselves in the culture of their people. Claiming to represent the authentic struggles of the people, this elite co-opts their resistance.

Fanon's task is both to demonstrate how these processes work and to further the transformation of internalization and resistance into an authentic appropriation of history. When a person is suffering from a neurosis because he or she is told to turn white or disappear, Fanon argues, the psychoanalyst should not unveil the desire to change color and advise the patient to accommodate to the situation. On the contrary, the analyst must help the patient both "to become *conscious* of his unconscious" and "to act in the direction of a change in the social structure; . . . my objective, once his motivations have been brought into consciousness, will be to put him in a position to *choose* action (or passivity) with respect to the real source of the conflict—that is,

---

78. *WE*, p. 53; *DT*, p. 19. Though the black bourgeoisie suffers from a type of social neurosis, the colonized individual from this and other classes is not immune to individual neurosis rooted in his or her own particular unconscious and family situation. René Maran creates the autobiographical character Jean Veneuve apparently in order to analyze the phenomenon of colonial racism. Maran's real problem, Fanon states, is that he is an abandonment neurotic: if he did not have the excuse of his color he would have invented some other excuse to explain his closed psychic structure (*BS*, pp. 78–79; *PN*, p. 63).

toward the social structures" (*BS*, p. 100; *PN*, pp. 80–81). One comes to grips with one's psychological problem only through "a leap to consciousness [*une prise de conscience abrupte*]" of the social and economic realities (*PN*, p. 8, my translation; see *BS*, p. 11;). There is no question here of pragmatically accepting an alienating social system. One overcomes one's "neurosis" by consciously and actively changing the system in which it is presented. To put it in the Hegelian terms so fundamental to *Black Skin, White Masks*, one demands mutual recognition.

Fanon's works, therefore, are historical points of departure for a liberating consciousness. The social contradictions in the Third World, the problems of colonial exploitation, domination, and racism, are presented in such a way that one is brought to a conscious relation with one's historical horizons and the necessity of realizing one's freedom in that situation. Fanon says in *Black Skin, White Masks* that he hopes his book will be "a mirror with a progressive infrastructure," where the black person can find himself again "on the road to disalienation" (*BS*, p. 184; *PN*, p. 148). The book is, in part, autobiographical: it traces Fanon's own attempt to understand racial alienation and overcome it. Still, it is not concerned with one man's alienation; it is addressed to the alienated black person in the Caribbean, and particularly to the dependent black bourgeoisie. By implication, however, it is the colonized intermediary and elite classes in general whose story is told. The book is a mirror in which they can reconstruct their own stories, according to their own particular situation. But the story of the colonized does not exist in isolation from the story of the colonizer. The book challenges the colonizer, too, to see through the system of oppression and his or her own alienation in it. The book is ultimately grounded in the Kantian categorical imperative:

> I find myself suddenly in the world and I recognize that I have one right alone: That of demanding human behaviour from the other.
> One duty alone: That of not renouncing my freedom through my choices. [*BS*, p. 229; *PN*, p. 186]

It is the task of the reader, whoever he or she may be, to appropriate the message and realize its meaning according to his or her own situation. Rather than being a conclusion, the last chapter of *Black Skin, White Masks*, entitled "By Way of Conclusion [*En Guise de*

Conclusion]," is a gripping poetic demand for the completely new beginning that comes with a revolutionary leap. It is Fanon's call for the kind of love that comes with understanding and action: I want, he says, to be able "to discover and to love [*vouloir*] man, wherever he may be" (*BS*, p. 231; *PN*, p. 187).

Fanon's works culminate with *The Wretched of the Earth* and always the message remains the same. "Come, then, comrades," he wrote on his deathbed, "the European game has finally ended; we must find something different" (*WE*, p. 312; *DT*, p. 230). The style of the conclusion to *The Wretched of the Earth* is very similar to that of *Black Skin, White Masks*. "For Europe, for ourselves, and for humanity, comrades, we must turn over a new leaf [*faire peau neuve*], we must work out new concepts, and try to set afoot a new man" (*WE*, p. 316; *DT*, p. 233). Now, however, the concern of the revolutionary is not simply the alienated colonized bourgeoisie. The concern is for the peasant and lower classes of the Third World and their potential betrayal by the Third World bourgeoisie. The revolutionary call in *Black Skin, White Masks* is carried to a new dimension and uttered to all of the oppressed. *The Wretched of the Earth* plots the revolutionary process of decolonization and the birth of the nation. It is an expression of national consciousness that demands that the colonized liberate themselves in and through responsible, thoughtful action. National consciousness, liberated from the chauvinism of nationalism and the tyranny of the bourgeoisie, is a particular form of historical consciousness. *The Wretched of the Earth*, as a communication of national consciousness, is a form of liberating narrative.

Much of Fanon's early work dealt with the experiences of a black man growing up in the French Caribbean. He analyzed the black and white myths that deformed Caribbean culture, and he used authors such as Nietzsche, Kierkegaard, Hegel, and Sartre to pose the alternative of liberation from colonial alienation. Fanon's later works were written out of the Algerian experience but had implications for the Third World as a whole. They analyzed colonial myths and countermyths, addressed the problem of decolonization, and emphasized the importance of national culture and national consciousness in the liberation process. Fanon wrote little about the growth of national culture in the Caribbean. Yet, he saw Caribbean plantation societies as basically conforming to his model of colonialism. The problem was how to transform a repressed West Indian national consciousness into the historical consciousness associated with liberating political action. Algeria, he thought, was setting an example; so too was Cuba, a territory in the Caribbean itself.[79] Fanon's untimely death from cancer left him without the opportunity to go further in his analysis of Caribbean culture. However, his work was, in part, a response to the Caribbean situation, and it influenced the development of a liberating historical consciousness in the Caribbean.

From the point of view of Caribbean culture, Fanon's narrative of liberation moves in two related directions. On the one hand, Fanon draws from the European tradition of liberating narrative to analyze in detail the dialectic of social totality, the movement from slave ethics to history, from master-slave struggle to liberation. On the other hand, he comments on the culture of the colonized and the growth of a national culture in relation to this movement to history. Fanon's work is indispensable for understanding the dynamic of Caribbean culture today.

79. See Fanon, "Aux Antilles, naissance d'une nation?" *RA*, pp. 87–94 (omitted from *AR*); "Blood Flows in the Antilles under French Domination," *AR*, pp. 167–69 (*RA*, pp. 169–71); and Fanon's comments to Bertold Juminer quoted in Geismar, pp. 125, 127.

Chapter 2

From the Drama of Colonialism to the History of Liberation

> There never was a greater event,—and on account of it, all who are born after us belong to a higher history than any history hitherto!
>
> FRIEDRICH NIETZSCHE, *Joyful Wisdom*

> The advent of peoples, unknown only yesterday, onto the stage of history, their determination [*volonté*] to participate in the building of a civilization that has its place in the world of today give to the contemporary period a decisive importance in the world process of humanization.
>
> FRANTZ FANON, *Toward the African Revolution*

D RIVEN by the demand for precious metals, raw materials, labor, and markets, European nations took military control of most of the non-European world between the sixteenth and the nineteenth centuries. Europeans pursued their economic interests with cannons and soldiers, defeated and subjugated nonwhite peoples, and commenced a process of systematic colonial exploitation. Non-European national and community leaders were killed, their peoples raped, their cultures forced underground; human dignity was brutally denied. In the creation of a colonial world, precolonial life and horizons were totally transformed and shattered. European colonies were established through violence. From the beginning, non-Europeans resisted the process of colonization. Once defeated, they struggled to rebuild their own culture in opposition to that of the colonizer. This is the drama of colonialism. It remains a major feature of the modern world. Drawing from the European tradition of liberating narrative,

Fanon analyzed this drama in its uniqueness and presented the process of liberation as an alternative through which a new history of humanity could be inaugurated.

Fanon uses the metaphor of a divided, compartmentalized space to capture the dramatic nature of the colonial situation:[1]

> The colonizer's town is a strongly built town, all made of stone and steel. It is a brightly lit town; the streets are covered with asphalt, and the garbage cans swallow all the leavings, unseen, unknown and hardly thought about. . . .
> The town belonging to the colonized people, or at least the native town, the Negro village, the medina, the reservation, is a place of ill fame, peopled by men of evil repute. They are born there, it matters little where nor how; they die there, it matters not where, nor how. It is a world without spaciousness [*sans intervalles*]; men live there on top of each other, and their huts are built one on top of the other. [*WE*, p. 39; *DT*, p. 8]

This spatial separation implies lines of force: the "dividing line, the frontiers are shown by barracks and police stations." It is this violent split that renders the two zones reciprocally exclusive. They are not opposed in the service of a higher unity, but, on the contrary, follow the rules of "pure Aristotelean logic" (*WE*, pp. 38–39; *DT*, p. 8).

One's place in the colonial world is based on perceived racial traits. The colonizer paints the colonized as "the quintessence of evil" and uses stereotyped imagery to turn a human being into an animal: "the yellow man's creeping motions, the emanations of the native town, the hordes, the stench, the swarming, the crawling, the gesticulations." This is a "Manichaean" world: one race is human, the other is not. The colonizer's vision determines how the colonized will be treated and acts as an ideology justifying the use of force in the exploitation of the colonized. The consequence of the politics of race is the priority of race over class in the formation of the colonial social structure: "you are rich because you are white"; you are oppressed and exploited because you are not white (*WE*, pp. 39–42; *DT*, pp. 8–11).

The correlate of spatial coercion is temporal alienation. The col-

1. Ato Sekyi-Otu, "Frantz Fanon's Critique of the Colonial Experience," Ph.D. dissertation, University of Toronto, 1977, p. 178, and "Form and Metaphor in Fanon's Critique of Racial and Colonial Domination," in *Domination,* ed. Alkis Kontos (Toronto: University of Toronto Press, 1975), pp. 146–47.

onized are deprived of an active relation to history. According to Fanon, it "is the colonizer who has *made* and who *continues to make* the colonized" (*DT*, p. 6, Fanon's emphasis, my translation; see *WE*, p. 36). Colonialism is a total process that seeks to empty the brain of the colonized "of all form and content" (*WE*, p. 210; *DT*, p. 144). It distorts the cultural life of the colonized and reduces action to resentful reaction: either frantically acquire the culture of the occupier (the turncoat), or defensively formalize and stereotype precolonial tradition (the substantialist) (*WE*, pp. 236–37; *DT*, pp. 166–67). At the extreme, the colonized become "spectators crushed with their inessentiality"; the person becomes the "colonized 'thing'" (*la "chose" colonisée*).[2] "The colonizer makes history; his life is an epic, an Odyssey," argues Fanon. The colonized suffers history, forming an almost "inorganic background" to the activities of the colonizer (*DT*, pp. 17–18, my translation; see *WE*, p. 51). In *A Dying Colonialism*, Fanon describes a father who has experienced the brute power of colonialism and who has fatalistically resigned himself to a "universe of infinite waiting and resignation" (*DC*, p. 103; *SR*, p. 87). The colonized, Sekyi-Otu comments, emerge "not as agents, but as actors of enforced roles."[3]

The Manichaean and violent nature of colonial domination sets the stage for resistance and violent reaction on the part of the colonized as they attempt to take charge of time and reconquer lost space: "For the colonized," Fanon states, "life can only spring up again out of the rotting corpse of the colonizer" (*WE*, p. 93; *DT*, p. 51). If there is an epic of the colonizer, there is also an epic of the colonized: "the two systems directly confront each other: the epic of the colonized society, with its specific ways of existing, in the face of the colonialist hydra" (*DC*, p. 40; *SR*, p. 22). The colonized, far from succumbing, are ready and waiting. Underneath the roles into which they are forced, the colonized preserve a human identity and temporal being through the recollection of the past in terms of a vision of the future. Across the spatial domination of colonialism, temporal possibilities reveal themselves and erupt into lived history.

The absence of reciprocity between the colonizers and the col-

2. *DT*, p. 6 (my translation); see *WE*, pp. 36–37. For references to the colonized person as a "thing," see also *WE*, p. 51 (*DT*, p. 17); *AR*, p. 14 (*RA*, p. 20); Frantz Fanon and C. Geronimi, "L'Hospitalisation de jour en psychiatrie," *La Tunisie Médicale*, 37 (December 1959), 727 (*L'Information Psychiatrique*, 51 [December 1975], 1125).

3. Sekyi-Otu, "Fanon's Critique," p. 178.

onized manifests itself in mutual misunderstanding between the two groups. Fanon discusses this divide in some detail in his psychiatric writings. The Arab charged with a crime in colonial Algeria would not confess to colonial authorities. According to the Algerian School of Psychiatry this resistance was due to the Arab's congenital immorality. In contrast, Fanon argues in an article written with R. Lacaton that confession, under normal circumstances, is "the ransom" for the criminal's "reinsertion into the group." By refusing to confess in the colonial situation, the Algerian indicates his or her nonrecognition of the colonizer's authority.[4] Fanon and another colleague, Charles Geronimi, observed a similar pattern of nonrecognition in the response of Muslim women to the Thematic Apperception Test. Muslim women were unable to make any sense of the images, not because they lacked imagination, but because the marginalization of Muslim society had induced an obscuring of vision and a lack of interest in things European.[5]

Fanon's writings on medicine and politics are particularly useful for demonstrating the political implications of the reciprocal misunderstanding that exists between the colonizer and the colonized. In "The North African Syndrome," Fanon discusses the attitude of the French professionals to North Africans in France. The North African, French doctors say, arrives "enveloped in vagueness" and does not trust the doctor. The doctor cannot find a lesion and concludes that the patient is suffering from "the North African Syndrome": primitive in mentality, the patient only imagines that he or she is sick. The patient-doctor relationship is constituted by a political relationship in which one race dominates another (*AR*, pp. 4–13; *RA*, pp. 10–19).

A Dying Colonialism discusses medicine in similar terms. The patient is not a patient but one of the colonized; the doctor is not a professional but a colonizer. The patient is diffident and lacking in trust; the doctor is impatient and quick to condemn. Unable to make contact through questioning, the doctor examines the body only to

4. Frantz Fanon and R. Lacaton, "Conduites d'aveu en Afrique du Nord," *Congrès des Médecins aliénistes*, 53d session, Nice, September 5–11, 1955, p. 657 (*L'Information Psychiatrique*, 51 [December 1975], 1115; my translation). See also J. Postel and C. Razanjao, "La Vie et l'oeuvre psychiatrique de Frantz Fanon," *L'Information Psychiatrique*, 51 (December 1975), p. 1064.

5. Frantz Fanon and C. Geronimi, "Le T.A.T. chez les femmes musulmanes: Sociologie de la perception et de l'imagination," *Congrès des Médecins aliénistes*, 54th session, Bordeaux, August 30–September 4, 1956, p. 368.

find it equally impenetrable. The pain, the doctor concludes, is dif-
fuse, as in an animal. The doctor and the clinical staff quickly come
to the conclusion that they have to be veterinarians. When medicine is
prescribed, the patient refuses to follow the doctor's orders. Even the
Arab doctor is seen as someone on the side of the colonizer, like the
Arab police and colonial officials. "There is always an opposition of
exclusive worlds," Fanon concludes, "a contradictory interaction of
different techniques, a vehement confrontation of values" (*DC*, p.
131; *SR*, p. 119). The opposition is inherent in the Manichaeism of
the colonizer-colonized relation.

In the section of *The Wretched of the Earth* entitled "From the Criminal Impulsivity of the North African to the War of National Liberation," Fanon presents, in more detail, the colonial ideology of French
magistrates, policemen, journalists, and others.[6] The Algerian was
born a criminal. The universities taught that the Algerian was a savage killer who acted without a motive. Professor Porot and the Algerian School of Psychiatry elaborated this ideology in "scientific"
terms. North Africans were intensely aggressive and had a predatory
instinct. They could not be trusted, were insensible to shades of
meaning, could not reason logically, and were incapable of self-disci-
pline. North Africans lacked emotivity and curiosity, were credulous
and obstinate. Lacking true moral conscience and inner life, they rid
themselves herself of worries by attacking other people. The problem
was biological: North Africans were congenital impulsives. According to Porot, "the native of North Africa, whose superior and cortical
activities are only slightly developed, is a primitive creature whose
life, essentially vegetative and instinctive, is above all regulated by his
diencephalon." Racism is scientifically justified. The conclusion of
the Algerian school was similar to that of Dr. A. Carothers of the
World Health Organization: the African, every normal African, is a
"lobotomized European" (cited in *WE*, pp. 300–302; *DT*, pp. 221–
22).

In his analysis of the Algerian school, Fanon offers some very
important insights into the psychology of the colonized and the nature of their resistance to colonialism. "Scientific" theories conven-

6. The French chapter heading "De l'impulsivité criminelle du Nord-Africain à la
guerre de libération nationale" is translated by Farrington as "Criminal Impulses
Found in North Africans Which Have Their Origin in the National War of Liberation" (*DT*, p. 215; *WE*, p. 293).

iently legitimated the activities of the colonizer. The psychiatrist perceived and defined the mental existence of the colonized through the lens of the colonizer. There was a certain element of truth in the claims of the colonial psychiatrists, but the significance of this truth was totally misunderstood. That "laziness" and all the other dehumanizing stereotypes that go with the term might be the "conscious sabotage" of a system perceived to be illegitimate was not considered (*WE*, p. 294; *DT*, p. 216). Psychosomatic disorders such as muscular contraction, argues Fanon, are not proof of a primitive mentality but "the postural accompaniment to the reticence of the colonized"; they are proof of the patient's "refusal with regard to colonial authority" (*WE*, p. 291; *DT*, p. 212). Implosive violence is the result of the fact that a colony is like a "concentration camp": men kill for a bit of bread; they fight each other because of the repression they suffer under colonialism.[7]

Psychosomatic disorders and acts of violence directed against one's own relatives are individual ways of living a common sociogenetic disorder. The colonized are forced into a reactive posture. What is most significant about the phenomenon of reaction, however, is the resistance of the colonized as a group to their oppression. Fanon's study of colonialism reveals that resistance is fundamental to the way the colonized understand their world and act in it. It is resistance that characterizes the North African's attitude to the doctor. In *The Wretched of the Earth*, the problem of resistance is examined primarily in terms of the upsurge of violent opposition to the colonized. However, this rebellious violence is always latent in more subdued forms of opposition. It is present, Fanon argues, in the persistent, clandestine attachment to traditional culture, for through this action the colonized make manifest their "refusal to submit." According to Fanon, this "persistence in cultural forms which are condemned by colo-

---

7. *WE*, pp. 307–308; *DT*, pp. 226–27. See Fanon's discussion of spontaneous violence in *WE*, p. 54; *DT*, pp. 19–20. See also Bachir Ridouh, Lucette Jarosz, and Edouard Cadour, "Approche épidémiologique psychiatrique de la criminalité algérienne," *Revue Pratique de Psychologie de la Vie Sociale et d'Hygiène Mentale*, no. 3 (1969), for a study of postrevolutionary criminality in which the thesis of the Algerian school (Porot and his colleagues) is attacked. The authors question the effectiveness of totalitarian institutions (traditional hospitals and prisons of colonial Algeria) in treating criminality (p. 164) and emphasize the importance of social, political, and economic conditions in the resolution of these problems (p. 169).

nial society is already a manifestation of the nation" (*DT*, p. 167, my translation; see *WE*, p. 237). In one article, Fanon briefly refers to this process in the West Indian context: African religion in the Caribbean was a form of resistance; the creole language was a "means of expressing the West Indian consciousness" (*RA*, pp. 89–90, my translation; omitted in *AR*). (Recent scholarship on Caribbean culture has emphasized the phenomenon of resistance and its twin variables: rebellion and pragmatic resistance.)[8] The attachment to tradition may result in a defensive formalism at the manifest level. Underneath this inertia, however, there bubbles and sometimes erupts "a much more fundamental substance which itself is continually being renewed [*en plein renouvellement*]" (*WE*, p. 224; *DT*, p. 155).

The problem with the culture of resistance is that it tends to understand social experience in Manichaean terms; it also tends to become formalized. According to Fanon, forms of popular culture that emerge out of the people's immediate experiences, out of their resistance to colonialism, or that appeal to a nationalism lacking in social and historical consciousness, lead to a blind alley if they fail to address the problem of freedom in history in a decisive way. These forms will be laughed at by the colonizer or encouraged as exotic distractions. They do not touch the reality of colonized existence (*WE*, pp. 224–25, 236–37; *DT*, pp. 154–56, 166–67). They are based on a mythical understanding through which the people turn back into themselves.

Fanon describes the Manichaean conflict between the colonizer and

8. See, for example, Orlando Patterson, who analyzes the pragmatic resistance of the Quashee type and other forms of passive and active resistance (*The Sociology of Slavery: An Analysis of the Origins, Development, and Structure of Negro Slave Society in Jamaica* [London, 1967; rpt. Kingston, Jamaica: Sangster's Book Stores, 1973], pp. 174–81, 260–83). Sidney Mintz and Richard Price argue that, although the master's control imposed limits on the culture of the slaves, the slaves were able to create a new, creole culture that was separate from, and in opposition to, the master's culture (*An Anthropological Approach to the Afro-American Past: A Caribbean Perspective,* ISHI Occasional Papers in Social Change, no. 2 [Philadelphia: Institute for the Study of Human Issues, 1976], pp. 20, 24–26). Monica Schuler develops this analysis and emphasizes the role of religion in resisting slavery ("Afro-American Slave Culture," in *Roots and Branches: Current Directions in Slave Studies,* ed. Michael Craton, Historical Reflections, Directions, 1 [Toronto: Pergamon Press, 1979], pp. 121, 131, 135–37). In his commentary on Schuler's analysis, Edward Brathwaite emphasizes the "double—or complex—competence of the slave's culture": on the one hand is Tacky, the rebel; on the other, Quashee, the pragmatic resister (Craton, *Roots and Branches,* pp. 154–55).

the colonized using literary terms. Colonialism is an "absurd drama [*drame absurde*]."⁹ The drama of colonialism consists, on the one hand, of the "epic" of the colonizer (the subjugation of the colonized); and, on the other hand, of the "epic" of the colonized (surviving, resisting, and fighting against the system). Both the colonizer and the colonized are trapped in the colonial system and understand themselves in terms of mythical narrative. It is this fundamental dualism of two peoples, two races, two castes, that Fanon calls "the tragedy of the colonial situation" (*DC*, p. 40; *SR*, p. 22). Drama, for Fanon, is a form based on Greek tragedy. It consists of irreconcilable antinomies. The law of the colonizer is supreme and the colonized live their fate as "damned" creatures, even in resisting.¹⁰

The Nietzschean idea of resentment and the Kierkegaardian notion of the ethical help to elucidate Fanon's understanding of the colonial drama in its mythical dimension and may have influenced Fanon's formulation of the problem.¹¹ Referring to Nietzsche's *Will to Power*, Fanon distinguishes action from reaction, stating that "there is always resentment [*ressentiment*] in a *reaction*" (*BS*, p. 222; *PN*, p. 180). Nietzsche argues that slave ethics takes the form of resentment (rancor):

9. For Fanon's use of the term *drame* (drama) and related imagery in this strong sense, see *BS*, pp. 145, 150, 186, 197 (*PN*, pp. 36, 118, 122, 151, 159); *DC*, p. 125 (*SR*, p. 111); *AR*, pp. 6, 48 (*RA*, pp. 12, 47); *WE*, pp. 36–37 (*DT*, p. 6); "Altérations mentales, modifications charactérielles, troubles psychiques et déficit intellectuel dans l'hérédo-dégénération spino-cérébelleuse: A propos d'un cas de maladie de Friedreich avec délire de possession," Thèse de médecine, Lyons, 1951, p. 15. (All translations from this work are mine.)

10. For this sense of the word *tragédie* (tragedy), see *DC*, pp. 40, 121, 125–26 (*SR*, pp. 22, 107, 113–14); *AR*, pp. 99, 147–48 (*RA*, pp. 103, 149); *WE*, pp. 148, 239 (*DT*, pp. 95, 168). Charles Markmann translates *malheur* as "tragedy" in *BS*, pp. 10, 231 (*PN*, pp. 8, 188). Fanon does equate tragic action with revolutionary action when he describes the coming to consciousness of the Algerian woman as an "authentic birth" in which she "rises directly to the level of tragedy" (*DC*, p. 50; *SR*, p. 33).

11. Critics such as David Caute argue that Fanon's early work is "existentialist" in orientation without clarifying exactly what they mean. Fanon read Nietzsche, Kierkegaard, Jaspers, and Hegel at the *lycée* in 1946. Fanon's brother, Joby, and friend, Manville, both cited his admiration for Nietzsche. Peter Geismar argues that Fanon was deeply influenced by Nietzsche's emphasis on action rather than theory and suggests that Fanon was a superman in the Nietzschean sense. Gendzier's response to Geismar is that *Thus Spoke Zarathustra* is not about the triumph of action per se but about values and the quest for freedom. She herself leaves the issue of Fanon's relation to Nietzsche poorly defined. There has been no comment on Fanon's connection to Kierkegaard. See Caute, *Fanon* (London: Fontana-Collins, 1970), pp. 35–36; Peter Geismar, *Fanon* (New York: Dial Press, 1971), pp. 3–4, 11, 43, 51, 149–50; Irene L. Gendzier, *Frantz Fanon: A Critical Study* (London: Wildwood House, 1973), p. 13.

"Slave ethics . . . begins by saying *no* to an 'outsider,' an 'other,' a non-self, and that no is its creative act. This reversal of direction of the evaluating look, this invariable looking outward instead of inward, is a fundamental feature of rancor. Slave ethics requires for its inception a sphere different from and hostile to its own. Physiologically speaking, it requires an outside stimulus in order to act at all; all action is reaction."[12] The slave blames the other person or the oppressor for all suffering, makes him or her the symbol of evil and object of vengeance, and is rebellious. Revolt, however, remains reactive. The slave does not act on his or her own terms, but in opposition to the other's terms. Nietzsche argues that resentment indicates a failure to accept responsibility for one's own existence. If carried to the extreme, blaming the other person can lead to total passivity. So powerful are the oppressors and their system of oppression that it is impossible to resist. Nietzsche calls this the "pessimism of indignation": one assumes that one can do nothing because one is wretched, and one blames someone else for one's wretchedness.[13]

Nietzsche argues that the ascetic ("Christian") priest turns hatred of others, or hatred of the oppressor, into self-hatred, and slave rebellion into acquiescence. He cultivates a consciousness of guilt among his followers and teaches them to blame themselves for their suffering. Internalizing his teaching, they learn to hate animality, humanity, the senses, life, reason, everything that is part of themselves. Human experiences are characterized as evil and contrasted to the good of heavenly morality.[14] This self-hatred is another form of resentment, of slave ethics. In *The Will to Power*, Nietzsche indicates the ideological significance of asceticism: the ruling classes have upheld the cult of selflessness and the gospel of the lowly because it "suppresses feelings of rivalry, of *ressentiment*, of envy—the all too natural feelings of the underprivileged—it even deifies a life of slavery, subjection, poverty, sickness, and inferiority for them under the ideal of humility and obedience."[15]

At the manifest level Nietzsche appears himself to be resentful of

12. Friedrich Nietzsche, *The Genealogy of Morals* in *"The Birth of Tragedy" and the "Genealogy of Morals,"* trans. Francis Golffing (New York: Anchor-Doubleday, 1956), pp. 170–71.

13. Friedrich Nietzsche, *The Will to Power*, trans. Walter Kaufmann and R. J. Hollingdale, ed. Kaufmann (New York: Vintage–Random House, 1968), p. 400.

14. Nietzsche, *Genealogy*, pp. 264–63, 298–99.

15. Nietzsche, *Will to Power*, p. 201.

the slave. However, he separates himself absolutely from the priestly asceticism that perpetuates slavery. The criticism of both slave revolt and its moralistic (ascetic) transformation is not a justification of slavery or oppression but a call for liberation from the drama of resentment. It is the ascetic priest who justifies slavery.[16]

The struggle of the colonized, that is, of "the wretched of the earth," is the central theme in Fanon's work. To the extent that the colonized are caught in the Manichaean colonial drama, their struggle is based on slave ethics and demonstrates aspects of resentment. The colonized, Fanon states, see colonizers as "the others." They want to "wreck [*faire sauter*]" the colonial world, throw out the colonizer, take over his place. However, this resentment was originally that of the colonizer, who makes the colonized into the "quintessence of evil" (*WE*, pp. 40–41; *DT*, pp. 9–10). At best, the colonizer, like the ascetic priest, imposes his peculiar religious and ethical code on the colonized. The colonizer is joined by the junior priesthood culled from the ranks of the colonized elite. Having internalized the myth of the colonizer, they blame themselves and their people for their oppression. "What can I do but despair?" asks the male character in one play; "O heaven what a dread thing / being black" (quoted in *BS*, p. 215; *PN*, p. 174). Caught in the tragic drama of resentment, the elite too can explode. Fanon uses the example of Césaire's Rebel, a slave in *Et les chiens se taisaient*, to illustrate this drama of Manichaean resentment: "It was I, even I, and I told him so, the good slave, the faithful slave, the slave of slaves, and suddenly his eyes were like two cockroaches, frightened in the rainy season. . . . I struck, and the blood spurted; that is the only baptism that I remember today."[17] Tamed into colonial asceticism, the Rebel explodes when he sees that the master is going to make the slave's son into another obsequious being. Rather than freeing himself or his son, however, the Rebel's action is fated to bring about his own end.

Fanon's depiction of the tragedy of the colonial situation and its Manichaean ethics can also be linked to Kierkegaard. Ethics for Kierkegaard, as for Nietzsche, is a form of truncated morality that

16. Even Fredric Jameson's otherwise excellent discussion of *ressentiment* assimilates Nietzsche's position to that of the ruling class. See *The Political Unconscious: Narrative as a Socially Symbolic Act* (Ithaca: Cornell University Press, 1981), pp. 201–203.

17. Aimé Césaire, *Et les chiens se taisaient,* in *Les Armes miraculeuses* (Paris: Gallimard, 1970), p. 107; quoted in *WE*, p. 88 (*DT*, p. 47).

enslaves itself to a particular concept of the good. Kierkegaard distinguishes three platforms of existence: the aesthetic, the ethical, and the religious (that is, the existential or historical). The aesthetic platform is characterized by the self-interested individual who is concerned only with finite, worldly experience, entertainment, amusement, and gratification. More important for the study of Fanon are the ethical and historical positions. The ethicist is the person who resigns him or herself to the law and demands of a "higher" moral order and who identifies his or her particular concerns with those of that order.

Whereas Nietzsche finds in Dionysian tragedy a way out of slave ethics, Kierkegaard uses Greek tragedy in general to establish a paradigm of the ethical. According to Johannes de Silentio, Kierkegaard's pseudonymous author of *Fear and Trembling*, tragic drama is structured in terms of a conflict between the universal law binding the individual to the community and the particular laws binding him or her to a family or to personal concerns. Agamemnon is the noble hero who submits to the demands of the gods so that his mission will prosper: his daughter must be sacrificed for the welfare of the community. The tragic hero renounces all personal aspirations and identifies with the laws of a predestined social order.[18] The vengeance and rancor that Nietzsche identifies as resentment is sublimated in Greek tragedy, only to return in the form of the demands of the gods, or of the law. The law finds a scapegoat, or tragic victim, who bears the guilt of the community. The social world is dualistically divided into good and bad, with the bad always rearing its head; it is everyone's ultimate duty to seek endlessly to eliminate it. There is no way out of the Sisyphean dilemma.

Kierkegaard's ethical is directly and indirectly discussed in Fanon's work. Fanon says of the black person who is driven to deny that which is black that he or she has "an ethical position in the world [*une attitude éthique dans la vie*]" (*BS*, p. 214; *PN*, p. 173). By declaring that white is good and black is evil, the white person establishes a relation between ethics and skin color. The black person who faces this dualistic moral consciousness confronts an either–or situation: "Either I ask others to pay no attention to my skin, or else I want them to be aware of it." By means of an "ethical transit [*un glissement éthique*]," Fanon

18. Søren Kierkegaard, *Fear and Trembling*, in *"Fear and Trembling" and "The Sickness unto Death,"* trans. Walter Lowrie (Princeton: Princeton University Press, 1968), pp. 86, 68–69.

says, I may believe that I am white because I act morally regardless of my pigmentation. Or I may recognize that I am black and then try to give moral value to that which is black. In either case, I accept the oppressor's dualistic and mythical conception of morality and its relation to skin color (*BS*, pp. 192–94, 197; *PN*, pp. 155–56, 160).

Fanon captures Kierkegaard's notion of the tragic hero in a tragic drama in his depiction of two different social types. The first is the colonized who tries to wear the white mask, but fails; the second is the colonized who tries to wear the black mask, but likewise fails. *Black Skin, White Masks* focuses on the first type of masquerader. Fanon takes the first-person narrator of Mayotte Capécia's *Je suis Martiniquaise* as a paradigm of black alienation: "Mayotte loves a white man to whom she submits in everything. He is her lord. She asks nothing, demands nothing, except a bit of whiteness in her life. When she tries to determine in her own mind whether the man is handsome or ugly, she writes, 'All I know is that he had blue eyes, blond hair, and a light skin, and that I loved him.'"[19] Faced with the conflict between herself (her background, her black skin) and the demands of the white world, the narrator denies herself and tries to attain all that is white. Civilization is associated with white pigmentation and with the life-style of the wealthy whites in their mansions above the city. The narrator internalizes this myth and makes these finite attributes the source of an ethical orientation. This type of relationship is necessarily unsuccessful. Her dream of being white conflicts with the fact of her blackness. However, there is compensation in the fact that her grandmother was white. Like the tragic hero, she is willing to undergo perpetual unhappiness in order to adhere to the ethical norm. "I also accepted the fact that I was barred from this society because I was a woman of color; but I could not help being jealous" (quoted in *BS*, p. 43; *PN*, p. 35). The "lover" makes the "beloved" pregnant and then abandons her. Infinitely resigned, she accepts. "Today I believe in the possibility of love," comments Fanon, "that is why I endeavour to trace its imperfections, its perversions" (*BS*, p. 42; *PN*, p. 43).

Capécia (as first-person narrator) is an example of the colonized, male or female, who has internalized the myth of the colonizer. The tragic hero of the oppressed establishes and follows an ethical hier-

19. *BS*, p. 42; *PN*, p. 34. Fanon confuses Capécia as first-person narrator in the text with Capécia as author of *Je suis Martiniquaise* (Paris: Corréa, 1948), thus losing the ironical distance that Capécia as author uses to critique her character.

archy based on color. Anyone whiter than oneself is respected; anyone blacker is rejected. The African is further away from the light than the West Indian; the person from Guadeloupe is more "savage" than the person from Martinique (*AR*, pp. 20–21; *RA*, pp. 25–26). The myth is engendered by the colonizer, but it begins to affect the colonized. It is the urban intermediary classes that it primarily dominates, though it penetrates down the social structure.

The second main type of tragic hero in Fanon's work is the colonized who lives "the great black mirage" (*AR*, p. 27; *RA*, p. 31). Fanon states in "West Indians and Africans" that Martinicans confronted by the racism of French soldiers during the Second World War, and by the weakness of white France during the occupation, began to discover their blackness. With the death of the white "father," the West Indian turned to the black "mother," "eager to rediscover the source, to suckle at the authentic breasts of the African earth." Whereas Capécia's narrator despaired because she was not sufficiently white, the West Indian now said to the African, "Don't pay attention to my white skin, my soul is as black as yours, and that is what matters" (*AR*, p. 25; *RA*, p. 29). But the African rejected this deserter and betrayer, this impure and mixed offspring. Resentful of the colonizer, the West Indian made "black" culture into the ethical norm to which he or she subjected his or her particular existence in a form of ascetic renunciation. However, the ethical was incommensurable with the real and the West Indian suffered despair: haunted by impurity, imperfection, and guilt, he or she lived "the tragedy [*le drame*] of being neither white nor Negro" (*AR*, p. 26; *RA*, p. 30).

The Wretched of the Earth extends the analysis of these two types of West Indian tragic heroes to the colonized bourgeoisie in general. Fanon states that colonized intellectual, political, and commercial elites are permeated by the colonizer's way of thinking (*WE*, pp. 44–45, 59–60; *DT*, pp. 12–13, 24). Like the Martinican after the death of the "father," the colonized intellectual may begin to reject European values and immerse him or herself in the culture and life of the people. A racialized African culture is placed in opposition to European values in a desperate attempt to return to this "barbarous people [*peuple barbare*]." The intellectual, however, catches on only to the "outer garments" of the people and arrives at exoticism and exhibitionism. Instead of grasping his or her own history and the history of the community, he or she arrives at "a blind alley" (*WE*, pp. 214–24; *DT*, pp. 147–54).

The ethical and tragic conflict that is suffered by the dependent bourgeoisie is experienced by the colonized peasantry, lumpen proletariat, and proletariat as well, though in a different way. The colonizer's culture and his or her language, in particular, is the medium through which European values and life-style can be presented as the norm and the good, and in relation to which the colonized begin to define themselves. Still, the majority of the colonized, unlike the colonized bourgeoisie, are able to maintain a certain distance from these norms by resisting them and recreating traditional cultural patterns. The problem is that the tragedy of the colonial system remains. One has to define oneself in terms of one's opposition to the colonial system. One is a tragic hero caught in a perpetual struggle to maintain one's community in reaction to the onslaught of the colonizer.

As many critics have pointed out, Fanon draws from the Hegelian-Marxist tradition to analyze the struggle of the colonized in its social and political dimensions.[20] However, he reinterprets the tradition in terms of the concrete specificity of the colonial situation. Both the master-slave (bondsman) relation and the colonial drama are based on a primary conflict. Conflict ceases when one protagonist submits to the other and becomes a slave. By recognizing the master as master and serving him in fear, the Hegelian slave moves from selfish immediacy to one-sided universality. Through his labor, he enters into a one-sided relationship with his master and provides for their common wants (as defined by the master).[21] As in the case of Nietzsche's slave and Kierkegaard's tragic hero, the Hegelian slave submits to a "higher" tyrannical law. In Fanon's model, contact with Europeans at the commencement of colonization results in conflict. The non-European protagonist is forced to submit to the superior military force of the European, thus becoming the colonized. The colonized experience their own mortality in relation to the master's power over them. As in the relation between the Hegelian slave and master, there comes into existence here a one-sided and merely implicit universality. The temporal process of the struggle in the colonial situation takes on, in addition, a spatial dimension: two reciprocally exclusive zones are established.

20. See, for example, Gendzier, *Frantz Fanon*, pp. 23–27, and Renate Zahar, *Frantz Fanon: Colonialism and Alienation*, trans., Willfried F. Fenser (New York: Monthly Review, 1974), pp. 15–16, 78–92.

21. G. W. F. Hegel, *Philosophy of Mind*, trans. A. V. Miller and William Wallace, part 3 of *Encyclopaedia of the Philosophical Sciences* (Oxford: Oxford University Press, 1971), p. 174, and *Phenomenology of Spirit*, trans. A. V. Miller (Oxford: Oxford University Press, 1977), pp. 115–16.

This new relationship of subordination is inherently unstable, however, because a primal interest in freedom constantly reasserts itself in the willingness of the slave to accept the risk of death in challenging the master. Temporal activity constantly calls into question spatial exclusivity. The initial struggle for recognition resurfaces in violent confrontation throughout the colonial period. Even where the colonized have suffered setbacks and have been forced once again into the colonial mold, they still maintain a posture of resistance: the understanding of the finite nature of the oppressor's power is evident in their thought and action. Fanon makes this point emphatically, as early as *Black Skin, White Masks*: "For the Negro who works on a sugar plantation in Le Robert, there is only one solution: to fight [*la lutte*]. He will embark on this struggle [*lutte*], and he will pursue it, not as a result of a Marxist or idealistic analysis, but quite simply because he cannot conceive of life otherwise than in the form of a battle [*un combat*] against exploitation, misery, and hunger" (*BS*, p. 224; *PN*, pp. 181–82). Fanon likewise notes that the black American has for centuries struggled against oppression (*BS*, p. 221; *PN*, p. 179). This is the "spontaneous" and reactive violence that erupts in the first two chapters of *The Wretched of the Earth*. It is an expression of the primal struggle for recognition in the context of the colonial drama.

According to Fanon, decolonization begins with the unleashing of this Manichean violence. The colonized demand a "tabula rasa": "the replacing of a certain 'species' of men by another 'species' of men, . . . [in] a total, complete, and absolute substitution" (*WE*, p. 35; *DT*, p. 5). In an oblique reference to Hegel, Fanon states: "The naked truth of decolonization evokes for us the searing bullets and bloodstained knives which emanate from it. For if the last shall be first, this will only come to pass after a murderous and decisive struggle [*affrontement*] between the two protagonists" (*WE*, p. 37; *DT*, p. 6). Hegel's notion of primal immediacy and struggle is excessively Hobbesian and somewhat solipsistic. The slave is not presented in terms of his social relationships with other slaves. Marx and Fanon would deal with the specificity of class and race and with their relationship to the social totality as it is concretely lived, but they would also keep the basic dynamic of the master-slave struggle (slave as proletariat, colonized).

At the level of the social constituents of the colonial totality, Fanon's analysis of the drama of colonialism can be examined in terms of its relation to the Marxist tradition and to the Marxist works of Jean-

Paul Sartre in particular. According to the Marxist tradition, the primary social contradiction within the capitalist mode of production consists of the struggle between the workers, or proletariat, and the capitalist class, or bourgeoisie, who control the forces of production. One's socioeconomic status determines one's role and consciousness within the social totality. In his analysis of the colonial totality, Fanon amends the causal relations in accordance with the specificity of the colonial situation: the racially based colonizer-colonized relation. It is not one's economic status that determines one's role in the colonial totality but one's racial status; your economic situation is mainly determined by your race. "In the colonies," Fanon states, "the economic substructure is also a superstructure" (*WE*, p. 40; *DT*, p. 9). Colonialism violently disrupts the endogenous socioeconomic structure of the colonized society. Class relations among the colonized are transformed and subordinated to caste relations between colonizer and colonized by virtue of the political fact of domination and the ideology of racism, which justifies and sustains that domination. As Sekyi-Otu argues: "The primary contradiction in this socio-historical experience, the dichotomy between colonizers and colonized, is the primal cause of deformities in the social structure of the colonized world; for this contradiction expresses a logic of social hierarchy which is not a direct function of the internal, organic development of the means and relations of production."[22]

Fanon's analysis of the colonial situation is similar in some respects to that of Sartre, who was greatly influenced by the Algerian Revolution and, possibly, by Fanon himself.[23] According to Sartre, industrial capitalism is a form of simple exploitation in which contractual relations hide the underlying *praxis* of oppression. (This emphasis on the *praxis* of oppression distinguishes Sartre's work from more orthodox Marxist positions.) What is different about the colonial situation, according to Sartre, is that colonialism is built on violence and justified in terms of the racial inequality of human beings. Colonialism is a form of "super-exploitation" rather than "simple exploitation" because it obtains a surplus product through forced labor.[24]

22. Sekyi-Otu, "Fanon's Critique," pp. 308–309; see also pp. 195, 211.

23. Simone de Beauvoir, *Force of Circumstance,* trans. Richard Howard (New York: Putnam's Sons, 1965), pp. 591–98.

24. Jean-Paul Sartre, *Critique of Dialectical Reason,* trans. Alan Sheridan-Smith (London: New Left Books, 1976), pp. 726, 740.

In addition to the primary racial contradiction between the colonizer and the colonized, there arise class contradictions between the colonized themselves. These secondary contradictions are derivatives of the primary contradiction. Fanon argues that the "bourgeoisie" of colonial society is a dependent bourgeoisie, fundamentally unlike its European counterpart. In the colonial period, the bourgeoisie consists of a small Westernized administrative, merchant, and intellectual class that is dependent on the colonial system. It may agitate for independence and begin to name the nation when it sees in independence a way of gaining more power for itself. However, it does not challenge the external control of the economy by the colonial power. Fanon emphasizes that this national bourgeoisie differs from the European bourgeoisie because of its fundamental inability to accumulate capital. Even where political independence is achieved, the national bourgeoisie is involved in intermediary activities within the context of neocolonial exploitation: the liberal professions, small business, agriculture. It is unable to take over financial and industrial control of the economy. It maintains itself as a "transmission line" between the nation and capitalism, content to be the agents of multinational companies. Lacking the pioneer, inventive, and productive aspects of the Western bourgeoisie under early capitalism, it is "unable to constitute itself as a class" through control of the economy; it has to resort to military dictatorship, ethnic chauvinism, and racism.[25]

Like the Hegelian slave after the initial defeat, this class may reject the path of struggle and submit to the truth of the master as master. The colonial bourgeoisie, Fanon says in *The Wretched of the Earth*, are "slaves set free" (p. 67; *DT*, p. 30). His overly general comment in *Black Skin, White Masks* is primarily applicable to this class: "Historically, the Negro steeped in the inessentiality of servitude was set free by his master. He did not fight for his freedom [*Il n'a pas soutenu la lutte pour la liberté*]." It is the master's money, language, and expertise that directs the "freed" slave. There is no demand for mutual recognition and reciprocity (*BS*, pp. 219–21; *PN*, pp. 178–79).

Fanon argues that just as the colonized bourgeoisie lacks the revo-

25. *WE*, pp. 149–53 (*DT*, pp. 96–99). Farrington translates "incapable de se constituer en classe" (*DT*, p. 110) as "incapable of learning its lesson" (*WE*, p. 167), and "ne pouvant mettre à jour des relations sociales cohérentes, fondées sur le principe de sa domination en tant que classe" (*DT*, p. 108) as "unable to bring out the existence of coherent social relations, and standing on the principle of its domination as a class" (*WE*, p. 164). See Sekyi-Otu, "Fanon's Critique," pp. 67, 331, and 481.

lutionary potential of the early European bourgeoisie, the proletariat of colonized countries lacks the revolutionary power that Marx attributed to the proletariat in capitalist society. The colonized proletariat cannot be the primary agent of social transformation because it is not linked to productive forces that are transforming the structure of society and eliminating scarcity. Nor does the condition of the proletariat represent the universal condition of the society. Unlike in capitalist countries, Fanon argues, the proletariat of underdeveloped countries is generally in a comparatively privileged position; it "is the nucleus of the colonized population which has been most pampered by the colonial regime." Fanon defines the proletariat as those workers living mainly in urban areas who make the colonial regime run smoothly whether or not they are directly involved in the process of production (tram conductors, taxi drivers, miners, dockers, interpreters, nurses, and so forth). By virtue of their comparative privilege these workers are "bourgeois" and "individualistic" (*WE*, pp. 108–11; *DT*, pp. 64–66).

Whereas, in contrast, the European peasantry is considered by classical Marxist theory to be an individualistic and unrevolutionary force, Fanon finds in the colonial rural class a traditionalism, discipline, and altruism that constantly resists European domination and cultural impositions. Members of this class are suspicious of the traitors who accommodate the colonial system. It is the colonized peasantry, Fanon argues, who spontaneously join the armed struggle. It is they, rather than the proletariat, who become agents of social change. The rural struggle has as its urban spearhead all the dispossessed rural people who have moved to the slums of the city and who have not succeeded in deriving privileges from the colonial system. Being the wretched of the wretched, this lumpen proletariat has nothing to lose. According to Fanon, "that horde of starving men, uprooted from their tribe and from their clan, constitutes one of the most spontaneous and the most radically revolutionary forces of a colonized people." Like "rats," "decay," and "gangrene" in relation to the colonial system, these "idlers" will throw themselves into the struggle and through it, rehabilitate themselves (*WE*, pp. 129–30; *DT*, pp. 80–81).

Sartre has provided a model of sociopolitical struggle that helps put into perspective Fanon's analysis of the tragic drama of colonial struggle and conflict. Fanon describes the new nation in its formative period in apocalyptic terms that parallel Sartre's description of the group. According to Fanon, the nation first exists among the colonized peasantry in the form of a spontaneous collective ecstasy in which old quarrels are liquidated and the colonized are unified by their opposition to the colonizer. The center of the nation is the local group that is bound together in an armed struggle by a "mystical body of belief." The local group finds that its interests are the same as those of other local groups. Former rival groups pledge to help each other in the violent overthrow of the colonizer, and solidarity grows (*WE*, pp. 132–33; *DT*, p. 82). Urban radicals and the urban lumpen proletariat join the group and expand its common center.

In Sartre's *Critique of Dialectical Reason* the "fused group" is the social unit that forms in response to a perceived common danger: everyone transcends his or her individuality to become "an individual incarnation of the common person." The group is based on a mutual and reciprocal recognition of the others as the same as oneself: all are unified in opposition to another person or group. The other acts upon us as a single totality; we recognize this common unity and respond. No longer antagonistic individuals in a binary relation to each other (the "series"), we find ourselves unified by a ternary relation of reciprocity. Just before the Bastille was stormed, states Sartre, "everyone, as a *third party*, became incapable of distinguishing his own safety from that of the Others." Sartre defines the third party as the "interindividual reality," "the human mediator through which the multiplicity of epicentres and ends (identical and separate) organizes itself *directly*, as determined by a synthetic objective."[26] In Fanon's work, the formation of the group as nation in opposition to the colonizer is an example of the fused group and the reciprocity of the ternary relation.

The nation in formation exists as a reaction to the colonial system, or, in Hegel's terms, as the resurgence of the primal life and death struggle. Fanon argues that the formative nation is in danger of being defeated by the colonizer if practical realism does not take over. When armed and unarmed men, women, and children descend upon the colonizer's space, they are mowed down by machine guns. To overcome the danger of dispersal, individuals in the fused group must firmly pledge their unity. They may be required to seal the pledge by committing an irrevocable act against the colonizer (*WE*, p. 85; *DT*, p. 44). But the group must also organize itself into an army trained in

26. Sartre, *Critique*, pp. 357, 367–68.

the tactics of guerrilla warfare. It does this through the delegation of authority to leaders who plan an overall strategy and direct activity into specialized channels (*WE*, pp. 135–36; *DT*, p. 85).

Sartre's *Critique of Dialectical Reason* sketches in some detail the intelligibility of this movement from fused group to organization. In order to preserve itself from the possibility of disintegration, the statute or pledge is introduced into the group. By swearing his or her allegiance, each individual agrees to recognize the common individual (third) as limit to his or her own freedom. On the basis of the pledge, the group is able to transform itself into an organization. Like Durkheim's organic society, the organization is a structure that reintroduces individual differentiation into the group so that specialized functions can be carried out that realize details of the common praxis: "the individual transcends his common being in order to realise it." Leadership (organizing) is one such function. The group authorizes an individual or individuals to assume the function of regulatory third parties acting in accordance with the ternary relation and pledge of the group. The group gives itself orders through this regulatory third party.[27]

There always exists the danger that the regulatory third party will cease to represent the group and will begin to assert dictatorial control. Fanon sees this as a very real danger that the struggling nation must face. The leader, who may have embodied the aspirations of the people during the struggle for liberation, may reveal, at the onset of independence, his real purpose: "to become the general president of that company of profiteers impatient for their returns which constitutes the national bourgeoisie" (*WE*, p. 166; *DT*, p. 109). During the struggle for independence, the leader was the representative of a living party. The party was a national organization founded on popular participation and oriented toward the needs of the people. The problem is that the leadership of the party, to the extent that it is or has become a dependent national bourgeoisie, may lead the nation in the direction of neocolonialism. After independence, the party can turn into a mere "administration." Instructions are delivered from the summit, and democratic processes are abandoned (*WE*, p. 171; *DT*, p. 112). The party's new task is to mystify and coerce the people; its members become informers for the regime. It may organize a national-socialist or ethnic dictatorship. The army and police are the pillars

27. Sartre, *Critique*, pp. 461, 522–23.

of the regime; advised by foreign experts, they pin the people down, "immobilizing and terrorizing them" (*WE*, p. 174; *DT*, p. 115). Eventually, the army itself may take control of the regime and, with the help of the national bourgeoisie, run the country in the interest of the former colonial power.

The intelligibility of this type of transformation is presented by Sartre as a movement from the organization to the "institution." Because the group or its derivative, the organization, does not have an ontological status, there always remains the threat that it will disintegrate into its constituent individual elements. "There is a sort of internal vacuum, an unbridgeable and indeterminate distance, a sort of malaise in every community, large or small; and this uneasiness occasions a strengthening of the practices of integration, and increases with the integration of the group." The group attempts to preserve itself by institutionalizing sovereignty and prohibiting individuals from seceding: "fraternity has to be imposed by violence" and the consequence is "terror." The institution is the group in which the individual is no longer essential; one is defined simply in terms of one's function in the institution. Freedom appears as the "slave of necessity." Whereas in the group all members are the same and hence sovereign, in the institution "there is a common individual who, as a member of the group, is *other than all* because he cannot become a *regulated third party*"; only he or she is sovereign. Sartre argues that the institution as a totality exists in a sovereign relation to other members of the society. The state becomes the arm of the sovereign, and the "series" or nongrouped individuals in the society can be exploited.[28] The master-slave relationship is then reestablished, though in a new form. Fanon's national bourgeois dictatorship is one such state.

Fanon's analysis of colonial conflict is presented in terms of a war of national liberation against a colonial power. Fanon was familiar with colonial domination both in his Martinican homeland and in his adopted Algeria. As his model of the national bourgeois dictatorship indicates, however, many former European colonies, especially those in Latin America, had already won or been given formal independence from Europe. A national bourgeoisie, sometimes composed largely of European settlers, the colonizers, was in control, the economy was tied to the European and American economies, and the majority of the people remained powerless and exploited. This neo-

28. Sartre, *Critique*, pp. 583, 595–96, 606, 615, 636–38.

colonial mode of domination was, like the colonial mode, based on violence. The army ensured that the hostility of the people would be kept under control. However, Fanon saw this neocolonial situation as being essentially unstable. He states that under these circumstances the "moment for a fresh national crisis is not far off" (*WE*, p. 186; *DT*, p. 124). The implication is that the neocolonial regime, too, would have to be transformed through violent struggle. The intelligibility of this new level of struggle can be understood in terms of Sartre's notion of the ongoing conflict between the group and the institution.

In Sartre's analysis, the members of the series, confronted by the violence of the new ruling institutional group, may begin to recognize each other as the same. They regroup in opposition to an external danger thus potentially initiating the cycle from series to group and institution back to series. At the abstract level at which *Critique of Dialectical Reason* is written, there appears to be a necessary circularity inherent in the genesis and disintegration of the group. For Sartre this is only a formal necessity, however. Given the concrete contingencies of groups and series interacting under particular historical conditions of scarcity, there can be movement in any direction. The group need not develop into an institution or even an organization, and the institution may develop without going through these formal stages.[29]

Though Fanon's analysis of the colonizer-colonized relationship and the derivative class formations is based primarily on the experience of French colonialism in Algeria, it is of relevance to other Third World situations such as that in the Caribbean. The development of Caribbean plantation societies was tied to the expanding world economy. Plantation society, however, is essentially a colonial society based on the violence that was required to transform a racially distinct group into slave labor. In response to colonial violence, violent struggles erupted both in the form of slave revolts and in the form of rebellions in the postemancipation era. The most successful of these, the Haitian Revolution, occurred at the end of the eighteenth century. It was an emancipation movement that developed into a war of independence, but it only inaugurated what would become a new mulatto and black dominated neocolonial society. Emancipation came to the other countries, as Fanon puts it, "from without," through the actions of the master; the slave was acted on even in his or her struggle

29. Sartre, *Critique,* p. 676.

for freedom (*BS*, p. 220; *PN*, p. 178). Opposite to Haiti in terms of national development were the French (and Dutch) colonies that were eventually incorporated as junior partners in the metropolitan political system. However, citizens were still discriminated against on the basis of skin color, and the former colonies remained economically dependent and underdeveloped.

During the slave period, some slaves throughout the Caribbean, particularly those of mixed racial background, the mulattos, were given their freedom and gradually improved their social status. After emancipation, and throughout the nineteenth century, a middle class of mulattos and some blacks gradually acquired administrative positions on plantations and in government or became merchant intermediaries working for European and American capitalism. This middle class was essentially a dependent national bourgeoisie in Fanon's sense. On plantations, slaves became paid workers, that is, a rural proletariat still tied to the land and unlike the European industrial proletariat. Other blacks who were able to leave the plantations "reconstituted" themselves as a peasantry with small landholdings, still largely dependent on the plantation system for jobs, markets, and supplies.[30] The reconstituted peasantry along with the rural proletariat were caught in a lingering colonial plantation system based on racial domination. The violence of racial domination is the common colonial factor in the experience of both the Algerian peasant and the Caribbean black. East Indians, brought into the Caribbean as indentured laborers to replace blacks in some areas, likewise found themselves bound in the colonial relationship.

With the increasing penetration of capitalism in the twentieth century, many rural inhabitants entered the cities in search of jobs and joined the ranks of the ghetto lumpen proletariat. An urban proletariat began to develop, but, as in Fanon's analysis of the dependent Algerian proletariat, it was not tied to an indigenous industrial base like the European proletariat. In the British colonies in the Caribbean, labor unrest preceded the gift of independence, and urban labor leaders became politicians and rose into the ranks of the dependent bourgeoisie. The people were left to be exploited by foreign capitalism and its agents, the intermediary bourgeoisie. Using Fanon's work, A.

---

30. Sidney Mintz discusses the reconstituted peasantry and rural proletariat in several works, including "The Caribbean Region," in *Slavery, Colonialism, and Racism,* ed. Sidney Mintz (New York: Norton, 1974), pp. 61–62.

W. Singham has analyzed the authoritarian tendencies of this type of leadership in the Caribbean and the violent hostility with which oppressed sectors confronted it.[31]

The task of liberation is to break out of this circularity. To the extent that the actions of the colonized are reactive, to the degree that the tragic nature of slave ethics cannot be abandoned, the master-slave relation remains the fundamental model of the sociopolitical world. Fanon, like the theorists before him, argues that this situation can and must be transformed. Mythical narrative is the mode of the symbolic that sustains reactive ethics and tragic circularity. Liberating narrative, in contrast, issues the challenge of transformation.

Decolonization, Fanon writes, is the process whereby "spectators crushed with their inessentiality" are transformed into "privileged actors, with the grandiose glare of history's floodlights upon them" (*WE*, p. 36; *DT*, p. 6). The colonized rise above the Manichaean conception of the world as a tragic drama to assume a historical conception of the world as infinite possibility. They recognize human agency and responsibility in an open and unknowable history. Fanon's notion of the entry into history must be understood, not in Manichaean terms, but in terms of the stepping out of drama (mythical, tragic understanding) and the assumption of historical, national, and human responsibility.[32] He states that the colonized "thing" "becomes man during the same process by which it frees itself" (*WE*, pp. 36–37; *DT*, p. 6). The struggle of the colonized acquires a new kind of epic significance.[33] This does *not* mean that the colonized were not human beings, did not create a unique culture and history, or lacked epic significance. It means, rather, that people arrive at an understanding of the sociopolitical totality and their significance in its transformation. They understand the imperative of mutual recognition in particular historical circumstances. This consciousness manifests itself in what Sekyi-Otu calls a "cosmogonic" leap, inaugurating willed, authentic decolonization.[34] Lived history is radically

31. A. W. Singham, *The Hero and the Crowd in a Colonial Polity* (New Haven: Yale University Press, 1968), pp. 81–83.

32. See *DC*, pp. 31, 107 (*SR*, pp. 14, 92); *AR*, p. 84 (*RA*, p. 79); *WE*, pp. 69, 147, 200, 247, 315–16 (*DT*, pp. 32, 94, 135, 175, 232–33).

33. See *DC*, pp. 84–88 (*SR*, pp. 68–72); *AR*, pp. 109, 150 (*RA*, pp. 113, 152); *WE*, p. 241 (*DT*, p. 169).

34. Sekyi-Otu, "Fanon's Critique," p. 414.

transformed into liberating history. In this new beginning, the culture of survival and resistance of the colonial period does not disappear. It is transformed in a process that gives it a new, open, and liberating significance.

Just as Fanon's conception of a reactive drama of resentment can be linked to the work of Nietzsche and Kierkegaard, so too can the idea of a leap to history. In *Black Skin, White Masks*, Fanon makes two closely related references to Nietzsche. In his introduction, he states: "Man's tragedy [*malheur*], Nietzsche said, is that he was once a child. None the less, we cannot afford to forget that, as Charles Odier has shown us, the neurotic's fate remains in his own hands" (*BS*, p. 10; *PN*, p. 8). In his conclusion, Fanon repeats this thought:

> At the beginning of his life a man is always clotted, he is drowned in contingency. The tragedy [*malheur*] of man is that he was once a child.
> It is through the effort to recapture the self and to scrutinize the self [*de reprise sur soi et de dépouillement*], it is through the lasting tension of their freedom that men will be able to create the ideal conditions of existence for a human world. (*BS*, p. 231; *PN*, pp. 187–88)

Elsewhere in *Black Skin, White Masks* Fanon refers to Nietzsche's critique of resentment and then continues: "To educate man to be *actional*, preserving in all his relations [*circularité*] his respect for the basic values that constitute a human world, is the prime task of him who, having taken thought, prepares to act" (*BS*, p. 222; *PN*, p. 180). In these comments Fanon insists on a movement beyond reactive slave ethics and distinguishes his position from any form of vulgar existentialism that sees human experience as terrifying and tragic abandonment to the vicissitudes of irrationality, violence, and death.

To take fate into one's hands is not just the task of the child or the neurotic; all must participate in making a new order out of disorder. The apparently individual task of becoming a creator is very much a social act. Chance is transformed into meaning by creating a world that is shared. Zarathustra, who is distinguishable from the "ascetic priest" by his commitment to life, entreats his followers:

> May your bestowing love and your knowledge serve towards the meaning of the earth! . . .
> We are still fighting step by step with the giant Chance, and hitherto the senseless, the meaningless, has still ruled over mankind.

> May your spirit and your virtue serve the meaning of the earth, my
> brothers: and may the value of all things be fixed anew by you. To that
> end you should be fighters! To that end you should be creators.[35]

The challenge is to become, like Zarathustra, a lover, a bestower of
virtue, who challenges others to encounter their own freedom and
partake of the creation of meaning. Zarathustra foresees a time when
the superman will live and a "house of healing" will be created on
earth.[36] Fanon dedicated his whole life, both in his medical and in his
political career, to the creation of this house of healing.

Fanon recognized that the Nietzschean leap from reactive drama to
history is not a romantic or abstract closure of lived contradictions.
At the beginning of his medical thesis is a dedication quoting Zarathustra: "I speak only of *lived* affairs and do not portray cerebral
mechanisms."[37] The quotation is striking, for it comes at the beginning of a medical thesis on an apparently neurological disorder. Like
Zarathustra, Fanon is concerned with living people in their concrete
existence rather than with scientific abstractions. The thesis focuses
on the social dimension of psychic disorder while recognizing the
totality of human existence as both biological and social. The work
therefore parallels the Nietzschean critique of dualism. A human
being cannot separate him or herself from his or her bodily needs and
desires through abandoning him or herself to "superterrestrial
hopes." Yet he or she is more than mere animal and transcends the
biological: "Man is a rope, fastened between animal and Superman—
a rope over an abyss," says Zarathustra.[38] "Man always exists in the
process of doing," states Fanon in his thesis.[39] The irrational is ever
present in the rational, error is the condition for knowledge. "Misfortune" carries with it the possibility of greatness: "The child," states
Zarathustra, "is innocence and forgetfulness, a new beginning, a spo-
rt, a self-propelling wheel, a first motion, a sacred Yes."[40] It is the
child in the adult that preserves creativity and regenerates humanity.

Nietzsche distinguishes noble, aristocratic behavior from the slave

---

35. Friedrich Nietzsche, *Thus Spoke Zarathustra: A Book for Everyone and No One*,
trans. R. J. Hollingdale (Harmondsworth: Penguin, 1969), p. 102.
36. Nietzsche, *Zarathustra*, p. 103.
37. Fanon, "Altérations mentales" [p. vii].
38. Nietzsche, *Zarathustra*, pp. 42–43.
39. Fanon, "Altérations mentales," p. 15.
40. Nietzsche, *Zarathustra*, p. 55.

ethics characterized by resentment. Slave ethics is any form of human consciousness that denies its own humanity, fails to accept the totality of its human responsibility, and proclaims its inability to act. The slave, socially defined by a system of oppression, is a noble aristocrat in the Nietzschean sense if he or she ceases to define him or herself reactively in slave terms and begins to confront his or her freedom actively. Likewise, the noble ruler is no more than a slave when he or she subjects him or herself to the laws of a system of oppression and harbors resentment against the lower classes.

Dionysian tragedy is the liberating narrative that brings one into relation with one's fellow person and with one's physical and spiritual being. In *Joyful Wisdom*, Nietzsche writes:

> Every art and every philosophy may be regarded as a healing and helping appliance in the service of growing, struggling life: they always presuppose suffering and sufferers. But there are two kinds of sufferers: on the one hand those that suffer from *overflowing vitality*, who need Dionysian art, and require a tragic view and insight into life; and on the other hand those who suffer from *reduced vitality*, who seek repose, quietness, calm seas, and deliverance from themselves through art or knowledge, or else intoxication, spasm, bewilderment and madness.[41]

Discourse based on slave ethics is mythical narrative. The person who is filled with resentment suffers from reduced vitality. Dionysian tragedy—which must be distinguished from Greek tragedy in Kierkegaard's sense—transcends pessimism through joyful wisdom to bring humanity into history. As Dionysian hero, Zarathustra is the bringer of the condition of freedom. "One repays a teacher badly if one only remains a pupil," he says; "Now I bid you lose me and find yourselves."[42] In the plunge into the abyss of infinity, one is challenged to transform the burden of one's life into the eternal activity of freedom: freedom to act nobly and responsibly with regard to the freedom of one's fellow person.

Liberating narrative reaches its peak in Nietzsche with the madman's revolutionary speech: "God is dead! God remains dead! And we have killed him! . . . There never was a greater event,—and on

---

41. Friedrich Nietzsche, *Joyful Wisdom*, trans. Thomas Common (New York: Ungar, 1960), p. 332.

42. Nietzsche, *Zarathustra*, p. 103.

account of it, all who are born after us belong to a higher history than any history hitherto!"[43] However, even the killing of God can be done out of resentment: one can react against a God whom one blames for one's existence by becoming an atheist.[44] Unless one is able to accept the madman's message and assume the task of "higher history," one has failed to liberate oneself. It is not in the infernal racket of "great events" that transformation occurs, but in the still hours, when new values are invented.[45] Yet higher history is not isolation from activity or withdrawal from the noisy world. It is "fellowship in joy." The revolutionary movement is the fellowship of creators who take up the reins of history and challenge others to join them.[46]

In Fanon's work the death of the colonizer takes on the significance of the death of God. The end of the colonizer means the beginning of the possibility of a new history for the colonized. Césaire's Rebel kills his master. Whereas in *The Wretched of the Earth* Fanon situates this episode from *Et les chiens se taisaient* in the context of the drama of resentment, in *Black Skin, White Masks*, he uses the passage in his discussion of the task of moving beyond the colonial drama. The act of killing the colonizer is not in itself liberating. As in the case of Césaire's Rebel, the act may be based on resentment, the actor caught in the colonial drama. In his discussion of colonial war and mental disorder, Fanon shows how the killing of the colonized can drive one insane (*WE*, p. 251; *DT*, pp. 178–79). *Black Skin, White Masks* emphasizes the psychological dimension: the overthrow of the white value system that can destroy the colonized. With this act comes the challenge of Nietzsche's madman: the creation of a new history. However, this "internal revolution" as Fanon calls it, quoting Césaire's *Cahier d'un retour au pays natal*, can itself be a reactive phenomenon, a form of slave ethics. The internal revolution referred to in the *Cahier* is a plunge into the tragic and reactive drama of colonial endurance and struggle. This plunge may shake the world, but it does not in itself bring about a new history. The task, Fanon implies, again referring to the *Cahier*, is to "leap" into the "black hole" while also moving out to the universal. Only in this way can there be a move-

43. Nietzsche, *Joyful Wisdom*, p. 168.
44. Nietzsche, *Will to Power*, p. 400.
45. Nietzsche, *Zarathustra*, pp. 153–54.
46. Nietzsche, *Joyful Wisdom*, p. 268.

ment beyond the "absurd drama" of colonialism (*BS*, pp. 195–99; *PN*, pp. 158–61). This is the silence out of which comes the creation of new values. As in the Nietzschean schema, one must totally overcome a dramatic (mythical) conception of one's relation to existence (God, the colonizer).[47]

Fanon is more explicit than Nietzsche in his reappropriation of the content of history. In the revolutionary moment, it may be necessary not only to kill the oppressor in oneself but also to eliminate the oppressor in reality. Under some conditions, this may be the only way in which history can be actively reappropriated. Nietzsche leaves implicit and universal the circumstances of the reappropriation of history. For Fanon, these circumstances are specifically incorporated into a contextualized narrative of liberation, that is, into local determinate incarnations of the story of human self-creation.

Fanon's connection to Kierkegaard, as in the case of Nietzsche, rests primarily on a critical movement from the ethical position (Nietzsche's slave ethics) to history. In the essay "West Indians and Africans," Fanon states that in Europe irony protects a person from existential anguish, while in Martinique it protects the black person from the consciousness (*prise de conscience*) of his or her blackness (*négritude*). The black person who says that another person is very black is using irony to deny his or her own blackness. Fanon then makes a suggestive comment on Kierkegaard that is omitted in the English translation: "The task consists of removing the problem,

47. A. James Arnold has shown how *Et les chiens se taisaient*, like Greek tragedy, expresses the tragedy of human existence and makes possible the renewal of the community in its endless struggle for survival. He links this aspect of the play to Césaire's familiarity with Nietzsche's early work *The Birth of Tragedy* (1871). (See A. James Arnold, *Modernism and Negritude: The Poetry and Poetics of Aimé Césaire* [Cambridge: Harvard University Press, 1981], pp. 117–18.) This notion of tragedy as endless repetition and recreation (mythical narrative) is different from the notion of tragedy in the mature Nietzsche, who instead insists on a radically new creation, a willed and decisive transformation of the old (liberating narrative). (See Nietzsche's 1886 commentary on *The Birth of Tragedy* in *"The Birth of Tragedy" and "The Genealogy of Morals"*, pp. 3–15, and *Joyful Wisdom*, pp. 111–14, 269–70.) Fanon used the Bordas 1947 edition of the *Cahier* (pp. 64–65, 94–96); there are changes in the later editions. See *Cahier d'un retour au pays natal / Notebook of a Return to the Native Land*, in *Aimé Césaire, The Collected Poetry*, trans. Clayton Eshleman and Annette Smith, biling. ed. (Berkeley and Los Angeles: University of California Press, 1983), pp. 60–61, 84–85, and Lilian Pestre de Almeida, "Les Versions successives du *Cahier d'un retour au pays natal*" in M. a M. Ngal and Martin Steins, eds., *Césaire 70* (Paris: Editions Silex, 1984), pp. 35–36, 61.

putting the contingent in its place, and leaving the Martinican the choice of supreme values. One sees everything that could be said by envisaging this situation in accordance with the Kierkegaardian stages." (*RA*, p. 24, my translation; see *AR*, p. 19). The task is to move from values based on race to truly human values. Fanon is referring to the platforms of existence in the Kierkegaardian schema: the aesthetic (the contingent), the ethical (irony), and the historical (the authentically human). Either one is lost in the conflict between the contingent and the ethical, or one chooses to overcome this conflict by recognizing one's unique humanity and demanding mutual recognition.

Fanon refers specifically to Kierkegaard when he discusses the movement from enslavement in the ethical to freedom in history. Though the former slave has struggled for freedom, the struggle has always been defined in ethical terms. The slave has struggled for white liberty or in reaction to white oppression. Fanon states that the former slave "can find in his memory no trace of the struggle for liberty or of that anguish of liberty of which Kierkegaard speaks" (*BS*, p. 221; *PN*, p. 179). It is necessary to struggle in anguish in order to move from the ethical to the historical platforms of existence. Borrowing Kierkegaard's language, Fanon says that "the real *leap* consists in introducing invention into existence" (*BS*, p. 229, see also p. 199; *PN*, pp. 186, 161). One eliminates the ethical in oneself by taking responsibility for history. This is the conversion that the son and the daughter undergo in the process of the Algerian Revolution. The old man's infinite resignation is challenged by the daughter's "entry into history," writes Fanon (*DC*, pp. 102, 107; *SR*, pp. 87, 93).

Kierkegaard contrasts the knight of faith, the person who experiences history in the fullness of its ambiguity, with the tragic hero, or knight of infinite resignation (Agamemnon). The knight of faith is the person who, in fear and trembling, calls the law into question and assumes responsibility for it. In the Abraham and Isaac story, God asks Abraham to sacrifice his only son. According to de Silentio, Abraham finds himself outside of the certainty of the ethical world. The commandment "Thou shalt not kill" is suddenly suspended and the duty of the father to the son ruthlessly called into question. Abraham has a number of possibilities open to him. He can attempt to retreat to the ethical, either by establishing God's new command as part of a higher ethical law (duty to God), or by denying altogether God's new request and binding himself to the old commandment.

Because Abraham believes in God the giver of the commandments, however, he can accept neither of these alternatives. Ethically speaking, he faces a hopeless contradiction: God the giver of the commandments denies the validity of the commandments. In fear and trembling, Abraham could simply confront the yawning abyss of his freedom, and despair. All certainty is thrust away from him, and only endless doubt and absurdity remain. Abraham, however, confronts the anguish of his freedom and acts on the basis of faith. By virtue of the absurd, the impossible becomes a possibility. Abraham believes in God and is therefore willing to give up his son if required to do so. But Abraham believes that God will not require Isaac of him.[48] It is this ethically incomprehensible belief in an alternative possibility that distinguishes Abraham's faith from the blind certainty of the tragic hero. Merely to exist in a spatiotemporal world is to be free at a very primary level. It is easy enough to ignore this freedom (the aesthetic); it is more difficult to deny it (the ethical); it is terrifying to confront it, realize its implications, and exist in it in the way that Abraham does (the historical).

This bizarre confrontation with the absurd can be made more meaningful in terms of Fanon's work if we illustrate it with an equally bizarre example from Fanon. Fanon contrasts the terrorist— Agamemnon in Kierkegaard's work—with the *fidai*, the person in the Islamic tradition who is willing to make the ultimate sacrifice. Let us suppose that Abraham is a fidai. According to Fanon, the fidai is a freedom fighter who "has a rendezvous with the life of the Revolution, and with his own life. The fidai is not one of the sacrificed. . . . [A]t no moment does he choose death." Nevertheless, the fidai "does not shrink before the possibility of losing his life for the independence of his country" (*DC*, pp. 57–58; *SR*, pp. 40–41). It may turn out that what is perceived to be a faithful rendezvous with life may in fact turn out to be resignation to a higher ethical law: the fidai may regress to the level of tragic hero. The imperative of independence becomes an ethical law justifying tragic sacrifice. From the point of view of history, the question of national independence is not an ethically binding demand. Rather, it is a historically grounded imperative in accordance with which the fidai must decide what the possibilities are for authentic struggle. The risk of death can then be authentically accepted as the risk of life.

48. Kierkegaard, *Fear and Trembling*, pp. 46–48, 57.

The Abraham story communicates the dreadful experience of human freedom to create history: one becomes conscious of what it means to be an actor. In Kierkegaard's view, the lesson of the biblical tradition is that human beings bring freedom into the world. The human being is an expression of the divine in time. Hence, the paradox: "The eternal truth has come into being in time."[49] Since the human being is not necessarily aware of the nature of this divine relation, the biblical tradition provides examples such as Abraham and Christ. This deepens the paradox, for it means that one becomes aware of one's freedom through stories of historical actors. "*The paradoxical edification,*" writes Kierkegaard's Climacus, "*corresponds therefore to the determination of God in time as the individual man; for if such be the case, the individual is related to something outside himself.*"[50] Ultimately, then, the individual person becomes the condition or historical point of departure for eternal consciousness. History, authentically understood as the paradox of eternity in time, is the condition or point of departure for liberating consciousness. The person who enters history as the historical point of departure for an eternal consciousness lives truth. Truth is the person consciously existing his or her freedom.[51]

Sartre has eloquently captured Kierkegaard's contribution and the nature of his paradox: "Kierkegaard was perhaps the first to show that the universal enters History as a singular, in so far as the singular institutes itself in it as a universal." Sartre observes that if history is the point of departure for eternal truth, then historical man is transhistorical. Furthermore, transhistoricity belongs not just to Jesus but to Søren, "Jesus' witness," and to us, "Soeren's grand-nephews." "Each of us *is* Soeren," writes Sartre, "in our capacity as adventure."[52]

Three moments of history can be analytically distinguished in Kierkegaard's work: the Deity in time (Abraham, Christ) exhibiting the passionate inwardness of freedom in action; indirect or historical communication (the Bible, Kierkegaard's works) exhibiting inward appropriation in form and demanding that one realize one's freedom

49. Søren Kierkegaard, *Concluding Unscientific Postscript,* trans. David F. Swenson and Walter Lowrie (Princeton: Princeton University Press, 1968), p. 187.

50. Kierkegaard, *Postscript,* p. 498 (my emphasis).

51. Kierkegaard, *Postscript,* pp. 505–15.

52. Jean-Paul Sartre, "Kierkegaard: The Singular Universal," in *Between Existentialism and Marxism,* trans. John Mathews (New York: Morrow, 1976), pp. 163, 142, 167.

by becoming the Deity in time; the concrete individual who encounters the message and begins to live in it by becoming the Deity in time. The three mutually imply one another and form a dialectical unity. The Deity in time is the concrete individual who lives and communicates his or her freedom. Put differently, Kierkegaard's Christian is a freedom fighter. The authentic historical community is based on the mutual recognition of concrete persons who act to liberate themselves and others.[53]

Can the scenario of a nation achieving national independence be reconciled with the triumph of individual freedom, which is at the core of Kierkegaard? Is not Fanon obnoxiously sectarian and Kierkegaard embarrassingly individualistic? These questions pose a false antithesis. Kierkegaard's individual is not an individualist if by that is meant a solipsist who is merely interested in personal gratification. Such a person has not moved beyond the aesthetic level of existence. The knight of faith has sought, like the sectarian, to deny his or her individuality and to resign him or herself to the certainty of the ethical. However, he or she has found it necessary to go beyond the ethical too, not back into solitude, but forward into history. Without history there is no eternity (freedom). The historical point of departure presupposes a relationship with other human beings, that is, with the Deity in time. An eternal consciousness is possible only in a world in which I realize my own freedom by demanding (that is, through indirect or liberating communication) that the other realize his or her freedom. Paul Hollenbach has used Fanon's work to argue that Jesus, the knight of faith par excellence, practiced a form of social healing and was eliminated because it threatened to release the smoldering discontent resulting from Roman colonial rule in Palestine.[54] "Shall we not ourselves have to become Gods?" asks Nietzsche's madman.[55]

The essential types of the knight of faith in Fanon's work are the

---

53. Russell H. Davis has defended Kierkegaard's notion of community against the critics who find only individualism in Kierkegaard's work. He correctly points out that in "religiousness B" (the historical or truly religious) one returns to history and recognizes the divinity of the other. However, Davis fails to recognize the significance of indirect communication for liberating action. See "Kierkegaard and Community," *Union Seminary Quarterly Review,* 36 (Summer 1981), especially pp. 205, 213–15.

54. Paul W. Hollenbach, "Jesus, Demoniacs, and Public Authorities: A Socio-Historical Study," *Journal of the American Academy of Religion,* 49 (December 1981), 573, 583–84.

55. Nietzsche, *Joyful Wisdom,* p. 168.

liberated intellectual of *Black Skin, White Masks* and the revolutionary fighter of *The Wretched of the Earth*. The colonized intellectual can overcome the tragic drama in which he or she is caught only by overcoming psychological alienation. Fanon, the white trained, black doctor from Martinique, writes: "I have only one solution: to rise above this absurd drama that others have staged round me, to reject the two terms that are equally unacceptable, and through one human being [*un particulier humain*], to reach out for the universal" (*BS*, p. 197; *PN*, p. 159). The colonized person kills the white oppressor in him or herself and makes the leap:

> The body [*densité*] of history does not determine a single one of my actions.
> I am my own foundation. [*BS*, p. 231; *PN*, p. 187]

The peasant or rural worker who joins the revolution is Fanon's other knight of faith. Toward the end of *Black Skin, White Masks*, Fanon argues that a distinction must be made between the colonized intellectual who finds his freedom through reflective social and psychological analysis and the plantation worker in the West Indies for whom the only solution to exploitation is to fight (pp. 223–24; *PN*, p. 181). This struggle must not take the form of resentment. Fanon states that "[r]acism, hatred, resentment, 'the legitimate desire for vengeance' cannot sustain a war of liberation" (*DT*, p. 87, my translation; see *WE*, p. 139). The spontaneous and Manichaean violence that is so evident in the early stages of the revolution must be channeled, molded, and educated. "These lightning flashes of consciousness which fling the body into stormy paths or which throw it into an almost pathological trance where the face of the other beckons me on to giddiness, where my blood calls for the blood of the other, where by sheer inertia my death calls for the death of the other—that intense emotion of the first few hours, falls to pieces if it is left to feed on its own substance" (*WE*, p. 139; *DT*, p. 87). What is decisive for liberation is the *meaning* of the death of the tyrant. We must rely on ourselves; that is, we must face the anguish of liberty that comes with taking responsibility for our own actions. This is why Fanon says that the armed struggle may be "symbolic" (*WE*, p. 94; *DT*, p. 52). The consciousness of freedom that comes with the killing of the tyrant within, rather than violent action, is what constitutes revolutionary activity. Yet, the knight of faith is an actor. In the colonial situation he or she will find it necessary to enter into the struggle in all its dimensions.

Truthful anticolonial violence, that which has gone beyond Manichaeism, must be seen as what Kierkegaard (de Silentio) calls the "teleological suspension of the ethical."[56] Manichaean violence, as resentment, makes an ethical demand for liberation higher than the commandment "Thou shalt not kill." The revolutionary, however, does not have the certainty that his or her action will lead to the elimination of oppression. The suspension of the commandment "Thou shalt not kill" puts him or her in a terrifying situation. He or she cannot reassert the ethical by claiming that the imperative of liberation is a higher ethical law. Unable to justify killing in order to prohibit killing, he or she faces the yawning chasm of despair. Like Abraham, however, he or she does not despair but, instead, acts out of freedom. He or she believes that the experience of freedom is incommensurable with political domination and economic exploitation and acts on this belief.

The liberated black intellectual and the revolutionary peasant are the historical points of departure for an eternal (free) consciousness. Like Abraham or Christ in the biblical tradition, they communicate the spirit of freedom. Fanon himself combined both of these positions. He was a black intellectual who went through a process of self-discovery, but he also actively joined in the revolutionary struggle. Dr. François Tosquelles, with whom Fanon worked as a resident at Saint-Alban, describes Fanon in terms that evoke the image of the knight of faith. According to Tosquelles, Fanon incarnated liberty and respect for the other, hope and creativity. Tosquelles actually calls Fanon a tragic hero. However, it is clear from his description that he has in mind Nietzsche's Dionysian hero, or, in Kierkegaard's terms, the knight of faith.[57]

Liberating narrative in the colonial situation discloses the reality of human freedom in a particular historical form, the nation. In Fanon's later work, the liberated nation is the symbol of the totality of freedom in a temporal and spatial dimension. The truth of the nation is incarnated in what he calls an "illuminating and sacred communication" (*AR*, p. 145; *RA*, p. 147). Such a symbolic act parallels Kierke-

56. Kierkegaard, *Fear and Trembling*, p. 69.
57. François Tosquelles, "Frantz Fanon à Saint-Alban," *L'Information Psychiatrique,* 51 (December 1975), pp. 1073–74.

gaard's historical point of departure for an eternal consciousness.[58] At the level of Kierkegaard's first reflection, the what or content of freedom (individual and national) can be discerned in national culture. The second reflection, the how or form of discourse, must also be specified. A narrative of national freedom that claims to present the certain path to liberation does not go beyond the ethical. It would, moreover, be the work of an elite who failed to recognize the humanity of the people and the necessity for them to take responsibility for the reordering of their reality. According to Fanon, national culture has to address the historical situation of the community in such a way that people are put in a position to liberate themselves through their own sense of reality. The writer, for example, "ought to use the past with the intention of opening the future, as an invitation to action and a basis for hope" (*WE*, p. 232; *DT*, p. 162). National culture must in its own way face the peculiarity of Kierkegaard's double paradox: the paradox of truth as freedom realizing its freedom in time, and the paradox of this historical event as the source of the freedom of others (all of the colonized can free themselves according to their peculiar situations).

Decolonization, as the entry into time and challenge to the colonizer's domination over history, transforms the lost space of the colony into the space, reconquered, of the new nation. The struggle of Hegel's slave for recognition is one of the basic points of reference for Fanon's understanding of this process. Writing as a participant in the Algerian Revolution, Fanon states that "one must accept the risk of death in order to bring freedom to birth" (*AR*, p. 95; *RA*, p. 98). The dependent bourgeoisie fail to struggle. On the other hand, the majority of the colonized are engaged in resisting the system either through pragmatic resistance or outright rebellion. This violence, which is inherent in the colonial system, must be transformed into a struggle for national liberation.

Sekyi-Otu has shown that Fanon understood this transformation to be constituted by a willed entry into history; only a *"willed* interruption of historical tendencies" could lead to socialist transformation in the colonial situation: "Fanon concluded that the reconstitution of a political and moral community must be the offspring of a radical

---

58. Søren Kierkegaard, *Philosophical Fragments or a Fragment of Philosophy,* trans. David F. Swenson and Howard V. Hong (Princeton: Princeton University Press, 1967), p. 137.

choice, and a radical transformation of existing conditions: a leap 'from one life to another.'" By showing that colonialism denied the historical premise of a shared humanity, Fanon could justify the radical leap and extraordinary, violent nature of the revolutionary project. The revolutionary moment is the "cosmogonic" moment, the violent beginning when the colonized consciously enter history. The logic of transformation rests on a moral or categorical imperative, that is, on a radical change in consciousness; the revolution is nevertheless a vital necessity resting on a historical imperative, namely the material existence of the colonized.[59]

Sekyi-Otu argues that if the logic of struggle in Hegel's work is read in terms of an immanent development, then the idea of a willed entry into history represents a break with Hegel. Since the colonial system is based on "reciprocal exclusivity" (Manichaeism), there can be no immanent engendering of revolution. The decision to engage in a violent revolutionary struggle can be justified only on the basis of the specificity of the colonial situation: the racial denial of human beings that places the colonized in a realm unlike anything in European history.[60] What is most significant about Sekyi-Otu's argument is his emphasis on consciousness and, therefore, his critique of the applicability of the notion of immanent development to the colonial situation. Fanon breaks with any notion of immanent historical development. Decolonization is not the result of "the mechanical development of material forces," he writes; it is "the hand of the African and his brain" that make freedom possible (*AR*, p. 173; *RA*, p. 175). Fanon's comparison of the colonized with Hegel's slave suggests that he has a radical reading of Hegel based on the idea of freedom as a vital imperative rather than an immanent necessity.

Freedom, that is, mutual recognition, is for Hegel the realized essence of humanity. Hegel uses the idea of freedom to draw out the implications of Kant's categorical imperative: "Freedom demands, therefore, that the self-conscious subject should not heed his own natural existence or tolerate the natural existence of others; on the contrary, indifferent to natural existence, he should in his individual, immediate actions stake his own life and the lives of others to win freedom."[61] In *Philosophy of Mind*, Hegel suggests that this impera-

---

59. Sekyi-Otu, "Fanon's Critique," pp. 67, 363–65, 414.
60. Sekyi-Otu, "Fanon's Critique," p. 65.
61. Hegel, *Philosophy of Mind*, p. 171.

tive is true for humanity in any social situation that precludes mutual recognition. For the Greeks and Romans, "freedom still had the character of a natural state." Slavery existed and as a consequence "bloody wars developed in which the slaves tried to free themselves, to obtain recognition of their eternal human rights." According to Hegel, those "who remain slaves suffer no absolute injustice; for he who has not the courage to risk his life to win freedom, that man deserves to be a slave."[62] As in the case of Nietzsche's discussion of slave ethics, the point of this statement is not to justify slavery (which apparently it does) but, on the contrary, to emphasize in the strongest way possible the necessity of realizing freedom.

If the primal struggle between Hegel's two protagonists leads to the master-slave relation, a secondary struggle must take place for true universality and mutual recognition to be obtained. The secondary struggle for recognition must recommence the primary struggle so that the master is compelled by the slave to recognize their mutual freedom. The secondary struggle differs from the primary struggle, however, because the slave now recognizes both his own and the master's mortality and humanity. The slave is fighting for the triumph of human rationality, not domination.

The movement from primary to secondary struggle is not an immanent one; its necessity should be understood in terms of the imperative of freedom, or liberating narrative. The slave who recognizes the master's humanity but is also willing to risk his life for his own freedom is the slave who understands the social situation and the necessity of liberation through the transformation of the social totality. What is significant in terms of liberation is not struggle in itself but the consciousness of the sociopolitical totality that demands that struggle. Liberating political struggle is a demand of the categorical imperative rather than an immanent development.

Hegel sometimes appears to say that it is the slave's labor that gives birth to the consciousness of freedom. He states in *Phenomenology* that through "work" "the bondsman becomes conscious of what he truly is."[63] The moment of labor (the economic) must be seen, however, in relation to both the moment of struggle (the political) and the moment of consciousness. It is fear that provides the initial possibility of a movement to recognition and universality. Like Kierkegaard's

62. Hegel, *Philosophy of Mind*, pp. 174–75.
63. Hegel, *Phenomenology*, p. 118.

Abraham, the slave has been "seized with dread" and has trembled "in every fiber of its being"; he has "experienced the fear of death, the absolute Lord." The slave can attempt to abandon his own individuality and submit to the truth of his master. However, this solution merely perpetuates his experience of being unessential. His only other choice is to realize the experience of fear and trembling for what it really is: "the absolute melting-away of every thing stable," "absolute negativity, *pure being-for-self*."[64] The finite world is dissolved; only possibility is left.

This is the point at which the leap to historical consciousness is made. Realizing that the object is shaped by his own activity, his own negativity, "he destroys this alien negative moment, posits *himself* as a negative in the permanent order of things, and thereby becomes *for himself* someone existing on his own account."[65] His chains are forged by his own hands and are his own creation; they can be broken asunder. The slave recognizes that the master is not the independent consciousness that he appeared to be but, rather, a dependent consciousness bound to the slave for recognition and fulfillment of desire. It is the slave who is the independent consciousness, who recognizes his own universality, and who demands that the master likewise recognize it. Here the struggle for recognition reappears as liberating necessity. What is important about the moment of labor is the opportunity that it provides the slave to see his own freedom in existence. This does not mean that labor generates consciousness. It is the idea of freedom that does so. The slave becomes conscious—this is the task of liberating narrative—of his own power over the alien object and over an alien being. However, this idea of freedom becomes meaningful only through reflection into one's own transformative activity. Consciousness of freedom is the basis of liberating political struggle and economic activity.

It is not the act of violent struggle that is the key to decolonization but, rather, the revolutionary leap, the "willed" entry into history, the consciousness of the categorical imperative. What moves the Hegelian dialectic from a situation of mutually exclusive protagonists to one of mutual recognition, is the recognition of the other and the recognition of oneself as an active, freely creative being. One does not arrive at consciousness, however, simply through trembling in front

64. Hegel, *Phenomenology*, p. 117.
65. Hegel, *Phenomenology*, p. 118.

of a master or experiencing the creative transformation of an object. Such events do not immanently imply freedom. They are made meaningful only through the *consciousness* of freedom. They are finite events whose infinity can be grasped only within the context of a specific narrative of liberation. Hegel's slave must make the leap to totality, he must consciously grasp the social significance of his own activity, if his action is to be anything more than an endless, vicious struggle between the two protagonists (the primary struggle). Only the consciousness of freedom, as the leap to totality, can move a truncated dialectic beyond the particular to the universal that it implicitly is. Hegel, and following him, Marx, sometimes lose this moment in the incomprehensible notion of immanence, but like Kierkegaard and Nietzsche, Fanon holds onto it throughout. There is no immanent movement in history. There is only necessity—the necessity of freedom—necessity as the ordering of the past in terms of a narrative of liberation.

Neither an economic transformation brought about by labor nor the spontaneous violence of the colonized against the colonizer are in themselves revolutionary. Fanon says of the consciousness of freedom made manifest in Algeria: "Whereas the colonized usually has only a choice between a retraction of his being and a frenzied attempt at identification with the colonizer, the Algerian has brought into existence a new, positive, efficient personality, whose richness is provided less by the trial of strength that he engages in than by his certainty that he embodies a decisive moment of the national consciousness" (*AR*, pp. 102–103; *RA*, pp. 106–107). The key to the master–slave dialectic is recognition, that is, the consciousness of freedom, of the humanity of both protagonists. The revolutionary moment, the leap and the risk of self, is not a leap into macabre violence. It is, rather, an anguished recognition of the totality of one's historical situation and of the necessity of being an active person in that situation. But this does not mean that the specter of violence vanishes into the romantic unity of a liberal ideal. Hegel's protagonists must (that is, they *ought* to) "*recognize themselves as mutually recognizing each other*."[66] The power of the categorical imperative in history is terrifying. Those that do not fulfill its demands must bear the consequences.

66. Cited in *BS*, p. 217; *PN*, p. 176, Fanon's emphasis; Hegel, *Phenomenology*, p. 112.

Historical consciousness is true only as the reentry into the terror of history.

Violence as a quantitative force is an important factor in decolonization. What is really significant for Fanon, however, is the quality of violence. The primary spontaneous and rebellious violence ever present in the colonial situation (Hegel's primary struggle) must be channeled if it is not to end in a cathartic release of useless and destructive energy. Violence does not automatically initiate a process of liberation; it does not engender from within itself an immanent flowering of freedom. Spontaneous violence is the Manichaean truth of colonialism: "The colonized replies to the living lie of the colonial situation by an equal falsehood. His dealings with his fellow-nationals are open; they are strained and incomprehensible with regard to the colonizers. Truth is that which hurries on the break-up of the colonial regime; it is that which promotes the emergence of the nation; it is all that protects the colonized, and ruins the foreigners. In this colonial context, there is no truthful behaviour: and good is quite simply that which is evil for 'them'" (*WE*, p. 50; *DT*, p. 17). This one-sided truth manifests itself in what Fanon calls "the cult of spontaneity"; it is based on a "strategy of immediacy." In a process of national "collective ecstasy," the colonized in each locality assemble into groups for the purpose of cleansing the nation of foreigners. Fanon links the consciousness of this confraternity to "the illusion of eternity"; the rebels are fearless, the atmosphere utopian. The problem with this apocalyptic moment, Fanon argues, is that fearlessness implies thoughtlessness (*WE*, pp. 131–34; *DT*, p. 183). Hannah Arendt accuses Fanon of having "glorified violence for violence's sake," but her polemic confuses certain tendencies in the student and Black Power movements of the 1960s with the problematic in Fanon's texts. What she misunderstands is precisely the dialectic of violence and liberating consciousness in Fanon's work. As she herself states, as an afterthought, Fanon was "much more doubtful about violence than his admirers."[67]

Fanon considers that it is only the idea of freedom as a concrete, national, political, and economic reality that can render violence meaningful (Hegel's secondary struggle). Limited and localized tacti-

67. Hannah Arendt, *On Violence* (New York: Harvest–Harcourt Brace Jovanovich, 1969), pp. 65, 14n19.

cal maneuvers must be reconciled with a national revolutionary strategy. Politics is discovered as a method of intensifying the struggle
and preparing the people in the art of self-government. Manichaeism
is overcome in the realization that what is significant in the struggle is
not the death of all enemies but recognition: the struggle "will be
ended not because there are no more enemies left to kill, but quite
simply because the enemy, for various reasons, will come to realize
that his interest lies in ending the struggle and in recognizing the
sovereignty of the colonized people" (*WE*, p. 141; *DT*, p. 89).

The Marxist tradition, and the Marxist works of Sartre, in particular, develop the Hegelian dialectical tradition by analyzing the interaction of specific groups and social units in the struggle for liberation.
In the Marxist schema of history, the working class (proletariat),
although it is initially fragmentary, is able to and must recognize its
class interests and transform the society. Under capitalism the development of the forces of production makes it possible to bring an end
to exploitation. This development of the productive forces, however,
is constrained by existing class relations. The dominant class, the
bourgeoisie, must, therefore, be overthrown. This is the task of the
proletariat because the proletariat is the class that is directly related to
the development of the forces of production through its labor; the
interests of the proletariat as a class are the universal interests of the
society as a whole. Marx generally presents this movement as though
it were immanent. The consciousness of the proletariat, "the communist consciousness," appears to be automatically generated out of the
tension between the possibilities brought about by the forces of production and the restrictions resulting from the existing relations of
production. Sometimes this consciousness is enlightened by those
"bourgeois ideologists, who have raised themselves to the level of
comprehending theoretically the historical movement as a whole."
Consciousness, however, only makes explicit what is already implicit
in the social totality.[68]

Marxist theorists such as Georg Lukács and Jürgen Habermas try to
liberate this model from a strict determinism by elaborating the role
of consciousness in social change. However, in their work conscious-

68. Karl Marx and Friedrich Engels, *The German Ideology*, part 1, in *The Marx-Engels Reader*, ed. Robert C. Tucker (New York: Norton, 1972), pp. 156–57; *The Communist Manifesto*, in Tucker, p. 343.

ness remains bound by the economic structure of society that it must objectively know. According to Lukács, there is only one objective understanding of the social totality: that of the proletariat, the "subject-object of history." Habermas emphasizes the role of social theory in "the critique of ideology." Humanity frees itself from illusion only by recollecting "the self-formative process of the species as a movement of class antagonism mediated at every stage by processes of production" and by recognizing human consciousness "as the result of the history of class consciousness."[69] A liberated consciousness has a role to play only within the given developmental process.

The deformation of the capitalist developmental process, the consequent specificity of the colonial situation, and the notion of a willed imperative make this model inappropriate for colonial territories. Colonial history is the result of the violent interaction of the colonizer and the colonized. The task is to transform the fragmentary resistance to colonialism of a *colonized peasantry* into an organized and conscious liberation movement. Localized groups come together, the peasantry unifies and is joined by some professionals and intellectuals, the lumpen proletariat enters the struggle, a new nation is embodied.

Like Fanon, Sartre recognizes the nature of violent conflict in the colonial situation: "The violence of the rebel *was* the violence of the colonialist; there was never any other."[70] Sartre adheres to the Marxist philosophy of history to the extent that he sees history as a totality that develops by virtue of the interaction of individuals and groups in relation to the material conditions of existence. For Sartre, however, this interaction is conceptualized in terms of human actions or projects oriented toward overcoming scarcity on the basis of given conditions.[71] Political activity, as *praxis*, always retains priority over economics in Sartre's model. As in the work of Lukács and Habermas, the traditional Marxist focus on the mechanisms of history is also displaced by the emphasis on understanding that history (consciousness). For Sartre, however, history cannot be reduced to an

69. Georg Lukács, *History and Class Consciousness: Studies in Marxist Dialectics,* trans. Rodney Livingstone (Cambridge: MIT Press, 1971), pp. 199, 208–209; Jürgen Habermas, *Knowledge and Human Interests,* trans. Jeremy J. Shapiro (Boston: Beacon, 1971), pp. 61–62.

70. Sartre, *Critique,* p. 733. See also Sartre's preface to *WE,* pp. 17–18.

71. Jean-Paul Sartre, *Search for a Method,* trans. Hazel E. Barnes (New York: Vintage–Random House, 1968), p. 91.

external, known, a priori dialectic in which the particular is already located and dissolved. (Sartre accuses Lukács of this error.)[72]

Sartre's abstract phenomenological analysis of the genesis of the group into the institution leaves implicit the imperative of recreating and preserving the group as a democratic entity in a specific historical context. We are left with the formal circularity of the movement from series to group to series, rather than with the historical totalization that would unify them. Still, Sartre's notion of "quasi-sovereignity" goes a long way in explicating a liberating democratic politics. At the core of the group is a paradoxical idea: the unity of the identical third is, in concrete terms, a unity of separate thirds. In the pure (abstract) fused group, the regulatory act of the third party, that is to say, the act that unifies the group, arises in all as the same. Through the organization, however, the individual thirds can be given separate functions while still remaining united in the group. This can be possible only if each third is both the same and different. The regulatory act performed by individual A does not arise in individual B and yet it defines the practice of the group. B understands the meaning of the act through a reciprocal grasp of the common field and therefore carries out his or her common function in accordance with it. In one sense, the person whose regulatory act unifies the material field is sovereign. A totalizes B and the others in the group. However, this sovereignty is limited by its reciprocity. B totalizes A at the same time and is also sovereign. In the group, therefore, one is really only quasi-sovereign; one is quasi-sovereign and quasi-object at the same time. The group is constantly being totalized; it is never a finished totality to anyone in the group.[73]

Jameson argues that Sartre's notion of the group is "profoundly democratic."[74] If the phenomenological intelligibility of the group rests on the assumption that human beings are free by virtue of being human, then the inference is that the freedom of all must be concretely recognized. Intragroup relationships are based on this categorical imperative. This is the meaning of the third, of the ternary relation. If these bonds of reciprocity dissolve into the isolation of seriality under the institution, then the group must be reformed in a

---

72. See, for example, Sartre, *Search*, pp. 26–28.
73. Sartre, *Critique*, pp. 576–81.
74. Fredric Jameson, *Marxism and Form: Twentieth Century Dialectical Theories of Literature* (Princeton: Princeton University Press, 1971), p. 253.

cosmogonic act. Thus the external dialectical circularity of the movement from group to institution to group must give way to action based on the categorical imperative and hence the affirmation of reciprocal recognition. Everyone is a responsible, sovereign agent who must recognize the sovereignty that is his or her own in the other. This is not Hobbesian "individualism" and "treacherous reciprocity" as Marxist critics argue.[75] One can distinguish, argues Jameson, the "relationship to objects which in human terms translates into a generosity or a freedom with respect to other men" from "work for another man" and "oppression by him." Freedom for Sartre, Jameson writes, is defined positively as responsibility, as "total political responsibility."[76]

In contrast to Sartre, Fanon writes from the position of a participant in a struggle with a precise goal, full decolonization. As participant, he must totalize the historical situation and draw conclusions relating to practical action. The task of political education, Fanon says, "is to make the totality of the nation a reality to each citizen" (*WE*, p. 200; *DT*, p. 135). The key to decolonization is the member of the group (nation) who retains his or her quasi-sovereignty through a practical understanding (totalization) of the movement of the nation. Quasi-sovereignty, that is, the concrete and responsible totalization of history by each person, is the truth of history. Fanon makes it absolutely clear not only that the institution can be prevented, but that it must be. Fanon realized that the most important task of the struggling nation, and one of the most difficult tasks it would face, would be to avoid the tragic circularity that would turn the new nation into a regime of terror. This is why Fanon emphasizes the necessity of maintaining and strengthening the democratic process within the group as it engages in struggle and as it undertakes the task of constructing a new nation.

The political, which is at first manifested in the spontaneous violent outbreaks of the group, must be rediscovered in its fullness in the process of struggle against the colonizer (or the colonizer's neocolonial agent, the national bourgeoisie). Through an education process that is concretely related to the reality of the struggle, the people

75. See, for example, Wilfrid Desan, *The Marxism of Jean-Paul Sartre* (New York: Doubleday, 1965), p. 286; Pietro Chiodi, *Sartre and Marxism* (Sussex: Harvest Press, 1976), p. 87.
76. Jameson, *Marxism and Form*, pp. 239–40, 287–88.

come to an awareness of their mutual responsibility to each other. They learn that the struggle cannot be understood in racial terms. "The people who at the beginning of the struggle had adopted the primitive Manicheism of the colonizer—Blacks and Whites, Arabs and Christians [*Roumis*]—realize as they go along that it sometimes happens that you get Blacks who are whiter than the Whites and that the fact of having a national flag and the hope of an independent nation does not always tempt certain strata of the population to give up their interests or privileges" (*WE*, p. 144; *DT*, pp. 91–92). "The scandal explodes" when some of the colonizers go over to the other side, "become Negroes or Arabs, and accept suffering, torture, and death" (*WE*, p. 145; *DT*, p. 92). Power cannot be given to a colonized bourgeoisie who will set up a neocolonial dictatorship. The people must vigilantly guard their own power in order to prevent a leader from becoming a "driver" who treats them only as a herd. They must be able "to meet together, discuss, propose, and receive directions." They must decide on the policy of the government. The party must remain "a tool in the hands of the people," and must be "decentralized in the extreme" (*WE*, pp. 195, 184–85; *DT*, pp. 131, 123).

The process of building the nation is not just a political process, however. There are social relations and a whole underdeveloped, dependent economy to be transformed. The national bourgeoisie identifies in spirit with the metropolitan bourgeoisie, but it is economically dependent and hence unable to develop the economy in the interest of the nation. Fanon argues that its way must be barred (*WE*, pp. 174–75; *DT*, p. 115). He emphasizes that once people have learned how the economy works against their interests, and once they have regained control over the means of production, they can truly work to build the economy and their own standard of living. He provides the example of liberated zones during the Algerian Revolution where production per acre greatly increased, calorie intake improved, and new foodstuffs, formerly exported, suddenly became available for consumption (*WE*, p. 191; *DT*, p. 128).

Fanon does not explore a detailed and systematic plan for economic reconstruction. He merely gives a few hints of what could be done: the nationalization of the trading sector, the establishment of democratically run wholesale and retail cooperatives, the redistribution of land to peasants (*WE*, pp. 179–80, 190–91; *DT*, pp. 119–20, 128). The possibilities would depend on the unique conditions in each liberated nation. What is ultimately important is that this economic

process be based on the assumption of human liberty. National reconstruction must not become a form of forced labor justified by the
economic progress it brings the state: "slavery is opposed to work,
. . . work presupposes liberty, responsibility, and consciousness"
(*WE*, p. 191; *DT*, p. 128). So firmly does Fanon believe in the fundamental priority of consciousness and freedom over other human experiences, including labor, that he states: "If the building of a bridge
does not enrich the awareness [*conscience*] of those who work on it,
then that bridge ought not to be built and the citizens can go on
swimming across the river or going by boat" (*WE*, pp. 200–201; *DT*,
p. 135). Independence makes it possible for truly liberated men and
women, as masters of the material means of their existence, to transform society radically (*WE*, p. 310; *DT*, p. 228).

Fanon has been accused of being an idealist. Fanon's problem,
argues Norman Klein, is his attachment to humanitarian values and
democratic methods over economic growth. Klein has learned from
history that if "the primary problem remains industrialization, some
degree of political coercion to achieve this end has been required."
Klein *knows* that national democracy "is a luxury of the advanced
industrial nations."[77] These considerations are Klein's a priori: development, whether it be the case of the English industrial revolution, or
of Soviet or Chinese development, is a process encompassing certain
events (urbanization, centralization of factors of production, separation of peasantry from land, and disciplining them for factory labor).
For Klein, the end justifies the means. Repression is necessary and
tolerable for the time being. Klein is an apologist and legitimator of
the neocolonial myth.

In contrast Fanon makes the wager that there is an alternative path
to human development that is based on a liberating national consciousness. A concrete consciousness of the sociopolitical totality is an
essential ingredient. The struggle of Hegel's slave, both in relation to
other persons and to nature, is liberating only to the extent that it is
consciously understood in terms of an experientially grounded, open-
ended narrative of liberation. Likewise, the violent struggle of the
colonized against the colonizer, and the continuous struggle against
the dependent bourgeoisie, can be liberating only if consciously understood in terms of an ever-enriched, historically specific narrative

77. Norman A. Klein, "On Revolutionary Violence," *Studies on the Left,* 6 (May–
June 1966), 81.

of liberation. In the colonial situation, this type of historical under-standing takes the form of national consciousness. The key to liberat-ing political, social, and economic decolonization is a national con-sciousness that is aware of the developing totality of the nation, of the global totality within which the nation situates itself, and of the total-ity of the human that sustains both of these.

Fanon distinguishes liberating national consciousness from na-tionalism. Nationalism is compatible with internal domination with-in the society and Manichaean opposition in relation to other groups or societies. The task of the national movement is to "create a pros-pect that is human because conscious and sovereign men dwell there-in." National consciousness goes beyond individual and group nar-cissism to a recognition of other individuals and national groups; it is accompanied "by the discovery and encouragement of universalizing values" (*WE*, pp. 203–205, 247; *DT*, pp. 137–39, 175).

National culture is the medium that makes liberating consciousness possible. Fanon states that culture is the expression of national con-sciousness, and national consciousness "is the most elaborate form of culture" (*WE*, p. 247; *DT*, p. 174). The ideology of the colonizer seeks to destroy the political and cultural reality of the nation and to reduce the colonized to an animal status. The culture of the colonized recalls the unity and history of the nation that has struggled and continues to struggle against oppression. National culture subverts the foreign ideologies imposed on the nation in the name of liberation and demystifies the mythologies imposed by indigenous elites. Liber-ating national culture is an open-ended totalization of the political, social, and economic dimensions of experience, from the point of view of the idea of freedom, in the language and forms of the people. As liberating narrative, authentic national culture makes possible the transformation of the drama of colonialism into the history of liberation.

Chapter 3

Mythology and Resistance: Vaudou

Papa Legba,	Papa Legba,
Come from Guinea,	Sorti lan Guinée,
That we may pass.	Pou' nou' passé.
Papa Legba,	Papa Legba
Open the gateway for us	Ouvri barrière pou' nou'
. . . . .	. . . . .

Ritual Invocations, MELVILLE HERSKOVITS,
Life in a Haitian Valley

It is the fight for national existence which sets culture
moving and opens [*débloque*] to it the doors of creation.
FRANTZ FANON, *The Wretched of the Earth*

AFRO-CARIBBEAN peoples came from traditional African societies with fundamentally religious cultures: religion provided the foundation for knowledge about the natural and social world. Religion legitimated political authority, but it could also be used to subvert it. After the colonial rupture, religion continued to play a fundamental role in the construction and reconstruction of the social world. African-based religions were at the heart of resistance and rebellion against a plantation society founded on violence. In colonial Saint Domingue, vaudou contributed in a vital way to the only slave rebellion in the Americas completely to overturn the colonial plantation order and achieve both emancipation and national independence. However, the tragic history of vaudou in the postindependence period showed that vaudou in the hands of the Haitian bourgeoisie could also legitimate neocolonial oppression. A form of mythical narrative, vaudou always remained bound to the drama of colonialism and its neocolonial aftermath.

Fanon mentions religion in brief passages in his discussion of the colonial drama and the struggle for national liberation. He distinguishes the culture of the colonized, which forms in reaction to colonialism, from true national culture. Whereas culture under colonialism is transformed into defense mechanisms, national culture is a dynamic, innovative movement, an assembling of the colonized for action. The culture of the colonized is forced into secrecy, and it may shrivel and become inert. Yet, the culture of the colonized, Fanon insists, is a form of resistance, an implicit manifestation of the nation (*WE*, pp. 236–37, 243; *DT*, pp. 166–67, 172).

In his discussion of colonial violence, Fanon states that the religious rituals of the colonized, particularly the ritual of possession, are muscular orgies of an escapist nature; in them "the most acute aggressivity and the most impelling violence are canalized, transformed, and conjured away" (*WE*, p. 57; *DT*, p. 22). This interpretation contrasts with Fanon's brief comment on religion in an article on the West Indies: African religions, he states, were a "form of resistance to Western, Christian oppression" (*RA*, p. 89, my translation; omitted in *AR*). Norman Klein has correctly criticized Fanon for presenting religious rituals as though they were merely cathartic processes for the "release of pent-up feelings." Religious experience in the form of millenarianism, Klein points out, is oriented not toward catharsis but toward the creation of a radical alternative where injustice is eliminated.[1] Michael Taussig, in his monumental study of the devil and commodity fetishism, demonstrates how the symbol of the devil, with all its ambivalence, expresses resistance to oppression and exploitation in South American plantations and mines. Fanon exaggerated the problem of conformity, Taussig writes: "In a myriad of improbable ways, magic and rite can strengthen the critical consciousness that a devastatingly hostile reality forces on the people laboring in the plantations and mines. Without the legacy of culture and without its rhetorical figures, images, fables, metaphors, and

---

1. Norman A. Klein, "On Revolutionary Violence," *Studies on the Left*, 6 (May–June 1966), pp. 64–68. Klein is discussing only *The Wretched of the Earth* and seems unfamiliar with Fanon's social critique of biologism (the libido) in *Black Skin, White Masks* and in the psychiatric writings.

other imaginative creations, this consciousness cannot function."[2] In the first chapter of *The Wretched of the Earth*, in particular, Fanon tends to underemphasize the creative and protest elements in religion and to reduce complex religious processes to psychological terms. Even here, however, there are indications that Fanon's work goes far beyond this rationalist position. He states that in dance and possession "may be deciphered as in an open book the huge effort of a community to exorcise itself, to liberate itself [*s'affranchir*], to explain itself" (*WE*, p. 57; *DT*, p. 22). In other words, the dance has a symbolical meaning that unifies the group, however unconscious it may be. Rather than being a merely cathartic process, dance is a celebration of the story of the community in opposition to the colonizer.

Despite his criticism of Fanon, Taussig recognizes the importance of Fanon's analysis. Phantoms of the spirit can indeed create divisions and conformism. A "nonfetishized mode of understanding human relations and society is necessary for human liberation," writes Taussig, and therefore "both precommodity and commodity fetishism stand condemned." Paul Hollenbach suggests that Fanon understood how colonial religious phenomena combined escapist and protest elements, whether they occurred in Fanon's Algeria, in Haiti, or in Roman-dominated Palestine two thousand years ago. What Fanon highlights by using psychological language is the extent to which the culture of the colonized must be demystified. Only then can the process of "social healing," as Hollenbach refers to it, really take place.[3] From the point of view of the imperative of liberation, mythical expression can be interpreted as an illusory attempt by the community to understand itself and resist the colonizer. The processes of understanding oneself and one's world, and of resistance, are significant cultural processes. However, they are *distorted* demands for liberation, bound by the Manichaean terms of the colonial drama. Authentic national culture goes beyond this reaction to colonialism to assemble the nation in a struggle for liberation.

2. Michael T. Taussig, *The Devil and Commodity Fetishism in South America* (Chapel Hill: University of North Carolina Press, 1980), p. 232.

3. Taussig, p. 230; Hollenbach's very suggestive use of Fanon to interpret the phenomena of religion and healing in Roman Palestine does not, however, adequately distinguish the mythical aspects of exorcism from social healing proper, that is, from liberation. Paul W. Hollenbach, "Jesus, Demoniacs, and Public Authorities: A Socio-Historical Study," *Journal of the American Academy of Religion*, 49 (December 1981), pp. 575–76, 584.

Vaudou consists essentially of different West African religions that have been brought together, altered, and syncretized with elements of Catholicism to create a uniquely Haitian creole religion. With its structural similarity to other African-based religions in the Americas (Santería in Cuba, Shango in Trinidad, Pocomania in Jamaica, Macumba in Brazil, Voodoo in the United States, ancestor worship and spiritual practices in other islands), vaudou is the classic example of the mythical encoding of experience in the Caribbean.

At the center of vaudou is the ritual of possession by means of which *loa* (vaudou divinities) descend into their followers in order to communicate with human beings. Taken together, the loa constitute a set of narrative structures ordering temporal experience. They are supplemented by various lesser spirits, especially the dead. The loa have as their ultimate point of reference Bon Dieu (God), who has been substituted for the Fon high god, Mawu. As in the tradition of the African high god, Bon Dieu is a remote being who has left his affairs in the hands of the other spiritual beings, the most important of whom are the loa. It is mainly by incarnating themselves in the bodies of *serviteurs*, through possession, that the loa present their stories, give advice, offer help, and reprimand their followers.[4]

The loa are the chief actors in a ritual drama. Victor Turner has argued that the dramatic component of ritual consists of a narrative structure that attempts to make sense of temporal experience and social crisis. Ritual has a redressive role in relation to what Turner calls the social dramas of everyday life. Ritual processes are invoked in response to a mounting social crisis in order to increase social reflexivity. The narrative component consists of "a distanced and generalized reduplication of the agonistic process of the social drama." The narrative structure of ritual drama provides a symbolic

4. Laënnec Hurbon, *Dieu dans le vaudou haïtien* (Paris: Payot, 1972), pp. 121–25. (All translations from this book are mine.) For summaries and classifications of the loa, see Hurbon, *Dieu,* pp. 106–109; Melville J. Herskovits, *Life in a Haitian Valley* (New York: Anchor-Doubleday, 1971), pp. 313–23; Alfred Métraux, *Voodoo in Haiti,* trans. Hugo Charteris (New York: Schocken, 1972), pp. 100–119; Harold Courlander, *The Drum and the Hoe: Life and Lore of the Haitian People* (Berkeley and Los Angeles: University of California Press, 1960), pp. 317–31; Maya Deren, *The Voodoo Gods* (Frogmore, Herts.: Granada-Paladin, 1975), pp. 84–85; Harold Courlander, *Haiti Singing* (1939; rpt. New York: Cooper Square, 1973), pp. 30–46; George Eaton Simpson, *Religious Cults of the Caribbean: Trinidad, Jamaica, and Haiti,* Caribbean Monograph Series, no. 15, 3d ed. enl. (Rio Piedras, Puerto Rico: Institute of Caribbean Studies, 1980), pp. 248–49.

matrix through which the group can "scrutinize, portray, understand and then act on itself."[5] Thus ritual gives rise to the possibility of either the reintegration of the disturbed social group or the social recognition that a breach is irreparable.

Though Turner highlights the social drama in which there is a distinct phase of crisis and factional struggle between groups, it should be emphasized that the narrative structure of ritual brings meaning to all the diverse experiences of everyday life, however minor the tensions and conflicts created by these experiences. Life, itself, is a social drama. Essentially, then, ritual recollects the storehouse of knowledge and meaning in a community so that it can be used to integrate lived experience. Ritual brings cultural order to social disorder. The ordering process is open-ended because new insights or new experiences can transform traditional understanding. The vaudou loa are the repositories of meaning who appear ritually to resurrect knowledge and provide new understanding.

Turner's model of narrative must be expanded in accordance with broader sociopolitical horizons if ritual processes are to be brought into relation with a critical narrative of liberation. Situated in the context of colonialism, vaudou can be analyzed as a response to colonial domination and exploitation. Remembering and celebrating a different precolonial life in Africa, the loa unify the colonized in opposition to the colonizer and consolidate the process of resistance. However, the loa are witnesses to the tragic misadventure of neocolonialism. They work for all who invoke them, and when a new ruling class pays them tribute, they become the ideological prop for an exploitative regime.

Unlike the mythology of many peoples, Haitian mythology is not generally related in the form of stories. As Alfred Métraux indicates, there are few actual myths to be heard in Haiti. This is because of the disruption brought about by the Middle Passage. Haitian mythology remains implicit; the center of its presentation is the ritual process itself, particularly possession. Followers of the loa know how their loa dress, talk, act, and even eat; they know their ritual symbols and sacred drawings, the music and the songs to which the loa respond.

5. Victor Turner, "Social Dramas and Stories about Them," in *On Narrative*, ed. W. J. T. Mitchell (Chicago: University of Chicago Press, 1981), pp. 152, 158. For an interesting use of Turner's analysis in Afro-Caribbean worship of the dead, see Jay D. Dobbin, "The Jombee Dance: Friendship and Ritual in Montserrat," *Caribbean Review*, 10 (Fall 1981), 28–31, 51.

Out of all these manifestations the mythological nature of the loa can be reconstructed. Religious songs, in particular, preserve the tradition by describing the loa and telling stories about them. As the "holy word" of vaudou theology, songs make use of aesthetic devices to recollect and recreate the "living memory" of vaudou tradition.[6] However, without the unifying influence of a priestly hierarchy, the vaudou text developed in different ways in different areas and remained open to a variety of expressions.

Possession, the climax of vaudou ritual, is the point at which a loa acts his or her mythological role (*mythos*) so that it can be brought to bear on reality (*mimesis*). The scene is set by the appropriate music, song, dance, and prayer. The loa appears on the divine stage in ritual costume to perform the sacred act and to receive the required libation and sacrifice. In a "fusing of horizons," to use Hans-Georg Gadamer's expression, the horizons of the living open onto the vistas of the venerated ancestors and guiding deities.[7] Meaning is retrieved in this perpetuation of tradition. Deren describes possession as the "central point" from which "surges the lavish arterial river of ancestral blood which bears all racial history forward into the contemporary moment."[8] The body of the serviteur is made into a sacred temple in which the language and word of the universe can be spoken. The ritual drama is a text in which a story is told, and it is this narrative that members of the community interpret in terms of the current events and social dramas they are experiencing. The concrete embodiment of myth in the ritual process, and its interpretation, are rule-governed cultural responses to concrete social situations. Because possession is such an important part of a community ritual, grounded in tradition, it cannot be reduced to the psychopathology of the individual.[9]

The loa are not limited to simply manifesting themselves. They are often requested to deal with specific events or social crises, or they may take it upon themselves to deal with these even if not specifically requested to do so. Deren remarks that vaudou must be pragmatic, given the harsh conditions of Haitian life. "It must do more than

6. Métraux, p. 114; Herskovits, p. 318; Michel S. Laguerre, *Voodoo Heritage,* Sage Library of Social Science, vol. 98 (Beverly Hills: Sage Publications, 1980), pp. 21–22.

7. Hans-Georg Gadamer, *Truth and Method,* trans. Garrett Barden and John Cumming (New York: Continuum-Seabury, 1975), pp. 269–74.

8. Deren, p. 233.

9. Métraux, pp. 132–36; Herskovits, pp. 147–48; Hurbon, *Dieu,* pp. 140–41.

provide a reason for living; it must provide the *means* for living."[10]
Loa are required to advise on planting, to give practical council on
social issues such as marriage or conflict, to provide protection, to
prescribe treatment for sickness, and, in the case of the Petro nation of
loa, in particular, to bring harm to others. Their task is to regulate
and control social relationships and relationships with nature.

Guérin Montilus states that the situation of oppression should be
taken as the point of departure for the analysis of Haitian culture.
Vaudou mythology can, indeed, be seen as a symbolic transformation
of colonial plantation society and its neocolonial legacy.[11] A spatial
metaphor of colonial oppression is present in the Haitian legend of
Trou Forban, the fearsome plantation on which zombies work as
slaves for their sorcerer-masters.[12] A zombie, according to Haitian
religion, is a human being whom a sorcerer has killed, raised from the
dead, and restored to bodily form; the soul and will of the zombie are
completely controlled by the sorcerer. In Africa, sorcery was understood as the major source of evil, whether in the form of disruption of
the community or in the form of natural misfortune.[13] The disruption of African communities, the collective enslavement of black people, and their transportation from their African homeland were such
catastrophic events that they were presumed to be the result, in part,
of sorcery. The white master was an evil sorcerer who used his power
to control his slaves by turning them into zombies. The legend of the
Trou Forban and the idea of the zombie lived on in the neocolonial
period as a response to the rise of exploitative and repressive indigenous elites. The legend is a narrative recollecting alienation under
slavery and political and social oppression in the neocolonial period.[14]

10. Deren, p. 76.

11. Guérin Montilus, "Mythes, écologie, acculturation en Haïti: Essai sur la réin-
térpretation des mythes du Golfe de Guinée dans le vaudou haïtien sous l'influence des
Fon du Bas-Dahomey" (Ph.D. diss., University of Zurich, 1973), p. 192. For a
general discussion of the failure of functionalist anthropology to deal with the colonial
system, see, in particular, Peter Forster, "Empiricism and Imperialism: A Review of
the New Left Critique of Social Anthropology," in *Anthropology and the Colonial
Encounter*, ed. Asad Talal (London: Ithaca Press, 1973), pp. 23–38.

12. Courlander, *Haiti*, p. 88.

13. The other source of misfortune was the contravention of group regulations and
religious obligations. See John S. Mbiti, *African Religions and Philosophy* (London:
Heinemann, 1969), pp. 213–15.

14. Métraux, pp. 281–85; Laënnec Hurbon, *Culture et dictature en Haïti: L'imaginaire
sous contrôle* (Paris: Harmattan, 1979), p. 129. Focusing on the Jamaican situation,
Schuler has also noted the conception of master as sorcerer in "Afro-American Slave

The zombie-sorcerer relationship encodes the Manichaean conflict between the colonizer and the colonized. By depicting the master as a sorcerer, Haitian culture presents him as an evil, powerful person who must be feared, but who, because he is in the wrong, also deserves to be severely punished. Maximilien Laroche argues that the state of slavery is not taken for granted in the myth of the zombie. If the zombie is given salt, he or she will become conscious of enslavement and destroy the master. Thus the state of enslavement is to some extent reversible.[15] Furthermore, the oppressed Haitian could also avail himself of the spiritual powers in existence. To counter the master's power, the Haitian cultivated a close relationship with traditional deities, and resorted to aggressive action in the form of sorcery and antisorcery (healing) rituals and techniques.[16]

Vaudou divinities encode the temporal processes sustaining the colonial drama of domination and resistance. The loa, like most aspects of the African religions that came to Haiti, were transformed and creolized through contact with other African divinities and with the Catholic saints that the slaves were forced to or chose to adopt and adapt. Catholicism taught that the African loa were manifestations of the devil; devil worship had to be replaced by Christianity. The slaves resisted this cultural attack by syncretizing elements of their own religion with compatible elements of Catholicism. Vaudou loa were sometimes given the names of Catholic saints: Legba, guardian of the crossroad and gateway, was syncretized with Saint Peter, who opens the gate to Heaven. This process of creolization was facilitated by the traditional openness of West African religions to new rituals, beliefs, and deities. Hurbon stresses that the masking of the loa is a rein-

---

Culture," in *Roots and Branches: Current Directions in Slave Studies,* ed. Michael Craton, Historical Reflections, Directions Series, no. 1 (Toronto: Pergamon Press, 1979), pp. 130–32. New research indicates that there is more than symbolic truth in the belief in zombies: Haitian sorcerers use special medicines to put their victims into a state of simulated death; then they bring their captives back to life under their control. See Jacques Pradel and Jean-Yves Casgha, *Haïti, la république des morts vivants* (Monaco: Editions du Rocher, 1983), and Art Candell, "Zombies Are for Real," *The Caribbean and West Indian Chronicle,* August–September 1984.

15. Maximilien Laroche, "The Myth of the Zombi," in *Exile and Tradition: Studies in African and Caribbean Literature,* ed. Rowland Smith, Dalhousie African Studies Series (London: Longman and Dalhousie University Press, 1976), p. 56.

16. The tension between the oppressor as sorcerer and the use of sorcery-healing to resist oppression is an important theme in the novel *The Beast of the Haitian Hills,* by Philippe Thoby-Marcelin and Pierre Marcelin, trans. Peter C. Rhodes (London: Victor Gollancz, 1951), pp. 61–66, 195–99.

terpretation of Christianity in terms of traditional African belief. Even though vaudou incorporated elements of Christianity and in this way protected itself, Christianity remained a separate religion, an "other," in the eyes of the followers of vaudou. Vaudou provided the slaves and their descendants with ways of understanding their new world that were different from the understanding of their oppressors. It allowed them to consolidate their identity as an exploited group in opposition to a racially and culturally distinct exploiter group.[17]

The crossroad complex of deities (particularly Legba, Carrefour, and the Gede loa) illustrate some of the ways in which vaudou orders Haitian social and political experience in terms of resistance. Fon myths relate how Mawu gave Legba the gift of understanding different languages; she made him into the messenger and means of communication between herself and the gods and between the gods and human beings. While the Haitian Legba has retained this connection with the crossroad, he has lost to other loa in Haiti the Fon Legba's power over divination and destiny, healing and sorcery, and he is no longer a typical trickster. In Haiti, Legba is perceived to be a wise, fatherly king from Guinea who guards all entrances, dwelling places, roads, and crossroads. Legba's power comes from his control of crossroads and entrances, the sacred spaces where the human and the divine worlds meet. At the beginning of ceremonies, he is requested to "open the gate [*ouvri barrière*]" so that the other loa may pass through. As intermediary between the human and the divine, Legba assures the community that order itself is possible and opens the way to that order.[18]

---

17. Hurbon, *Dieu*, pp. 219–22. Sidney W. Mintz and Richard Price discuss in general terms the process by which a new and vital Afro-American culture was created in *An Anthropological Approach to the Afro-American Past: A Caribbean Perspective*, ISHI Occasional Papers in Social Change, no. 2 (Philadelphia: Institute for the Study of Human Issues, 1976), pp. 24–26; see also Schuler's response, "Afro-American Slave Culture," pp. 120–24, 129, the responses of Richard Price and Edward Brathwaite to Schuler, also in Craton, *Roots and Branches* (pp. 146 and 155, respectively), and David Trotman, "The Yoruba and Orisha Worship in Trinidad and British Guiana: 1838–1870," *African Studies Review*, 29 (September 1976), 12–13.

18. Melville J. Herskovits and Frances S. Herskovits, *Dahomean Narrative: A Cross-Cultural Analysis*, Northwestern University African Studies, no. 1 (Evanston: Northwestern University Press, 1958), pp. 125–26, 139–40, 142–48 (particularly p. 147), 176–79; Herskovits, p. 174; Deren, p. 98; Laguerre, *Voodoo Heritage*, p. 52; Courlander, *Haiti*, pp. 35–36; Courlander, *Drum*, p. 133; Métraux, pp. 101–102, 360–61; Emmanuel C. Paul, *Panorama du folklore haïtien* (1962; rpt. Port-au-Prince: Fardin, 1978), p. 265.

The Haitian Legba, in comparison to the youthful, phallic Fon (and Yoruba) Legbas, is a limping, old man. Deren argues that it is the transformation from free person to slave that is symbolized in this change: "It is as if, in coming westwards, the Africans had left behind the morning and noon of their destiny, the promise and power of their own history."[19] Montilus sees in Legba's infirmity a symbolic representation of the wretchedness of the peasant. Legba smokes a peasant pipe and carries on his shoulders the sack that the peasant takes into the fields. The sack contains the peasant's smoked green banana and cassava, not the ripe boiled banana and wheat of the bourgeoisie. Yet, supported on his crutch or cane, his apparent weakness hides an inner strength: he is still a powerful loa who descends with great force into the body of the possessed.[20]

Many of Legba's characteristics were transferred onto new deities in Haiti. Maître Carrefour (crossroad), also known as Kalfou or Legba Petro, is a deity distinct from Legba yet related to him. Carrefour has retained from the Fon Legba power over healing and sorcery, particularly when they take place at the crossroad. However, he exercises his power at night. Songs describe him as a magician and a dangerous spirit. His domain is magic, both benign and malevolent, for healing and sorcery.[21]

Some mythological aspects of the Fon Legba are also associated in Haiti with the Gede. The Gede family, and particularly leading members like Baron Samedi and Gede Nibo, are crossroad loa associated with death and the dead, sorcery, healing, eroticism, and the disorderly behavior typical of the trickster. Songs describe the Gede in funereal terms, invoking images of the cross and the cemetery. Some Gede dress as corpses, and Baron Samedi wears the black hat and dress coat of an undertaker. Whereas the Rada loa are addressed through the mediation of Legba, the ancestors ("the dead") are addressed, and ancestral council is sought, through the mediation of the Gede.[22]

The Fon Legba is linked to sorcery and healing. In Haiti, Baron Samedi, like Carrefour, guides the malevolent work of sorcerers and

19. Deren, p. 99.
20. Montilus, pp. 161–63.
21. Deren, p. 101; Courlander, *Haiti*, p. 99; Laguerre, *Voodoo Heritage*, pp. 117–18; Herskovits, pp. 233–40; Herskovits and Herskovits, *Dahomean Narrative*, pp. 139–44.
22. Montilus, p. 17; Laguerre, *Voodoo Heritage*, pp. 95, 100–102, 208; Herskovits, p. 166; Métraux, pp. 113–14; Deren, p. 103.

secret societies at crossroads or at the crosses in cemeteries. When they are ready to raise a zombie from the coffin, they ask Baron Samedi to "hold that man [*quembé n'homme na*]." Through Baron Samedi, the sorcerer can transform himself into an animal or change others into animals. Like Carrefour, Baron Samedi and other leading members of the Gede family have power over healing and can restore the dying to life. This ability to preserve life or to decide when death will come gives Baron Samedi some of the power over destiny characteristic of the Fon Legba.[23] Devotees sing: "If you need *wanga* [charms], where do you go? To the house of Guédé. If you want advice where do you go? To the house of Guédé. If you need treatment where do you go? To the house of Guédé."[24] The Gede remind the community that death is real and that evil exists, but they also give access to the forces of life and, therefore, control over destiny.

The Gede are also associated with the erotic and indiscriminate behavior typical of the trickster and of the Fon Legba in particular. One of the recurring images of Legba in Fon mythology is the image of a never-satisfied male with an erect penis who tries to take any woman at hand. The Fon Legba avoids being reprimanded for his antisocial behavior through cunning, deceit, and magic. He even outwits and humiliates his mother, Mawu. In Haiti the Gede often appear toward the end of ceremonies dancing the erotic *banda* dance and singing about genitals and sexual intercourse. The Gede are also greedy, disruptive, and quite comical. Songs describe them as vagabonds and troublemakers. The Gede are terrifying, yet ridiculous; they are sources of trouble, yet they give protection.[25] As in the case of the Fon Legba, disruptive and disorderly behavior is tied to human intercourse, healing, and the renewal of life. In a statement relevant to the Haitian Gede, Pelton describes Fon Legba mythology as a "foray into the formless, which simultaneously gives human shape to the dark and fearsome and new life to a structure always in danger of becoming a skeleton."[26]

23. Herskovits, p. 225; Laguerre, *Voodoo Heritage*, p. 104; Courlander, *Haiti*, pp. 87–88; Deren, pp. 111–12.

24. Métraux, p. 115.

25. Herskovits and Herskovits, *Dahomean Narrative*, pp. 142–50, 173–76; Laguerre, *Voodoo Heritage*, pp. 97, 102–103, 106; Métraux, p. 113; Deren, pp. 104–105; Herskovits, p. 167.

26. Robert D. Pelton, *The Trickster in West Africa: A Study of Mythic Irony and Sacred Delight* (Berkeley and Los Angeles: University of California Press, 1980), p. 94.

Legba, Carrefour, and the Gede meet at the crossroad. The cross, symbol of the crossroad, is prominent in their symbolic drawings. The crossroad is the point of intersection between the visible and the invisible, the living and the ancestors, the devotees and the loa. Legba, Carrefour, and the Gede are three aspects of one mythological complex. Legba gives access to the mythological realm, but he has become a limping old man. Carrefour is a virile young man who aggressively takes charge of sorcery and healing. The Gede go beyond Carrefour to descend into the abyss and retrieve new potency. Deren has underscored the connection between Legba and the Gēde (particularly Baron Samedi, whom she equates with Gede Nibo). Legba opens the ceremony and gives access to the life source. The ceremony concludes with salutations to Gede, who gives access to souls of the dead. If Legba is Lord of Life, Gede is Lord of Resurrection. According to Deren, the cosmic abyss "is both tomb and womb." "In a sense," she states, "Ghede is the Legba who has crossed the cosmic threshold to the underworld, for Ghede is now everything that Legba once was in the promise and prime of his life." Gede "is the cosmic corpse which informs man of life."[27]

The transformation of Legba in the colonial world made of him a powerful but suffering tragic hero. However, the Gede appropriated from the Fon Legba the power over life and laughter, which could turn the suffered contradiction into a painless one. Missionaries in West Africa regarded Legba especially, with his grand phallus, to be a manifestation of Satan.[28] On the slave plantation in Haiti, Legba would not be allowed to stand outside the doorway exhibiting his manly power. This loss is compensated in Haitian mythology through Carrefour and the Gede, who adopt some of Legba's original vigor and virility. Carrefour and the Gede could operate more secretively, often under the cover of darkness, thus eluding the missionaries. Still, the significance of the Gede does not lie simply in this feature of camouflage. By transferring onto the Gede attributes of the Fon Legba, Haitians encoded an important approach to their situation. In their erotic behavior, the Gede are symbols of fertility. With their healing powers, they are symbols of regeneration. They are

27. Deren, pp. 102, 43–44.
28. Pierre Verger, *Notes sur le culte des orisa et vodun à Bahia, la Baie de tous les saints, au Brèsil et à l'ancienne Côte des Esclaves en Afrique*, Mémoires de l'Institut Français d'Afrique Noire, no. 51 (Dakar, 1957), pp. 109, 120–25; Herskovits and Herskovits, *Dahomean Narrative*, pp. 150–51.

symbols of the resurrection that turns death into new life. Legba has encountered the death that is slavery and is reborn in the Gede as the struggle for survival and life. Deren eloquently captures this element of the Legba–Gede relationship: "If Legba was once Lord of Life, Ghede is now Lord of Resurrection, and the difference between them is Death, which is Ghede. It is the knowledge of death that has transfigured Legba, and has given to all that they have in common the particular colour and accent which is Ghede."[29] Knowledge about death and about the possibilities of recreating a new life give believers some control over slavery and postemancipation oppression.

The Gede are symbols of the resistance to slavery that makes individual and group life possible. In their comic behavior the Gede are tricksters who defy social restriction, unmask contradictions, and blunt the bitter edge of oppression. As death that levels all, and as death transcended, the Gede have an unmatched capacity to resist the colonizer and heighten recognition of social conflict. The movement from life to new life, from Legba to the Gede, is indicated in the order of possession in most Rada ceremonies. As Bastide points out, there is both a tragic and a comic component. The service moves from the tragic, beginning with Legba, opener of the symbolic world, to the comic, ending with the Gede, guarantors of the power of the symbolic in the struggle for survival.[30]

Métraux provides some good examples of the Gede as comic demystifiers of social and political reality in the contemporary period. It is a Gede who rebukes and shames two loa, Siren and Whale, when they snobbishly affect elegance and begin talking French. In another instance, Gede parody the Catholic catechism and the Haitian military and political elites. Mimicking a catechism class, Gede break out into a typical Gede song crudely describing coitus; for their contributions to the class, they are rewarded with military, political, or ecclesiastical titles.[31]

During the American occupation of Haiti (1915–34), there occurred a dramatic incident involving the Gede loa. *Houngans* (vaudou priests) possessed by Gede loa marched up to the presidential palace accompanied by a large crowd. They were ritually dressed (tall silk hats, long black tailcoats, smoked glasses—clothes suitable for a visit

---

29. Deren, p. 102.
30. Roger Bastide, *African Civilizations in the New World,* trans. Peter Green (New York: Torchbook–Harper & Row, 1971), p. 140; see also Deren, p. 43.
31. Métraux, pp. 104, 334–35.

to a president), carried flags, waved ceremonial handkerchiefs, and shook sacred rattles. The surprised palace guards waited helplessly while the Gede demanded money from a president reputed to be secretly sympathetic to vaudou. President Borno feared the houngans, but he also feared the antivaudou bourgeois class that backed him. Eventually he gave in, sent out money, and then ordered the guards to disperse the crowd.[32]

True to their image as demystifiers of social and political reality, the Gede march dramatized the conflict between the poor, oppressed peasant masses in the neocolonial period, and the wealthy national bourgeoisie, headed by a president working for American capitalism. The ritual process, that is, the march, is a narrative episode encoding the sociopolitical contradiction. The resolution has a romantic aspect to the extent that the ritual culminates in a gift of money that symbolically resolves the immediate conflict. Yet the contradiction between the people and their leader is dramatized in the subsequent event: the guards are ordered to disperse the crowd. In spite of the tragic overtones that this final circumstance connotes, the entire incident becomes comic. The Gede, with their peculiar clothing and behavior, their daring disregard for all protocol, and their relative success, ensure that such is the case.

When the government-backed Catholic clergy attempted to eliminate vaudou in the "antisuperstition" campaigns of the early 1940s, the Gede again resisted. In one instance, as Catholic priests uprooted and burned crosses in family burial grounds, Baron Samedi and other members of the Gede family possessed women bystanders and uttered the following threat: "Do you really think you can get rid of us like this? All you are burning is wood. Us, you will never burn. Today you throw these crosses into the fire but soon you will see another kind of fire burning in this valley."[33]

This sense of identity and resistance is captured in the symbol of Africa in vaudou mythology. Guinea, the Congo, or other African nations are referred to as the ancestral home. The name of a particular African nation, usually Guinea, came to symbolize not merely that geopolitical entity but Africa itself, the homeland. From there loa journey to meet their devotees in Haiti; to Africa the dead return. The

32. Courlander, *Haiti*, p. 85; see also Deren, p. 106; Laguerre, *Voodoo Heritage*, p. 106.
33. Métraux, p. 348.

community affirms that it is the privileged bearer of an African tradition that is distinct from, and opposed to, the European colonial structure and its neocolonial heir. African tradition, however transformed and creolized, remains as the primary spiritual sustenance that guides actions and makes survival possible.

Sometimes an African nation is presented as a true home and the colonial world as an alien land. One vaudou song goes so far as to demand that the deity Ouangol (Roi Angola) repatriate his followers: "Ouangol, bring me back to Africa [Congo]. . . . This country is not mine [*Min ninm alé o Ouangol adié Congo. . . . Pei sa pa pou moin*]."[34] It is not difficult to imagine slaves in the colonial period in particular, many of whom were African-born, expressing in earnest this desire to return home. One way of returning to the ancestors was to die deliberately, through suicide, thus depriving the slave owner of labor. The belief that the dead dwelt in Africa could also be cultivated as a weapon of battle: it encouraged some slaves to risk their lives in challenging the slave owner, for should death strike, they would return to Africa.[35] Above all, however, Africa was a pragmatic symbol of a living Afro-American tradition and community aware of its identity and struggling for its survival in opposition to the colonizer.

Vaudou went beyond limited forms of symbolic and actual resistance to play a role in rebellions aimed at transforming the system of oppression altogether. Religious symbolism, myth, and ritual unified the slave community against its owners and induced slaves to believe that they could not be harmed by bullets or that they would return to Africa if they died on the battlefield. The transformative dimension of Vaudou reached its peak in the Haitian Revolution. Nevertheless, the revolution cannot be reduced to vaudou. The slaves fought against the immediate forms of oppression that they faced and, in doing so, made use of what they were familiar with, including their religion. As C. L. R. James has shown, the revolution was also a response to tensions between mulattoes and whites, French and British, and between the French ruling classes themselves. Very important, as well, was the influence of the French Revolution and the discourse of liber-

---

34. Laguerre, *Voodoo Heritage*, p. 112.

35. Métraux, pp. 43–44; Orlando Patterson discusses suicide in the Jamaican situation in *The Sociology of Slavery: An Analysis of the Origins, Development and Structure of Negro Slave Society in Jamaica* (London, 1967; rpt. Kingston: Sangster's Bookstores, 1973), pp. 264–65.

ty that gripped leaders like Toussaint L'Ouverture.[36] In the Haitian Revolution, a slave rebellion was transformed into a successful struggle for emancipation and national independence, but this only made room for the tragic rise of conflicting black and mulatto military elites, who would become a dependent bourgeoisie in the neocolonial period. For the slaves and their leaders, national consciousness remained merely implicit. The tension between a restorationist-oriented rebellion, based on Afro-Haitian culture and religious tradition, and a European-influenced revolution, led by the slave, free black, and mulatto elites, was never resolved.

In 1757 the African-born Macandal led a group of maroons against white slaveowners with the intention of driving whites out of Saint Domingue. The rebels poisoned white masters and pillaged plantations. According to the eighteenth century French historian Moreau de Saint-Méry, Macandal persuaded the slaves that he was the mouthpiece of a loa, that he was immortal, and that he should be worshiped. When he was caught and burned, many slaves refused to believe that he had perished. Popular tradition relates that he was possessed by a loa and escaped. His name has become a term used for poison or poisoner.[37]

Some decades later, another rebel leader appeared, Boukman, a Jamaican-born houngan. Boukman was the headman on his plantation. Along with other slave conspirators, he planned an elaborate slave revolt that developed into the Haitian Revolution. James comments on the connection between vaudou and the conspiracy: "Voodoo was the medium of the conspiracy. In spite of all prohibitions, the slaves travelled miles to sing and dance and practise the rites and talk; and now, since the [French] revolution to hear the political news and make their plans."[38]

Historians have reconstructed the ritual events preceding Bouk-

36. C. L. R. James, *The Black Jacobins: Toussaint L'Ouverture and the San Domingo Revolution,* 2d ed. (New York: Vintage-Random House, 1963), pp. 81–82; see also Eugene Genovese, *From Rebellion to Revolution: Afro-American Slave Revolts in the Making of the Modern World* (Baton Rouge: Louisiana State University Press, 1979), pp. 123–26.

37. Louis-Elie Moreau de Saint-Méry, *Description topographique, physique, civile politique et historique de la partie française de l'île Saint-Domingue* (1797; rpt. Paris: Société de l'Histoire des Colonies Françaises et Librairie Larose, 1958), vol. 2, pp. 629–31; Métraux, pp. 46–47; Odette Mennesson-Rigaud, "Le Rôle du vaudou dans l'indépendance d'Haïti," *Présence Africaine,* February–May 1958, pp. 54–55; Simpson, *Religious Cults,* p. 235.

38. James, p. 86.

man's revolt using the limited documentary evidence and drawing heavily from the oral tradition. These reconstructions remain hypothetical both because of the necessarily covert nature of any such religio-political undertaking and because of the transformations that the oral tradition may have undergone, particularly in response to varying Haitian intellectual and ideological climates. When twentieth-century Haitian scholars argue that the achievement of independence in 1804 was the work of vaudou, they are oversimplifying one complex aspect of the revolutionary struggle.[39] Nevertheless, the evidence suggests that vaudou did a play an important role in the revolution.

According to the reconstructions, Boukman assembled his supporters in the secrecy of the Bois Caïman on a stormy night in 1791. He stated that the high god of the slaves (Bon Dieu) had ordered vengeance and would assist the slaves in their task. He continued: "Throw away the symbol of the god of the whites who has so often caused us to weep, and listen to the voice of liberty, which speaks in the hearts of us all! [*Jetez portraits Dieu blanc / Qui soif d'l'eau dans yeux nous / Coutez la liberté qui nan coeur à nous tous!*]" In the middle of the ceremony, an old priestess appeared dancing wildly with a cutlass. She plunged it into the neck of a black pig. The slaves drank the blood and swore allegiance to Boukman and solidarity to each other in their attempt to exterminate the white masters. Shortly after the ceremony, Boukman gave the signal to set on fire the plantations in the north and kill all white men, women, and children.[40]

Boukman was killed in battle, but other leaders took over. Armies

39. See, for example, Michel S. Laguerre, "Voodoo as Religious and Revolutionary Ideology," *Freeing the Spirit,* 3, (1974), p. 25; Mennesson-Rigaud, p. 56.

40. James, pp. 86–88; Mennesson-Rigaud, pp. 58–60. See also Laguerre, "Voodoo as Ideology," pp. 25–26; Métraux, pp. 42–43; Montilus, pp. 92–93; Jean Price-Mars, *Ainsi parla l'oncle* (Ottawa: Lemeac, 1973), pp. 93–94. That such a speech was actually heard at that time is questioned by David Geggus in "Slave Resistance Studies and the Saint Domingue Slave Revolt: Some Preliminary Considerations," Occasional Papers Series, no. 4, Latin American and Caribbean Center of Florida International University, Winter 1983, p. 15. Most commentators accept that the Bois Caïman ceremony itself did occur in some form. Geggus (p. 16) aruges that though probable, there is only a slender thread of historical evidence for it: A. Dalmas, *Histoire de la révolution de Saint-Domingue* (1814), which mentions neither Boukman nor the priestess, and B. Ardouin, *Etudes sur l'histoire d'Haïti* (1853) in which they first appear. However, the reconstruction of the ceremony is based not only on these sources but also on the folk tradition; see Mennesson-Rigaud, p. 59. The link between religion and resistance in Jamaica has been traced in various works by Monica Schuler; see, for example, "Afro-American Slave Culture," pp. 128–36.

under black generals were organized, and conflict ensued until independence was won on January 1, 1804. In a complex process full of ironic twists, the slaves of Saint Domingue eventually threw off their yokes and joined black and mulatto freedmen to defeat Napoleon's army, eliminate the French plantocracy, and destroy the colonial system in Saint Domingue. In the tradition of Macandal and Boukman, guerrilla leaders used religion in the struggle. Biassou, for example, surrounded himself with religious specialists and held ceremonies in the middle of the night prior to attacking the enemy. At the peak of the ceremony, he announced that he was divinely inspired and that anyone who was killed would return to Africa. Then he led his forces out to battle. Derance, advised by houngans, led his troops with shouts that the bullets were merely dust. Ducoudray ran through his ranks waving the tail of a bull and shouting, like Derance, that the bullets were made of dust; his forces were told that they would return to Africa, if killed. Halaou had healers in his band and carried a white cock under his arm claiming that it transmitted to him the desires of the loa.[41]

Some scholars have suggested ways in which particular mythological structures lent significance to the revolutionary process. Which loa were influential in the revolution and why? Was it Ogoun, the loa of war; the Gede, who understand the meaning of death and the processes for counteracting sorcery, or the Petro loa, who understand both sorcery and fiercely aggressive antisorcery healing techniques?

Deren argues that it was the Petro nation of loa that provided the moral force and organization that initiated the Haitian Revolution. Even today, she states, the words *vive la liberté* occur regularly in Petro ritual songs. The aggression and malevolence of Petro loa symbolize the violent anger of transported slaves protesting their enslavement: "Petro was born out of this rage. It is not evil; it is the rage against the evil fate which the African suffered, the brutality of his displacement and his enslavement. It is the violence that rose out of that rage, to protest against it. It is the crack of the slave-whip sound-

---

41. Métraux, pp. 43–44, 47; Simpson, pp. 235–36; Mennesson-Rigaud, pp. 63–64; Laguerre, "Voodoo as Ideology," p. 27; Vittorio Lanternari overemphasizes the messianic nature of vaudou in *The Religions of the Oppressed: A Study of Modern Messianic Cults,* trans. Lisa Sergio (Toronto: Mentor–New American Library of Canada, 1965), pp. 139–41. One of the main sources of these descriptions is Thomas Madiou's *Histoire d'Haïti* (1847–48). Geggus (p. 17) questions the accuracy of some of Madiou's descriptions.

ing constantly, a-never-to-be-forgotten-ghost, in the Petro rites. It is the raging revolt of the slaves against the Napoleonic forces. And it is the delirium of their triumph."[42]

The Petro nation was founded by an eighteenth-century houngan, Don Pedro, who has become a vaudou deity, Dan Petro. The Petro cult developed into an aggressive rite, distinct from the Rada rite, with an emphasis on sorcery-healing. Petro loa are described as powerful, violent, and malevolent. Petro adherents sing: "When enemies try to harass me, I shall order a malevolent spirit to take care of them [*Jou mangagé malagé ion gro loa nan dè ié io*]." Jean Petro is asked: "How many little men have you eaten [*combien ti mounes ou mangé*]?" Songs identify Carrefour, Legba Petro, as a powerful accomplice of Dan Petro. Deren convincingly associates Petro rites with the revolution. The aggressiveness of the Petro loa, their connection with the techniques of sorcery and healing, and the use of gunpowder in Petro ritual give credence to the idea that Petro rites were closely tied to the revolution.[43]

Deren attributes the aggressive characteristics of the Petro nation to the Amerindian (Carib) influence on Black Maroons. She argues that the Amerindian religious system offered a decentralized, dynamic, and aggressive ethos, emphasizing magic and sorcery, which the Dahomean tradition lacked, and which the Africans found to be particularly appropriate to the new experience of enslavement in the Americas. The Dahomean Ogoun, Deren concludes, was too honest and chivalrous a warrior for the colonial situation. Only wily and ruthless deities, who could sponsor guerrilla tactics and provide magical protection, were appropriate for the initial stages of the revolution.[44]

The problem with Deren's argument is that she overemphasizes the contrast between the African and the Indian ethos and the impact of the latter on Petro rites. In traditional African religions, sorcerers were held to be the source of the disruption of the community: the response to sorcery was aggressive antisorcery (healing), often having recourse to the same techniques as sorcery, but in the interest of the

42. Deren, pp. 66–67.
43. Moreau de Saint-Méry, vol. 1, p. 69; Métraux, pp. 39, 118; Courlander, *Haiti*, pp. 48, 132; Herskovits, p. 151; Laguerre, *Voodoo Heritage*, pp. 48, 113–15, 124, 144; Deren, p. 116.
44. Deren, pp. 67–71, 131.

community. Furthermore, as Deren herself points out, Petro ritual is also influenced by non-Dahomean African ritual. Congo slaves, in particular, had a reputation for aggressive ritual and *marronage*, that is, running away. In contrast to Deren, Métraux hypothesizes that the Petro rites are derived from an unknown African source.[45] Most likely, Petro is an adaptation based on different African sources and New World influences.

Deren's discussion of Petro rites is influenced by the work of the Haitian scholars Lorimer Denis and Odette Mennesson-Rigaud. Using vaudou tradition, particularly ritual song, Denis and Mennesson-Rigaud reconstructed a vaudou version of the events of Boukman's Bois Caïman ceremony. The songs were in agreement that it was a Congo-Petro ceremony. The Rada deities did not participate in the ceremony, but they lent their support in the ensuing struggle. The Rada loa could not help when first addressed because they did not have the right to make blood flow. However, the Congo-Petro loa came to the rescue. The Rada loa could then send those members of their nation who were connected with fire, thunder, or tempests to join the Petro loa in their struggle. Gede-L'Oraille transmitted the plans of the great council of Rada loa to the battlefield.[46] This reconstruction can be faulted for painting the Rada in such benevolent terms that mention of their participation in the revolution becomes problematic. Nevertheless, the movement from secrecy to rebellion follows the logic of guerrilla struggle. Once the battle had broken out, the Rada loa, particularly those related to battle such as Ogoun, would become significant again.

The role of the Gede in the revolution derives from their connection with death, sorcery, and healing. Though the Gede are generally considered to be Rada loa, this connection brings them into relation with the Petro nation. Baron Samedi, in particular, is important to sorcerers and healers. (Hurbon and Barrett consider all Gede members to be Petro loa.) With their power over life and death and their control of spiritual and physical means of harming and helping people, they could play an important role in an incipient struggle against oppression. Inasmuch as their story represents the transformation of

45. Deren, pp. 72–74; Métraux, p. 86.
46. Mennesson-Rigaud, pp. 59–60. Even if the reconstruction is historically inaccurate, it indicates the importance with which twentieth-century vaudou adherents regard the revolution and the manner in which they associate it with the work of particular deities.

life through death, and the renewal of life against all adversities, they could order and inspire the types of activities of which a vicious war between master and slave was composed. Barrett observed a vaudou ceremony in Gede's honor in which Gede appeared, dressed in red and black, with a pistol in his pocket. Gede acted out a ritual drama with the *hunsis* (initiates), who were dressed in eighteenth-century French military uniforms. When the hunsis charged against Gede, he pulled out his pistol and fired; all fell to the ground. This ritual drama was a reenactment of the war against the French forces at the time of the revolution. Nearly two centuries after its occurrence, the revolution was being celebrated and participants in the ritual drama reminded of the history and promise of their nation, the first of the modern independent Third World countries.[47]

The role of the Ogoun family in the revolution is of interest because of its connection with the waging of war and, hence, with the processes of social and political transformation. If the crossroad is the point of ambiguity, the meeting place between order and disorder, warfare is one area in which this indeterminacy is manifested in history. The Ogouns share some of the ambiguity characteristic of crossroad loa. They are usually classified as Rada loa but have Petro manifestations. (Laguerre classifies the whole family as Petro loa.) Ogoun, the army strategist, goes to the crossroad deity Simbi for medicinal assistance. According to a rare Haitian myth, Ogoun Badagri is Gede Nibo's godfather. When Gede Nibo grew up, he pretended to be Ogoun's brother, which upset the general very much. Therefore, during ceremonies, Ogoun may chase Gede Nibo and make him kneel to beg for forgiveness. The myth suggests that there is an unresolved tension between the warring vigor with which Ogoun approaches life (and death) and the subtle comedy and ambiguous eroticism through which Gede transforms death (and life) at the crossroad.[48]

Vaudou songs identify Ogoun as a "bloody general [*jénéral sâglâ*]" and associate him with the ferocity of a thunder and lightning storm. He is described as being a "son of battle [*ga'çon la guè*]." A strong protector, Ogoun provides immunity against attack, and weapons

47. Leonard Barrett, "African Religion in the Americas: The 'Islands in Between,'" *African Religions: A Symposium,* ed. Newell S. Booth, Jr. (New York: NOK Publishers, 1977), pp. 203–204; Hurbon, *Dieu,* p. 108.

48. Courlander, *Drum,* p. 330; Laguerre, *Voodoo Heritage,* pp. 121, 131–37; Deren, pp. 115–16; Métraux, p. 114.

for war. His serviteurs sing: "Every time I remember you, / I have some consolation and gain more courage [*Kanm rété msongé Ogou Féray / Mconsolé aléman aléman ko-anie / Oua kitan oua kitan ko-anie / Mpa rélé aléman alémiso sobagi ma sié*]." Ogoun Ferraille is covered with iron knives and machetes. Ogoun likes rum and women; his color is red.[49] Ogoun's association with strength and metal weapons derives from Fon and Yoruba mythology. Mawu gave Ogoun her strength and made him master of the forge, producer of iron tools and weapons. One Dahomean myth relates that instead of a head a sword comes out of his neck.[50] In Haiti, Ogoun has taken on, in addition, the association with lightning and thunder that the Fon attribute to Hèbyosso and the Yoruba of Nigeria, to Shango. Hèbyosso has disappeared in Haiti. Shango remains and is often treated as a manifestation of Ogoun, Ogoun-Shango. Shango was a powerful warrior king. The Haitians related their fierce Ogoun to the warlike thunder and lightning of Shango rather than to that of Hèbyosso.[51]

Speaking through the mouth of a possessed person, an Ogoun once declared that his task was to watch over the security of the national territory and claimed that he and Shango (that is, Ogoun-Shango) were the principal protectors of General Dessalines. In the reconstruction of Denis and Mennesson-Rigaud, Ogoun-Ferraille was one of the Rada loa who came to the help of the Petro loa in the war of independence. (Mennesson-Rigaud further claims that Toussaint, though sometimes described as a devout Catholic, fought under Ogoun-Fer in the war of independence, but the evidence for this is weak.) Dessalines, who began as one of Toussaint's lieutenants, is said to have consulted the deities before any engagement. Dessalines dressed for battle in Ogoun-Shango's red clothes. Sometimes Ogoun-Shango possessed him and thus himself directed the combat.[52]

49. Métraux, p. 107; Courlander, *Drum*, p. 78; Courlander, *Haiti*, p. 80; Laguerre, *Voodoo Heritage*, pp. 133, 136.

50. Herskovits and Herskovits, *Dahomean Narrative*, p. 125; Harold Courlander, *A Treasury of African Folklore: The Oral Literature, Traditions, Myths, Legends, Epics, Tales, Recollections, Wisdom, Sayings, and Humor of Africa* (New York: Crown Publishers, 1975), pp. 194–96.

51. Montilus, p. 187; Herskovits, p. 320; Courlander, *Haiti*, p. 40; see also Courlander, *African Folklore*, pp. 205–10.

52. Paul, p. 278; Mennesson-Rigaud, pp. 59n29; 64–66; see also Laguerre, "Voodoo as Ideology," p. 27

The archival and oral based reconstructions of the role of vaudou in the revolution remain hypothetical, but they tell a relatively consistent story of loa participating in the struggle for emancipation and independence. The story in its basic dimensions becomes more convincing when it is recalled that religion played an important role in all the major slave revolts in the Caribbean. The slave acted out of an African-based religious worldview. Ritual beings participated in the process of social transformation by bringing order and meaning to actual social processes. Vaudou in the colonial period, in particular, was a cultural force that played a key role in the attempts of the Haitian slave to survive in a situation of oppression, to resist that oppression, and, ultimately, to bring about emancipation. As Hurbon puts it, "*Vaudou* appeared very early to the slaves as their own language, as their conscious place of differentiation from the world of their masters, and as the force which would increase tenfold their capacity to fight."[53] As carriers of cultural order, it was the loa who would see to it that the social disorder that was slavery would be eliminated. The social crisis was so profound that it had to be understood with the help of the most aggressive deities one could invoke.

Though vaudou continued to play a role in resistance during the postindependence period, it was rarely linked to strategies for social or political change. It is reported that in the Caco uprising against the American occupation, some rebels wore Ogoun's color, red, as their distinguishing color.[54] However, the history of vaudou in the postindependence period is largely a legacy of accommodation with oppressive neocolonial regimes.

During the nineteenth century, both the mulatto commercial elite and the rural, black military elite attempted to consolidate their political power and continued to exploit the black peasantry. They established economic and cultural ties with France again and with Britain, Germany, and the United States.[55] The power that vaudou had to

53. Hurbon, *Dieu*, p. 76.
54. Herskovits, p. 321. Rémy Bastien, however, argues that the role of vaudou in resisting the Americans was minimal; see "Vodoun and Politics in Haiti," in Harold Courlander and Rémy Bastien, *Religion and Politics in Haiti*, ICR Studies, 1 (Washington, D.C.: Institute for Cross-Cultural Research, 1966), p. 52.
55. This consolidation of neocolonialism is summarized in Micheline Labelle, *Idéologie du couleur et classes sociales en Haïti* (Montreal: Les Presses de l'Université de Montréal, 1978), p. 14, and in David Nicholls, *From Dessalines to Duvalier: Race, Colour, and National Independence in Haiti* (Cambridge: Cambridge University Press, 1979), p. 8.

unify Haitians was seen by the new national leaders as a threat to their hegemony. Once generals such as Toussaint, Dessalines, and Christophe had established their control, they attempted, unsuccessfully, to suppress vaudou. Bastien writes that vaudou "with its capacity to sway the masses, its secrecy and conspiratorial nature, was a challenge to the state that L'Ouverture could not tolerate."[56] Furthermore, having internalized many of the values of their colonial masters, the new leaders considered vaudou to be inferior to European religious forms.[57]

What most of the new leaders did not yet realize was that vaudou could be co-opted by the state in the interest of the new ruling elite. There was nothing intrinsic to the vaudou narrative order that demanded that the believer enter into a struggle for liberation. Even during the revolutionary war, vaudou religion could be and was used in the interest of the planters. Geggus argues that Hyacinthe, who is sometimes mistakenly represented as an anti-French slave leader, "led slaves into battle invoking the protection of magical charms, but as an ally of the white planters." Some of these planters themselves, such as Hanus de Jumécourt, made use of vaudou.[58]

The one nineteenth century national leader who understood the importance of vaudou to the new regime was General Soulouque (Emperor Faustin I, 1847–59). Soulouque is said to have openly practiced vaudou and to have organized ceremonies in the national palace in order to legitimate his own regime in the eyes of his black subjects. Soulouque set the pattern for vaudou in the twentieth century. Vaudou was retrieved, as Hurbon puts it, for mainly conservative political ends. Like Soulouque, President Antoine Simon (1906–11), brought vaudou into the presidential palace. When the ethnologist and physician François Duvalier came to power in 1957, vaudou was systematically co-opted in the interest of a repressive political regime.[59]

In response to the American occupation in the early twentieth century, many members of the Haitian elite began to champion Haitian creole traditions in opposition to European values. The rising black bourgeoisie, in particular, claimed to represent the black masses and their "African" ways of understanding the world. Duvalier came into

56. Bastien, p. 49. See also Nicholls, p. 32.
57. Nicholls, pp. 41–43.
58. Geggus, pp. 15–16.
59. Bastien, pp. 50–52, 57; Métraux, pp. 53–54; Hurbon, *Dieu*, p. 78.

power with a black nationalist (*noiriste-négritude*) ideology, supported by the black bourgeoisie and by black workers and peasants.[60] Haitian culture and religion were appealed to in order to legitimate the political ambitions of Duvalier and the socioeconomic aspirations of the new black bourgeoisie. Ironically, American economic penetration increased, and European culture remained the point of reference for "civilized" Haitians.[61] As the guarantor of a repressive neocolonial dictatorship, vaudou took on a new ideological significance.

Duvalier's ideology emphasized the creative role of blacks and black culture in the history of Haiti and stressed the difference between the black and white races. He and his followers claimed that he was the true representative of blacks in Haiti and of the black race in general. His supporters announced that he was divine and that he was the living embodiment of the five founders of the nation—Toussaint, Dessalines, Pétion, Christophe, and Estimé. His speeches used vaudou terminology, and through the name "Papa Doc" he cultivated paternalistic, priestly, and even divine images of himself. (The loa are frequently addressed as "Papa.") Duvalier linked himself not only to the heroes of Haitian independence but also to the tradition of sorcery in vaudou. When he appeared in public, he dressed like the revered Baron Samedi, Lord of the Dead, protector of sorcerers. In 1959 he is supposed to have hijacked the coffin of one of his political opponents and, with the power of Baron Samedi, to have turned the corpse into a zombie whom he could control. Some vaudou congregations and houngans accepted their new leader because he seemed to stand for the Afro-Haitian tradition of the ancestors and to represent the ordinary Haitian. Others saw him as a powerful sorcerer to be feared and obeyed.[62]

Vaudou had traditionally been a nonhierarchical religion centered in the local community. Duvalier brought it under his political and financial control. He established himself as the first chief houngan of

60. Nicholls, pp. 191–93, 210–11, 237.

61. Nicholls, pp. 236–42; Laënnec Hurbon and Dany Bebel-Gisler, *Cultures et pouvoir dans la Caraïbe: Langue créole, vaudou, sectes religieuses en Guadeloupe et en Haïti* (Paris: Harmattan, 1975), pp. 111–13. See also Boniface I. Obichere, who is sympathetic to François Duvalier though admitting that there was little economic change under his regime ("Black Power and Black Magic in Haitian Politics: Dr. François Duvalier, 1957–1971," *Pan African Journal*, 6 (Summer 1973), 110–11, 117–18).

62. Nicholls, p. 233; Robert I. Rotberg, "Vodun and the Politics of Haiti," in *The African Diaspora: Interpretive Essays,* ed. Martin L. Kilson and Robert I. Rotberg (Cambridge: Harvard University Press, 1976), pp. 362–65.

Haiti, and those houngans who tried to maintain their independence were liquidated. Many Christian priests were expelled. When necessary, Duvalier resorted to his armed militia and to his secret police, the Tonton Macoutes, to enforce his demands. Duvalier's son, Jean-Claude, became president-for-life when his father died, and perpetuated this tradition.[63]

It is in the sphere of sorcery that the relationship between an accommodating narrative and the repressive regime can most clearly be established. Hurbon argues that vaudou in the reign of Jean-Claude Duvalier underwent a symbolic crisis that manifested itself in an increasing fear of zombies and sorcerers. Bands of sorcerers (*san pouèl*) became more prominent and less secretive. Operating under the protection of the Gede, these sorcerers gathered around the mapou tree, residence of the Gede, particularly those mapou trees at crossroads, to hold midday or midnight ceremonies and dispose of their victims. In ceremonies dedicated to Petro loa, san pouèl would buy points for protection and to take advantage of the enemy: "I have bought the hook; it is for catching my fish. [*M-achté zin-an, sé pou-m kinbé pouason mouin.*]"[64] Hurbon argues that Haitians were finding that the Rada loa could not give adequate protection to their serviteurs, with the result that serviteurs, were increasingly turning to Petro loa. Sorcery was being used more and more in everyday life.[65]

Whereas in the revolutionary period religion was a source of symbolic support for the fighting slaves, in the era of the Duvaliers, religion was manipulated in order to create a climate of fear. Jean-Claude's regime, like that of his father, presented itself as though it had the protection of the most powerful and aggressive loa. The vaudou believer might accept this claim if only because the actual success of the regime suggested that its leader did indeed enjoy such protection. Political and economic power was held to be acquired by sorcery, and powerful persons were feared and respected because of their links with sorcery. In order to protect themselves, people had to buy charms, hold ceremonies, appeal to Petro loa, and generally use the enemy's techniques. Rather than be persecuted, it was better to

---

63. Nicholls, p. 234; Bastien, pp. 59–61; Harold Courlander, "Vodoun in Haitian Culture," in Harold Courlander and Rémy Bastien, *Religion and Politics in Haiti*, ICR Studies, 1 (Washington, D.C.: Institute for Cross-Cultural Research, 1966), pp. 19–20; Hurbon and Bebel-Gisler, p. 132.
64. Hurbon, *Culture et dictature*, p. 141.
65. Hurbon, *Culture et dictature*, pp. 133–45.

win protection for oneself by actually joining the bands of sorcerers. The regime had successfully appropriated the legend of Trou Forban and the mythology of the zombie controlled by the sorcerer in order to maintain its political domination.[66]

The accommodation of vaudou to the Duvalier regimes was not without its ambiguities, however. In the first place, that vaudou believers were turning to sorcery perhaps indicated a desire for aggression. Sorcery, Hurbon suggests, may in fact have represented a popular attempt to contest political power by using the enemy's techniques. Whether the rise of sorcery was an attempt to protect oneself by joining the winning side, or whether it was a popular contestation of power using the enemy's techniques, the Haitian who turned to sorcery found him or herself trapped in a vicious circle. Sorcery could be countered only by sorcery, and the state remained the strongest sorcerer. The san pouèl could offer only illusory protection. Hurbon argues that this vicious circle of sorcery is the language that vaudou used to depict the political, social, and economic crisis in Haitian society. It symbolized the clash between the national bourgeoisie and the peasant masses. Moreover, argues Hurbon, the growth of sorcery indicated a bursting apart of the traditional cultural system: "There is a generalized suspicion. The rules of the game are false."[67] Not only is the neocolonial system called into question, but the role of vaudou itself comes to be recognized as problematic.

Ironically, the idea of sorcery involves a critique of oppression: sorcery was considered malevolent, undesirable, and, implicitly, the regime was likewise judged.[68] The houngan who was tied to the dominant class might be suspected of practicing anticommunal activities for the benefit of this class. He becomes linked to sorcery. The family maintained intimate relations with the loa outside of his control and could thus create a protective religious space of its own. Still, the increasing importance of sorcery under Jean-Claude suggests that it is this very possibility of the community distancing itself from sorcery that is greatly reduced. Hence the severity of the symbolic crisis. Co-opted and controlled, vaudou tends to lose its ability to resist oppression. (One idea that Hurbon does not explore is the possibility that what were perceived to be secret societies of sorcerers

66. Hurbon, *Culture et dictature*, pp. 134–35, 138–39.
67. Hurbon, *Culture et dictature*, pp. 142–44.
68. Hurbon, *Culture et dictature*, pp. 133, 142.

might instead have been antisorcery groups aggressively seeking to recapture popular power in the community.)[69]

In the colonial situation, vaudou was predominantly meaningful to adherents in terms of their struggle to maintain their own identity and community and, ultimately, to transform the immediate situation of oppression. In the neocolonial situation, vaudou took on meaning in terms of accommodation to and acceptance of a new system of oppression. Manipulated by a dependent bourgeoisie, it became an instrument of oppression. Though one of these two ideological possibilities was prominent in each period, both possibilities are inherent in vaudou mythology.

The real ambiguity of vaudou is that its mythic, tragic structure orders both resistance to oppression and accommodation with the oppressor. According to the Greek conception of tragedy, fate or destiny is ultimately accepted, even in the process of valiantly struggling against it; nothing really ever changes, even though one is always engaged in a struggle for change. Hurbon argues that vaudou assumes the reality of evil (sorcery) as quasi-fatality, as the quasi-natural in human experience. Using the phenomenological language of Martin Heidegger and Paul Ricoeur, he states that it is impossible to escape evil because it is an ontological necessity: "Whether evil should assume a quasi-natural or quasi-fatal character, that implies that there will always be a residue which one will seek in vain to integrate unless History is totally abolished."[70] One can attempt to get helpful loa to neutralize the presence of evil, but evil, too, is in the hands of the loa and will therefore always be present in one form or another. Some loa bring humor to the community, thus ensuring that tragedy is put into perspective. Humor is a way of coping with tragedy, of making it painless, but the tragic contradiction remains.

Legba and Gede (Baron Samedi) are symbols of quasi-fatality par excellence. They represent the endless upsurge of the natural and the irrational into the cultural, the ever-present disorder out of which new order arises, the tragic and the comic. At another symbolic level, this deep tragic structure manifests itself in the tension between Rada and Petro nations of loa. To the extent that Rada represents benev-

---

69. Though all observers and commentators emphasize the religious influence of the Catholic church, traditional antisorcery activity also played a role in the overthrow of the Duvalier regime in 1985.

70. Hurbon, *Dieu,* p. 205.

olence and Petro malevolence, Legba's ambiguity is also the ambiguity between Rada and Petro. Crossroad loa such as Baron Samedi and Carrefour are implicated in sorcery, which is one of the distinguishing features of the Petro nation. Ontologically speaking, sorcery is the symbol of evil, and the sorcerer is the individual who is outside the normal bounds of the community. The sorcerer represents not only the perverse side of the human but, also, our own individualism.[71]

In relation to the social totality, the duality and interrelationship between good and evil take on a new dimension. The Petro nation joins with Rada forces to fight against the colonizer as evil sorcerer. The reality of evil, however, is such that the colonizer may not be overcome. Perhaps his sorcery is too powerful. Geggus cites a manuscript of the revolutionary period in which blacks are said to regard both rebel leaders and civil commissioners as sorcerers and hence invulnerable.[72] In social and political terms, the triumph of the slaves over their masters represents at a determinate point in time the triumph of good over evil. However, the tragic conception of vaudou is such that acceptance of the reality of evil implies a vision of the revolution as failure. Evil rears its ugly face once more in the guise of the national bourgeoisie.

The tragic irony is that the spiritual power that was directed against the colonizer turns back on itself. The Duvalier dictatorships are a vivid indication of this ironic reversal. Vaudou mythology acknowledged that certain loa might support the regimes and that the regimes might therefore be undefeatable. The fatality of evil reaches its most acute point with the upsurge of sorcery. To survive under the regime of sorcery, one either accommodates that sorcery or resists it through recourse to sorcery oneself. Thus arises the reductio ad absurdum, the vicious circle of sorcery that Hurbon calls the crisis of the symbolic order.

Roger Bastide argues that vaudou is an example of a "living" religion because it creatively responded and adapted to the Haitian situation. A "living" religion is both experienced or lived through (*vécu*) and alive or vital (*vivant*): "it changes and adapts itself to the changing world as a totality." Because there was no need for the Haitian to defend against cultural attack after the revolution, vaudou was able to evolve creatively and freely, unlike some other Afro-

71. Mbiti, pp. 200, 213; Hurbon, *Dieu*, p. 203.
72. Geggus, p. 16.

American religions. This process, Bastide says, was facilitated by the early break with Africa and African traditions when slavery was abolished in Haiti. (Bastide does not adequately deal with the conflict between the state and vaudou that was part of the postindependence Haitian experience.)[73] As illustrated by the example of the crossroad complex, Haitian loa are grouped differently from Fon loa; some of the loa have changed their nature; new loa have been created. Vaudou was a vital response to the situation of colonial oppression.

A living religion must be distinguished, Bastide argues, from a "preserved" religion. Though meaningful to adherents, a preserved religion is not living and vital. It is traditional and conservative, tied to formalistic rituals set down by ancestors. In words reminiscent of Fanon's discussion of culture as "custom" (*WE*, p. 224; *DT*, p. 154), Bastide argues that preserved religion is a type of sociopathological defense mechanism in which a culture defends itself from the onslaught of colonialism by binding its members in a tightly enforced, pre-given framework. Culture becomes hardened and fossilized. The process can be compared to a neurotic who defends himself from crisis by relying on a rigid pattern of behavior.[74]

The problem with Bastide's distinction between living and preserved religions is that it allows no room for a critique of mythology. A religion can be "living" and vital and, at the same time, essentially reactive. Bastide's distinction is rooted in a phenomenological tradition in which the criterion of cultural authenticity is openness to new experience rather than the demand for liberation. Though his terminology appears to resemble Fanon's distinction between culture as a defense mechanism (preserved) and liberating national culture (living), Bastide never makes the leap to authentic national consciousness.

According to Fanon, it is necessary to challenge radically the dehumanizing colonial structure that has turned traditional culture into a reaction to colonialism. Liberating national culture has the task of naming reality anew in an "invitation to thought, to de-mystification, and to battle" (*WE*, p. 227; *DT*, p. 157). Vaudou cemented the early rebels, but its mythology never provided the Haitian Revolution with the consciousness of history characteristic of Hegel's slave or Fanon's freedom fighter. No doubt, Fanon sometimes ignores the living, vital aspects of colonial and neocolonial culture, whereas Bas-

73. Bastide, pp. 130–32, 139–41.
74. Bastide, pp. 128–29.

tide is able to identify them in some religious forms. Bastide, however, ultimately ignores the question of whether or not vaudou critically appropriates the social and political totality in an authentic struggle for recognition. Fanon, in contrast, introduces the conceptual foundation for a culture that struggles for liberation not only from colonialism but also from any other form of domination and exploitation in the neocolonial period or in any other period.

James comments that Toussaint had to organize and train the insurgents, making of "untrained blacks an army capable of fighting European troops." Religious effervesence would not be sufficient condition for revolutionary social and political transformation.[75] As Fanon puts it in his critique of spontaneity, "The hard lesson of facts, the bodies mown down by machine guns: these call forth a complete reinterpretation of events" (*WE*, p. 134; *DT*, p. 83). Using the Haitian Revolution as an example of a failed anticolonial revolution, Nicholls argues that Fanon incorrectly linked violent struggle to decolonization.[76] Fanon's point, however, was that violence had to be ordered in terms of the narrative of liberation. Vaudou failed to provide this order. Toussaint went to the other extreme: he adopted the French revolutionary ideology and in so doing lost contact with his own country's popular culture.[77] Neither vaudou nor the new leadership that took up the revolutionary struggle escaped the mythical (black and white) misunderstanding of the colonial world.

Without a doubt, vaudou mythology can render meaningful the eventuality of social and political change. Because of its tragic structure, however, because it assumes the fatality of evil, the crisis of vaudou always remains implicit, and the way to truly transformative action, to real healing, is barred. The structure of mythical narrative does not presuppose the necessity of freedom. Though the loa will help emancipate their followers if requested, they are not interested in emancipation as such; they make no call for liberation as a universal demand or categorical imperative. Co-opted by the national bourgeoisie in the neocolonial period, vaudou sets the stage for the misadventures of national consciousness.

Liberal commentators have sometimes blamed the Haitian plight

75. James, p. 116.
76. Nicholls, pp. 250–52.
77. James, pp. 278–92; Genovese oversimplifies the complex relation between popular culture and French revolutionary ideology (pp. 85–92, 123–25).

on vaudou and suggested ways of eliminating it. According to Bastien, vaudou has lost its original revolutionary impetus and now inhibits social and economic progress. He believes that there is hope for development only if Haitians are "cured of folklore." Likewise, Courlander recommends policies aimed at educating and Christianizing the Haitian peasantry and generating social progress. To be sure, Bastien and Courlander recognize that vaudou once played an important role in unifying the black community and making life meaningful and tolerable. Courlander states that vaudou is not the cause of Haiti's backwardness but the result.[78] Yet both Bastien and Courlander ultimately approach vaudou from a positivist and developmentalist perspective: modernity will come with a secular and scientific understanding of the world, which, for them, means with a Western or European understanding. Thus vaudou is seen as an uncreative myth that has outlived its purpose and must be demystified and eliminated.

There is no point, however, in securing for Haiti increased Western cultural domination in order to facilitate the effectiveness of American imperialism as it attempts to "develop" the world. Vaudou, Hurbon argues, is among other things a quest for protection against capitalist economic and social oppression. In opposition to the white Christianity, which justifies exploitation, it emphasizes a fundamental relationship to creole culture. The notion of indivisible traditional family land can reduce the chances of the family losing its land through subdivision and sale. Vaudou tends to reject the discipline of the body that would transform the body into forced labor. It transgresses Western moral codes.[79]

The Marxist critic condemns vaudou, like the liberal critic. In a perceptive commentary on Hurbon's work, Gil Martinez argues that Hurbon accentuates one side of the Marxist critique of religion (religion as protest against real distress) but fails to recognize the other side (religion as imaginary protest and thus illusion). From the Marxist viewpoint, vaudou is alienation at the level of the superstructure and reproduces the fundamental alienation of the producer from the object he or she produces. Vaudou could play a role in the struggle for independence because of the particular social and political structure of the period. In the period of the Duvaliers, the social structure

78. Bastien, pp. 48, 66; Courlander, "Vodoun in Haitian Culture," p. 22.
79. Hurbon, *Culture et dictature*, pp. 123–30.

is different. Co-opted, vaudou no longer has a political potential. According to Martinez, the situation of vaudou in relation to the class struggle is determined by its relationship to "the evolutionary march of history." Today vaudou is an illusion that inhibits the struggle of Haitians for liberation. Martinez argues that it is that very quasi-fatality of evil and sense of destiny identified by Hurbon that constitutes religious alienation. For authentic liberation, concludes Martinez, religious alienation must be critiqued on the basis of scientific (Marxist) analysis.[80]

Though Martinez avoids Courlander's paternalistic offering of one form of religious alienation for another, he nonetheless demands demystification of illusion on the basis of modern, rational, scientific thought. What he does not understand is the role that such thought can play in the ongoing domination of the Haitian. If the language of development can legitimate American imperialism in Haiti, so too the language of scientific analysis can legitimate the domination over society of a supposedly revolutionary vanguard. In such a situation it is not difficult to envision vaudou becoming a form of resistance just as it is to aspects of American imperialism. Resistance to "zombification" can occur in either a capitalist or a "socialist" system if there remain political and social relations based on domination and exploitation.

The challenge facing vaudou is the challenge of finding an adequate mode of cultural discourse that actively calls for social transformation and liberation. More than any other commentator on vaudou, Hurbon has understood the nature of the challenge. Martinez, in spite of his tendency to see liberation in purely "scientific" terms, recognizes Hurbon's contribution. Hurbon's thesis, he states, reminds us that every revolutionary process must take seriously the language of the masses in order to enter into it critically and orient it.[81] Hurbon emphasizes that it is not possible to fight for political, social, or economic progress without taking popular culture seriously. In words echoing Fanon's comments on national culture, Hurbon states in *Dieu dans le vaudou haïtien*: "It is in one and the same movement that cultural and political struggle must be undertaken." Mobilization must not depend on disdain for one's tradition and language. Hurbon

80. Gil Martinez, "Vodou et politique," *Nouvelle Optique,* April–September 1972, pp. 198–200.
81. Martinez, p. 200.

returns to this theme in *Cultures et pouvoir*: it is necessary to encounter the popular classes where they encounter themselves, interpret their exploitation, and look for ways out. Through this encounter, the person who believes in vaudou is put in a position to criticize his or her religion for him or herself.[82] In the language of the narrative of liberation, the task is to incarnate the concrete universal, to give form and content to a new and specific historical point of departure; the task is to understand the problem of liberation through a culturally specific milieu.

82. Hurbon, *Dieu,* p. 250; Hurbon and Bebel-Gisler, pp. 116–17.

Chapter 4

The Story of Survival: Anancy

black iron-eye'd eater, the many eye'd maker,
creator,
dry stony world-maker, word-breaker,
creator . . .

EDWARD BRATHWAITE, *The Arrivants*

The contact of the people with the new movement gives
rise to a new rhythm of life and to forgotten muscular
tensions, and develops the imagination. Every time the
storyteller presents a fresh episode to his public, he
presides over a real invocation. The existence of a new
type of man is revealed to the public.

FRANTZ FANNON, *The Wretched of the Earth*

THE trickster tale in Afro-Caribbean folklore is a comment on
pragmatic modes of resistance in the colonizer-colonized encounter. If vaudou is a cultural structure with which the slave can
enter into battle, the Anancy tale is a story by means of which the
slave learns to rebel in more subtle ways. The rebel is the slave who
kills the master; in most cases the rebel slave, too, will be executed.
Anancy is the slave who survives by avoiding rash actions, without
giving in to the master. The trickster tale and vaudou are two aspects
of a deeply integrated cultural whole. Anancy, the spider trickster, is
Akan, whereas vaudou is primarily Fon in origin. Anancy is the
folktale hero of Jamaica and other English- (and Dutch-) speaking
Caribbean islands. Vaudou is the religion of Haiti. Yet, both Anancy
and Legba come from a common African cultural base, and both are
tricksters who become all the more important where order must be
created out of colonial disorder.

The mythical unity of Anancy and Legba is underscored by striking parallels between West African Anancy tales and Legba myths. In

one tale, Anancy tricks the Akan high god, Nyame, and shames him into leaving the earth. In a similar manner, Legba humiliates the Fon high god, Mawu, into leaving the earth and establishing herself in the sky. In another Akan tale, Anancy, disguised as a bird, discovers Nyame's secret and becomes responsible for Sun's relative importance over Moon and Darkness. Nyame rewards Anancy with the high god's sayings and words, thus giving him power over communication between human beings and Nyame's ultimate order. An Afro-American variant has God, who has retreated from earth, ask Anancy to spin a web linking heaven and earth. Legba, too, is an intermediary between the human and divine worlds. Mawu makes him report the happenings in the human world to her, in the sky, every night.[1] Legba and Anancy, mythology and folktale, are united as centers of the production of meaning out of chaos.

Fanon's psychiatric works, as well as his sociopolitical writings, are concerned in a fundamental way with analyzing how the colonized understand themselves and their relationship to the colonizer. One of the themes that he explores is the mode of behavior of the colonized who constantly resist the system of oppression while appearing to submit. This type of behavior is symbolized by the trickster in Caribbean folktales. In the Manichaean colonial situation dissimulative behavior is characteristic of the colonized in their relationships with the colonizer. Prior to the Algerian Revolution, an Algerian charged with a crime by French colonial authorities might deny guilt, even if he or she had previously acknowledged it, or if the evidence unquestionably implicated him or her. In France, a North African appearing before a French doctor might announce that he or she was about to die, his or her belly, throat, leg, everywhere, was aching. The colonizer interprets this behavior in accordance with preconceived racial stereotypes. According to the colonial magistrate, the North African is a liar, is lazy, and is cunning. The French doctor sees the Arab male as "a-man-who-doesn't-like-work"; "a simulator, a liar, a malingerer, a sluggard, a pretender, a thief," even a rapist. His ailment is

---

1. Robert D. Pelton, *The Trickster in West Africa: A Study of Mythic Irony and Sacred Delight* (Berkeley: University of California Press, 1980), pp. 47n.25, 50–51; R. S. Rattray, *Akan-Ashanti Folk-Tales* (Oxford: Clarendon Press, 1930), pp. 72–77; Melville J. Herskovits and Frances S. Herskovits, *Dahomean Narrative: A Cross-Cultural Analysis,* Northwestern University African Studies, no. 1 (Evanston, Illinois: Northwestern University Press, 1958), pp. 149–50; Enid F D'Oyley, *Animal Fables and Other Tales Retold* (Toronto:Williams-Wallace International, 1982), pp. 8–9.

merely imaginary; he is said to be suffering from "the North African syndrome." The psychiatrist provides what is supposed to be a biological proof that this behavior is characteristic of the North African: the Arab is intensely aggressive and has a predatory instinct; he is a congenital impulsive whose life is primarily vegetative and instinctive. Not only the North African but every African is supposed to be a "lobotomized European," quite unfit for French citizenship.[2]

The dissimulative behavior of the colonized in relation to the colonizer presupposes the absence of reciprocity and the mutual nonrecognition characteristic of the colonizer-colonized relationship. The Algerian criminal who refuses to confess, argues Fanon, is in fact refusing to accept the social contract that the colonizer has tried to impose. Even if he or she is forced to submit to the colonizer's power, this "cannot be confused with acceptance of this power." Likewise, argues Fanon, a trait such as laziness must be seen as "the conscious sabotage of the colonial machine."[3]

Most of the derogatory terms used to describe the North African have also been used to describe, among others, colonized people of African or mixed African and European descent. The North African stereotype is very close to the Sambo stereotype in the United States and the Quashee stereotype in the West Indies. According to Patterson, the master considered the black Jamaican slave to be a pathological liar; he or she was also distrustful, lazy, lacking in judgment, childlike, happy-go-lucky, cruel, and revengeful.[4] Though the slave often behaved in ways that seemed to justify the stereotype, particularly in relationships with the master, such behavior did not constitute the extent of the slave's personality. Criticizing Stanley Elkins's claim that the Sambo was a "personality-type," Roger Abrahams argues that the role was instead "a convenient mask to wear; in assuming this role consciously or reflexively, blacks could achieve aggression and protection at the same time." Likewise, Patterson

2. Frantz Fanon and R. Lacaton, "Conduites d'aveu en Afrique du Nord," *Congrés des Médecins aliénistes,* 53d session, Nice, September 5–11, 1955, pp. 657–59 (*L'Information Psychiatrique,* 51 [December 1975], 1115–16; all translations from this article are mine); *AR,* pp. 4–6 (*RA,* pp. 10–13); *DC,* p. 127. (*SR,* pp. 113–14); *WE,* pp. 302–303 (*DT,* pp. 222–23).

3. Fanon and Lacaton, p. 660 (*L'Information Psychiatrique,* p. 1116); *WE,* p. 294 (*DT,* p. 216).

4. Orlando Patterson, *The Sociology of Slavery: An Analysis of the Origins, Development and Structure of Negro Slave Society in Jamaica* (Longon, 1967; rpt. Kingston: Sangster's Book Stores, 1973), pp. 175–77.

notes that the slave "played upon the master's stereotype for his own ends." Edward Brathwaite, reversing Elkins's notion of the Sambo type, argues that this behavior is tied to the phenomenon of rebellion in a single personality complex that he calls the "Quashie/Tacky" or "Uncle Tom-the-Tiger" complex.[5]

In *Black Skin, White Masks*, Fanon highlights the symbolic form that best expresses this covert pragmatic resistance in Afro-America. Following Bernard Wolfe, he comments on the aggression directed against the white master by means of the trickster symbol in the oral tradition of the plantation blacks. Disguised as a rabbit, the black person protests domination and symbolically outwits or defeats the master (*BS*, pp. 173–76; *PN*, pp. 140–43). The colonized is a trickster, whether in Africa or the Caribbean, who resists the system of colonization without necessarily losing his or her own identity or internalizing the master's values.

Klein explains how systems of communication and cultural codes are employed "to deceive, confuse and humiliate administrators, missionaries, scholars, social scientists and others looked upon as representatives of colonial power." Such codes can appear in sculpture and art work, in stories and rituals, and in linguistic and behavioral forms. Often these codes can be interpreted only by insiders. Klein states: "They can convey certain social meanings under conditions in which these would normally be braked; they transmit information not available in the public media; they preserve secrecy and intimacy when there is no privacy. Collective use helps to unite and give morale to groups whose everyday life is atomized and demoralizing." The Kalela Dance of Rhodesia, argues Klein, appeared to be a ritual in which groups mocked each other. In reality, however, it was British authorities and Africans striving after a European life-style who were being mocked. Though Klein argues that Fanon underemphasizes the protest function of prenationalist culture, it is exactly this protest function that Fanon analyzes in the symbol of the colonized as trickster.[6]

5. Stanley M. Elkins, *Slavery: A Problem in American Institutional and Intellectual Life* (Chicago: University of Chicago Press, 1962), pp. 130–33; Roger D. Abrahams, *Positively Black* (Englewood Cliffs, N.J.: Prentice Hall, 1970), p. 7; Patterson, *Sociology of Slavery*, p. 180; Edward Brathwaite, commentary on Monica Schuler, "Afro-American Slave Culture," in *Roots and Branches: Current Directions in Slave Studies,* ed. Michael Craton, Historical Reflections, Directions, 1 (Toronto: Pergamon Press, 1979), p. 155.

6. Norman A. Klein, "On Revolutionary Violence," *Studies on the Left*, 6 (May–June 1966), 64–65, 72.

The "Quashee" or "Sambo" stereotype, the image of the bungling but obedient fool, lost in the quagmire created by the colonizer's domination of time, is nothing but a racist stereotype. On occasion, the colonized might internalize this image, losing themselves in the role. More often, the colonized merely pretend to be foolish; role-playing becomes a strategy for survival, a form of pragmatic resistance. Sambo and Quashee were tricksters whose activity was only one step away from rebellion, for they sought to outwit and dupe the master, though in a camouflaged way, so that they would not themselves be defeated in the process. It was in trickster folktales, in particular, that the cunning behavior of the trickster-slave was encoded and represented for the instruction of the community.

The Caribbean trickster tale is essentially African in its form, though it has been creolized and transformed in the Caribbean. Slavery resulted in the intermixture of different African cultures with European and Amerindian cultures, but in many cases African forms and structures were retained. Even if they underwent only minor changes in form in the Caribbean, however, folktales underwent a radical change in meaning. In Africa, folktales instructed young and old in the ways of the culture and functioned as a means of psychic relief and satire. They were aesthetic works that rendered reality meaningful and constantly opened up new insights into existence. In the Caribbean, folktales had similar functions, but they had to address, in addition, the problem of survival in a completely new social situation: the systematic domination and enslavement of one race by another on the Caribbean plantation. Anancy, the spider trickster of the Akan, had to spin a new web of meaning whenever he appeared in the fields, at social gatherings after dusk, or at wakes.

Cunning and deceitful behavior in relation to the colonizer or master is symbolized by trickster heroes in black narrative in the Americas (Anancy, Brer Rabbit, Ti Malice, John, and others). Human tricksters were more pragmatic and realistic than the animal tricksters, but all tricksters used guile to preserve themselves and to improve their situation in their struggle against the master.[7] As Fanon argues, beneath Uncle Remus's melancholic grin hid the cunning rabbit. The stereotyped grin of Sambo is transformed by means of the camouflaged aggression of the rabbit into what Wolfe calls a "cultural

7. Lawrence W. Levine, *Black Culture and Black Consciousness: Afro-American Folk Thought from Slavery to Freedom* (New York: Oxford University Press, 1977), pp. 131–32.

bludgeon."[8] The trickster tale is an aesthetic creation and performance that brings to the level of shared discourse and makes meaningful this particular form of behavior. Quashee's bizarre actions are represented in the tales so that the colonized person understands that such behavior is socially necessary, though only within culturally defined limits.

The aesthetic dimension of the trickster tales ensures the richness and communicability of the message and system of values in the tales. Elements of the master's culture and his language, in particular, are incorporated into the tales. However, these cultural elements are combined with African cultural patterns and fashioned into a new cultural unity in a process of creolization. At the same time, this aesthetic dimension preserves a form of cultural exclusivity by camouflaging the meaning of the tales from the colonizer.

The African storyteller was able to expose or ridicule a bad master or chief by substituting Nyame, the high god, or the name of an animal, for a real person in a real drama. He or she further protected him or herself by declaring that what was about to be said was fictitious. However, the trickster tale cannot be reduced to a particular event that is being satirized, for there is a more enduring mythic form underlying any particular trickster tale.[9] This mythic form allows for both the incorporation of new content and the possibility of pointed satire. In fictionalizing a particular event, a tale both camouflages that particular meaning and generalizes so that other events are encompassed by its meaning.

This is an important principle in the Caribbean trickster tale. The narrator tells us at the end of "Eating Tiger's Guts" that he or she has explained why tigers live in the forest and spiders in the roof of a house. The story actually tells us a great deal more than this. Jekyll comments that the refrain found at the end of many Jamaican tales, "Jack Mantora me no choose any," is a polite way of saying that the tale is not aimed at anyone in particular in the audience.[10] Recalling

---

8. *BS*, pp. 174–76 (*PN*, pp. 140–42). See also Bernard Wolfe, "Uncle Remus and the Malevolent Rabbit," in *Mother Wit from the Laughing Barrel: Readings in the Interpretation of Afro-American Folklore*, ed. Alan Dundes (Englewood Cliffs, N.J.: Prentice-Hall, 1973), pp. 524–40.

9. Rattray, *Akan-Ashanti Folk-Tales*, p. xi; Paul Radin, *The Trickster: A Study in American Indian Mythology* (New York: Schocken, 1972), pp. 154, 167.

10. Walter Jekyll, *Jamaican Song and Story: Annancy Stories, Digging Sings, Ring Tunes* (London, 1907; rpt. New York: Dover, 1966), p. 10.

her own childhood experiences, Louise Bennett states: "Annancy sometimes did very wicked things in his stories, and we had to let Jack Mandora (*sic*), the doorman at heaven's door, know that we were not in favour of Annancy's wicked ways."[11] The refrain is a concluding statement on the paradoxical status of fiction in the tale. Bennett's doorman is a type of censor who allows the storyteller to delve into the depths of the real in the medium of fiction. The narrator's performance enhances this fictive dimension. Anancy speaks "Bungo talk," the form of Creole containing the most Africanisms. In the presentation of the story, language unites with dramatic techniques, song, and dance in an opening to the fictional world and a redescription of the real world of human action.[12]

This artistic ordering of experience by the community allows the colonized to attack the colonizer symbolically. Jekyll remarks that language is for the black Jamaican "the art of disguising thought." Sympathetic as he was, Jekyll may not have understood that he was a white man under attack.[13] Religious expression could be curbed by the colonizer or driven off the plantation. By virtue of aesthetic camouflage, storytelling (as well as songs and other forms of verbal play) was available to be used by the slave, even under the overseer's watchful eye. Beneath the master's domination of plantation time, the slaves were able to recapture a symbolic space and plot the story of resistance.

In both African and Caribbean folktales, the trickster is a deeply ambiguous character. The African spider and hare have had the most influence on the Caribbean, though other trickster heroes such as the tortoise and the human trickster have also played a role. The African tricksters have many traits in common. They are cunning and wily, yet sometimes stupid; they are greedy and aggressive, indolent and unreliable. They have many negative traits, but their cunning and courage usually arouse admiration. The Bantu hare (Brer Rabbit or Ti Malice in the Americas) often outwits the hyena (Bouki or Zam-

11. Louise Bennett, "Me and Annancy," in Jekyll, p. ix.
12. For a good discussion of the performance of the tales and of their aesthetic elements, see Laura Tanna, "Anansi—Jamaica's Trickster Hero," *Jamaica Journal*, 16 (May 1983), 26–29. See also Roger D. Abrahams, *The Man-of-Words in the West Indies: Performance and the Emergence of Creole Culture* (Baltimore: Johns Hopkins University Press, 1983), p. 158, and Frederic G. Cassidy, *Jamaica Talk: Three Hundred Years of the English Language in Jamaica*, 2d ed. (London: Macmillan, 1971), pp. 275–76.
13. Jekyll, p. 53.

ba). Like the hare, the Akan and Caribbean spider, Anancy, often outwits stronger animals (especially the leopard or, in the Caribbean, Tiger). But he is sometimes stupid and ineffective. Paulme argues that the spider can be seen as a unity of the hare (positive) and the hyena (negative): "Everything takes place as if an original figure, to whom Spider even with his contradictions remains very close, was separated in two—Hare and Hyena being finally only the two faces of the same character."[14] Paulme implies that the key to the trickster is neither positivity nor negativity, neither morality nor immorality, but the ambiguous and accentuated human traits characteristic of Anancy.

The Caribbean trickster recreates cultural order out of the scattered events of social existence. Folktales deal with common human problems such as scarcity, sexuality, conflict, and oppression. Trickster tales in particular are vehicles for exploring both the deep ambiguities in the human predicament and pragmatic ways of dealing with concrete situations. It is not sufficient, however, to deal with Caribbean trickster tales in the abstract, ignoring their relationship to the primary contradictions and Manichaean social and political disorder characteristic of the colonial social totality. Colonial society is divided into two castes on the basis of phenotype and into derivative class formations. The culture of the oppressed caste addresses the problem of survival in this situation.

Lawrence Levine and Bruce Dickson have argued that the problem of survival in slave and postemancipation society is one key to understanding the American trickster tale. In order to survive, the slave has to be cunning and crafty in relationships with the master. He or she has to understand the art of pragmatic resistance. By means of cleverness and guile, the trickster is able to attain a limited victory over the master. In trickster tales, this type of victory is symbolized by the defeat of a large animal by the trickster. However, the tales are not wish-fulfillments in which the master is romantically defeated; the trickster does not invariably win (as even Fanon, among others, mis-

---

14. Denise Paulme, "The Impossible Imitation in African Trickster Tales," in *Forms of Folklore in Africa: Narrative, Poetic, Gnomic, Dramatic,* ed. Bernth Lindfors (Austin: University of Texas Press, 1977), p. 97. Harold Courlander makes a similar point in *The Drum and the Hoe: Life and Lore of the Haitian People* (Berkeley and Los Angeles: University of California Press, 1960), p. 171. See also Alice Werner, "African Mythology," in *Mythology of All Races* (Boston: Archaeological Institute of America, 1925), vol. 7, pp. 321–24.

takenly suggests). In his discussion of black American slave tales, Levine notes: "If the strong are not to prevail over the weak, neither shall the weak dominate the strong." Dickson states that the John and Old Master trickster tales of the American South were realistic and devoid of fantasy. They assumed an ongoing "fixed relationship of conflict between masters and slaves that defined the boundaries within which all characters were to act and in which both sides were equally capable of victory and equally vulnerable to defeat."[15] The black American trickster tales are ways of expressing the peculiar features of the slave's resistance to the master. A cultural order is created based on the slave's struggle for survival in a situation of social disorder.

Like the black American tales, Caribbean trickster tales take on a particular meaning in relation to the social totality in the Caribbean. The trickster represents an actor in a specifically colonial, plantation drama. As a narrative form, the Anancy tale is both a *mimesis*, or representation, of lived events and particular ways of acting in the Caribbean world, and a *mythos*, or plot, ordering these real experiences in terms of existing cultural codes. Ricoeur argues that in the narrative act a creative interplay occurs in which new experiences are interpreted through already given forms of understanding, while the given is itself transformed by the new.[16] In Anancy tales the colonized tell stories about the fundamental nature of their social situation, and about the way people behave in that situation. They do so in order to understand and communicate the meaning of their own actions, and in turn they act in response to the plots presented in the tales. The primary conflict between the colonizer and the colonized or between the slave and the master is represented, and the slave's response as the trickster (Quashee) is encoded. Rather than romantically dissolve the conflict, this cultural ordering of reality assumes the reality of social disorder and the constancy of struggle.

There are four narrative possibilities that, taken together, constitute the social ambiguity in the Caribbean trickster tale: (1) the trickster as successful hero (slave) who deludes the powerful character

15. Levine, p. 120; Bruce D. Dickson, "The 'John and Old Master' Stories and the World of Slavery: A Study in Folktales and History," *Phylon*, 35 (Winter 1974), 427.

16. Paul Ricoeur, "Explanation and Understanding: On Some Remarkable Connections among the Theory of the Text, Theory of Action, and Theory of History," in *The Philosophy of Paul Ricoeur: An Anthology of His Work*, ed. Charles E. Reagan and David Stewart (Boston: Beacon Press, 1978), p. 155.

(the master); (2) the trickster as successful villain (master); (3) the trickster as unsuccessful hero (slave) whose attempts to delude the powerful (master) fail; (4) the trickster as unsuccessful villain (master). The trickster as successful hero and as successful villain are the most common types of trickster tale. Success is always tinged with villainy and always remains tentative. The four structural possibilities combine in the tragic ordering of lived reality.

All four of these structures can be illustrated in the folktale "Eating Tiger's Guts." In this tale, the clever Anancy outwits the large Tiger and gets the small monkeys into trouble. Both Anancy and Tiger are chased away by the big monkeys who come to the rescue of their smaller relatives. The main theme is the successful attempt of Anancy, as hero, to outwit the more powerful Tiger. However, Anancy is a villain in relation to the small monkeys, who are deceived into suffering the brunt of Tiger's wrath. Anancy's success is only temporary, for the little monkeys enlist the help of the big monkeys, who chase away the intruders (the villains are defeated). Even Anancy's heroism in relation to Tiger is called into question, for, ultimately, the hero emerges beaten by the big monkeys.

Variants of this tale also indicate the trickster's ambiguity (the hero–villain) and the four narrative possibilities (success and failure for hero and villain). In Beckwith's version (b), Tiger kills all of the monkeys except one, who reveals Anancy's ruse. The possibility of the heroic little person (Anancy) being punished therefore arises. In version (a), the hero is very successful in the sense that Tiger dies. Ambiguity remains, however, for Anancy's success is marred by his crying child, who reveals him. In contrast to these Jamaican versions, the Herskovitses' Surinam version has Tiger killing some of the monkeys and Anancy eating others for supper. Anancy's heroism is marred by his villainy. As far as Tiger's feast goes, it is interesting that in another tale the monkeys are the ones who defeat and eat Tiger for supper.[17] Life is experienced as a constant encounter with oppression in which one is sometimes successful, sometimes not.

Many Caribbean tales depict the victory of the trickster over a larger animal. In "Eating Tiger's Guts" Anancy is a hungry person

17. Jekyll, pp. 7–10; Martha Warren Beckwith, *Jamaica Anansi Stories* (1924; rpt. New York: Kraus Reprint, 1976), p. 13; Melville J. Herskovits and Frances S. Herskovits, *Suriname Folk-Lore* (New York: Columbia University Press, 1936), pp. 215–17.

engaged in a desperate struggle for survival. Tiger is the person with surplus food: "as you are such a big man," Anancy exclaims.[18] The conflict becomes a power struggle between the weak and the strong and takes on a particularly political meaning. Anancy is the slave or oppressed; Tiger the master or overseer. Likewise in the "Riding Horse" tale, which is found both in Africa and in the Caribbean, the trickster successfully defeats a larger animal: Anancy tricks Tiger into becoming his horse and beast of burden. The story is very common in the Caribbean and takes on special significance there because of the dimension of power relations. It is a symbolic inversion of the principal relation of disorder in the Caribbean, racial oppression. The master-slave dualism is recast in terms of an inverted social order in which the master is symbolically defeated.[19] That this colonial conflict is drawn on racial lines is suggested in other stories such as "Gaulin," where Anancy cunningly says to his competitor: "As you being such a clean an' white gentleman I think you will succeed [in winning the woman]. So if you succeed, when you coming home back you must make me know; then you can take me to be your servant."[20]

In such tales, Anancy symbolizes, in Leonard Barrett's words, "the possibility of the underdog emerging triumphantly in a world which pits the weak against the strong."[21] Anancy's successful action is an encoding in narrative of Quashee's devious techniques of survival in particular situations. Anancy is Quashee, the master of "congo-saw," or double-talk. His aim is to protect himself by cringing before the white master, lying, avoiding the issue, and misleading him. When the master's back is turned, Quashee may strike out against him. Anancy appears to suffer from the disorder that the French colonialists called the North African Syndrome. He is the lobotomized European. He is also a great actor and a brilliant trickster who knows the value of pragmatic resistance. If the master considers his slave or

18. Jekyll, p. 7.

19. Beckwith, p. 5; Elsie Clews Parsons, *Folk-Lore of the Antilles, French and English* (1943; rpt. New York: Kraus Reprint, 1969), pp. 73–76. For African versions see Clement M. Doke, *Lamba Folk-Lore* (1927; rpt. New York: Kraus Reprint, 1976), pp. 61–63; A. B. Ellis, *The Yoruba Speaking Peoples of the Slave Coast of West Africa* (1894; rpt. Oosterhout, Netherlands: Anthropological Publications, 1970), pp. 265–67; Heli Chatelain, *Folk-tales of Angola* (1894; rpt. New York: Kraus Reprint, 1969), p. 203.

20. Jekyll, p. 73.

21. Leonard Barrett, *The Sun and the Drum: African Roots in Jamaican Folk Tradition* (Kingston, Jamaica: Sangster's Book Stores, 1977), p. 34.

servant to be an ignorant liar, then Quashee can play on the stereotype to his or her own advantage. Anancy teaches Quashee how to
act in accordance with the Jamaican proverb "Play fool to catch
wise."[22]

Even as the hero of the colonized, however, Anancy is not always
successful. In African tales, a large animal representing a given order
may triumph over a small animal who challenges that order. In the
Jamaican version of "Eating Tiger's Guts," Anancy ultimately fails to
defeat Tiger. In another Jamaican story, Anancy tries to trick Tiger in
order to get food from him. Instead, Tiger is the trickster, and Anancy is dragged over the stones by Cow.[23] The master, too, could be
devious. One terse and proverbial tale from Surinam shows how
easily defeat can come to the colonized:

> Anansi passed the Aboma [boa constrictor] everyday. "Friend," Anan-
> si asked the Aboma, "when do you eat?"
> "When God wishes."
> The next day when Anansi was passing, the Aboma grabbed him.[24]

Anancy's ups and downs are more than the general facts of life. They
are tragic reflections on the harshness of a dehumanized colonial existence. The colonized may win some battles against the oppressors,
others will be decisively lost. As popular manifestations of the black
myth, the tales teach the colonized how to survive and cope.

Although the Caribbean trickster generally represents the cunning
slave or black person struggling against the master, he may also
represent the cunning master (or other official of the plantation hierarchy) beguiling a weak slave. Anancy deceives the innocent little
monkeys so that they become Tiger's enemies; those that escape he
eats. In the Jamaican tale "Dry Bone," Anancy has a helpless old man
taken out to die in the woods. The tale is reminiscent of an Ashanti
tale in which a greedy king Anancy kills a dwarf and tricks an ant into
assuming his punishment. The tales comment on the existence of
unpunished crime and the irrational in general. The Jamaican tale
goes further, however, to address specifically the relation of domina-

---

22. Louise Bennett, "Me and Annancy," in Jekyll, p. ix. See also Patterson, *Sociology of Slavery*, pp. 178–81.

23. Beckwith, p. 11. For an African version of the defeat of the trickster by Lion,
see Doke, pp. 137–39.

24. Herskovits and Herskovits, *Suriname Folk-Lore*, p. 273.

tion in the Caribbean. The cruel overseer has the power to take the life of his old slave.[25] Patterson argues that "Dry Bone" is a parody of white plantation society: Rabbit, Guinea-pig, and Anancy were white people competing with each other to get rid of the old slave.[26]

As master, Anancy is not always successful, however. Anancy fails to beat the little monkeys when the big monkeys come to their assistance. In Jekyll's "Anancy and Cow," Anancy invites to his house the harmless brother Cow and then attempts to slaughter him. He fails and Cow escapes.[27] Beckwith reports a Jamaican tale in which Anancy tricks and eats a helpless old woman, leaving her children to cry. Hog, Goat, and Cow are too scared to help the children, but Jackass traps Anancy. He takes Anancy to the children who then burn the villain to death.[28] Like the tales about the defeat of a larger animal, this model of a more just world opens up new possibilities for the colonized. But all possibilities are circumscribed by the vicissitudes of reality that appear in other tales.

Besides referring to the colonizer-colonized relation, trickster tales also illustrate relationships between the colonized themselves. Some tales explicitly distinguish ways of acting toward the colonizer from ways of acting toward members of one's own group. In a tale called "Annancy, Monkey, and Tiger," Anancy claims to have enough common sense to take care both of himself and of his friend Monkey. When Tiger is about to eat Monkey, Anancy tricks Tiger into praying, at which point Monkey makes his escape. In another tale, Anancy helps the community defend itself against Fire and tricks Fire into burning the house of Tiger, the enemy.[29] Cunning and deceit is justified in relationships with the master, for the benefit of the oppressed community as a whole. The deceit is not directed against the

---

25. Jekyll, pp. 48–51; W. H. Barker and Cecilia Sinclair, *West African Folk-Tales* (London: George G. Harrap, 1919), pp. 63–67.

26. Patterson, *The Sociology of Slavery*, pp. 252–53. Patterson argues that "Dry Bone" was based on a satiric song actually directed at a cruel and murderous slave master. If this is the case, the tale shows how a particular event can be used to symbolize a typical situation transcending the individual event. Patterson's comment that the depiction of Anancy as a slave master is a displacement of the slave's own unpleasant features onto the white overseer has the very problematic implication that only slaves had negative traits. Of course, Patterson knows that this is not the case. See also Levine, p. 118.

27. Jekyll, pp. 63–65, 104–107.

28. Beckwith, pp. 48–50.

29. Jekyll, pp. 77–78, 129–31.

members of one's own community. Levine notes the distinction in American slave tales between "stealing" from fellow slaves, which was not condoned, and "taking" from the master what was owed to the slave.[30]

Other tales deal with intracommunity relationships. Beckwith reports a Jamaican story almost identical to an Ashanti tale about the institution of punishment. Anancy finds a magical calabash that provides him with as much food as he wants. He refuses to share it with his hungry family. They turn against him, and the calabash is destroyed. Anancy then finds a magical whip that beats him. He takes the whip home and the members of his family are beaten. As in the Ashanti version, Anancy is punished for his greediness, deceitfulness, and failure to share with his family. His family is punished in order to indicate the reinstitution of parental authority. A number of French and English Caribbean versions change the story so that a magical source of food is stolen from a friend and the thief receives a beating.[31] However, in both the African and Caribbean versions there is a situation of scarcity, a transcendence of that situation by a hero-villain (a trickster), and punishment for failure to share the food. The moral (cultural) order triumphs over the natural order, despite the situation of scarcity. The condition of slavery and its aftermath, however disruptive, does not reduce the trickster narrative to a mere reflection of the ruthless ways of a struggle of all against all for survival. Anancy's morality and immorality presuppose a morally functioning and basically unified black community.[32]

Commentators have usually overlooked the community aspect of the Caribbean trickster tale, sometimes arguing that the tale is a morally degraded form of narrative in relation to its African progenitor. According to this argument, colonialism created an artificial state of nature in which human beings were reduced to a struggle for survival

---

30. Levine, p. 131.

31. Beckwith, pp. 31–33; Paul Radin, *African Folktales* (Princeton: Princeton University Press, 1970), pp. 209–11; Barker and Sinclair, pp. 39–44; R. S. Rattray, *Hausa Folk-Lore, Customs, Proverbs, etc.* (Oxford: Clarendon, 1913), vol. 2, pp. 80–106; Parsons, pp. 223–25; Pelton, p. 38.

32. For a discussion of slave community, see Elsa V. Goveia, *Slave Society in the British Leeward Islands at the End of the Eighteenth Century* (New Haven: Yale University Press, 1965), p. 245; Sidney Mintz and Richard Price, *An Anthropological Approach to the Afro-American Past: A Caribbean Perspective,* ISHI Occasional Papers in Social change, No. 2 (Philadelphia: Institute for the Study of Human Issues, 1976), pp. 20–23.

against nature and against each other. Arthur Kemoli argues that the West African Anancy tale was a form of satiric irony based on the assumption of a moral order: those who diverged from this order were castigated in the tales. In contrast, under the reign of terror that characterized the Caribbean, the slave had to use basically immoral tactics of cunning, deceit, and treachery to outwit the oppressor. The slave satirized his or her own laziness and guile in a form of "self-defeatist irony." At the same time, the slave acknowledged the necessity of such behavior for survival. Morality, Kemoli concludes, became an "illusive mirage" in the Caribbean trickster tale.[33]

The hidden assumption behind Kemoli's argument is that the slave did in fact behave as depicted by the racist Quashee or Sambo stereotype and that Anancy reflected this behavior. There is no doubt that survival under very harsh conditions is an important feature of the tales. Pragmatic concern with a basic necessity of life, food, is a very common theme; Anancy is often hungry. This does not, however, make the tales immoral. In the tale about the institution of punishment, Anancy is punished for his transgressions. Jean-Pierre Jardel notes in his commentary on tales from the French West Indies that "ingenuity not sin [*débrouilla, pas péché*]" is the formula used to close some of the tales.[34]

Nor are the tales moralistic. Examining a number of African and Caribbean tales in which the theme of false friendship occurs, Lee Haring argues that the tales are based on a morphological sequence in which equilibrium replaces disequilibrium. According to Haring, the

33. Arthur Kemoli, *Caribbean Anansi Stories* (London: Commonwealth Institute, 1976), pp. 5–6. Basil C. Hedrick and Cezarija A. Letson state that one can find a moral in Rabbit's exploits in the Bahamas only by stretching the evidence; see *Once Was a Time, a Very Good Time: An Inquiry into the Folklore of the Bahamas,* Museum of Anthropology Miscellaneous Series, no. 38 ([Greeley, Colo.:] University of Northern Colorado, 1975), p. 34. Courlander argues that bad triumphs over good as frequently as good over bad in Haitian trickster tales (*Drum,* p. 173). Maryse Condé claims that the Antillean rabbit is as depraved as Zamba because a pedagogy of survival has replaced a moral code; there was no room for generosity or compromise among slaves; see *La Civilisation du bossale: Réflexions sur la littérature orale de la Guadeloupe et de la Martinique* (Paris: Harmattan, 1978), pp. 38, 43. Dickson makes a similar point when he argues that John's actions were products of circumstance. Dickson avoids the dehumanizing implications of this "situationalism," however, by arguing that the slave had many roles (husband, father, and so on) and was not bound by his role as slave (pp. 428–29).

34. Jean-Pierre Jardel, *Le Conte créole* (Montreal: Centre de recherches caraïbes de l'Université de Montréal, 1977), p. 17.

trickster embodies "the anti-social tendency" and must therefore be dismissed. The normal cultural order based on mutual friendship is restored.[35] Haring's evidence does not entirely support this conclusion. In the monkey and crocodile tale, the monkey deceives his "friend" the crocodile, but only in order to avoid being eaten by the crocodile. The monkey is the heroic trickster; the crocodile, the villain. The antisocial tendencies used by the monkey are necessary to survival. He uses guile in order to escape. Equilibrium is restored but only through activities that are immoral when considered in abstract terms. This ambiguity is fundamental to the meaning of the trickster tale.

Haring's mistake lies in the imposition on the African and Caribbean trickster tale of a structure that is applicable only to romance tales.[36] In some European fairy tales, villainy is liquidated by a virtuous hero (the good prince kisses the poisoned Snow White). A romantic narrative resolves the contradiction (villainy) in a sequence of events leading to a harmonious ending (equilibrium). Romance tales can be found in the Caribbean oral tradition, but they are less characteristic of the Caribbean than are the trickster tales and may be the result of European influence.[37] (Recent scholarship has shown that romance tales are far less characteristic even of the European folk tradition than was formerly thought.)[38] The trickster tale, though it *may* conclude with a temporary restoration of equilibrium, manifests a tragic ordering of existence: the hero is also a villain, and equilibrium always remains shaky.

Using the example of West African Anancy tales, Robert Pelton demonstrates the essential creativity that can be traced to Anancy's ambiguity and ambivalence. He argues that it is necessary to understand how the tales pull apart and reorder cultural reality so as to

35. Lee Haring, "A Characteristic African Folktale Pattern," in *African Folklore*, ed. Richard M. Dorson (Bloomington: Indiana University Press, 1972), pp. 178–79.

36. Haring, pp. 165–66. Haring notes that she has been criticized by Roger Abrahams for forcing a culture-bound model of narrative closure on the African and Afro-Caribbean trickster tale (p. 178n). See also Abrahams, *The Man-of-Words*, p. 186.

37. See, for example, the analysis of Ti-Jean tales in Condé, *Civilisation*, pp. 40–45.

38. Robert Darnton argues that French folktales are "far more rooted in the real" than their bourgeois retellers have made them out to be ("The Meaning of Mother Goose," *New York Review of Books*, February 2, 1984, pp. 41–47). Likewise, John M. Ellis describes the way that Grimm brothers distorted German folktales in *One Fairy Story Too Many: The Brothers Grimm and Their Tales* (Chicago: University of Chicago Press, 1983).

transform creatively the culture and open up new meaning. The storytellers, writes Pelton, "are conveying to their children, and reminding themselves, that life itself is a twisted story, a process in which the human mind and human words are always drawing forth from the rawness of the earth and the body a surprising pattern, which, however partial and dimly known, is charged with permanent value and meaning."[39]

Pelton examines a story from Ghana in which a jealous and sterile husband has prohibited his wife from any possibility of human intercourse. Anancy puts purgative in the husband's food, adopts for himself the name "Rise-up-and-make-love-to-Aso," and seduces the wife. The child of the adulterous union is killed by Anancy, cut into pieces, and scattered about to become the source of jealousy. Anancy appears to be an adulterer, a destroyer of the social order and equilibrium. However, argues Pelton, he is actually rescuing human intercourse from impotence and sterility. But the paradox goes deeper. Having destroyed jealousy, Anancy then restores it to its proper place in the cultural order. By scattering his son around, sexuality is restored to its rightful role and adultery prohibited.[40] Equilibrium is reinstated, but not as stasis: Anancy's ambivalence leaves no room for a moralistic comment on adultery. Nor are the tale's implications amoral. Adultery is not culturally legitimate, but it may be culturally necessary. Anancy, comments Pelton, "creates social intercourse by disclosing, plunging into, heightening, or even embodying the raw forces out of which human life is made."[41] The trickster tale orders social experience in terms of an ongoing creative process that enhances both the integrity of the community and the need constantly to reformulate and recreate that community.

It is this very ambiguity, at once destructive and creative, that is both the power of the trickster tale and its ultimate, tragic limit. The tales articulate a mythical conception of the world as a place of endless and ongoing struggle, of progress and regress, friendship and enmity. This mythical conception has implications for the meaning of the tales in relation to the colonial social and political totality. If there is

---

39. Pelton, p. 70. See the related discussion of the Winnebago trickster by Paul Radin (pp. 167–68), C. J. Jung (pp. 200, 203), Karl Kerenyi (p. 185) and Stanley Diamond (p. xx), in Radin, *The Trickster*.

40. Pelton, pp. 41–43. The story is found in Rattray, *Akan-Ashanti Folktales*, pp. 132–37.

41. Pelton, p. 50.

nothing permanent about the position of the master, there is also no necessary permanence in the community. One perverse implication (from the point of view of the community) is that the trickster-slave may indeed turn his skills against his own people in order to benefit himself and become like the master.[42]

The tales capture and are a part of the tragedy that Fanon calls the colonial "drama." They are part of a cultural order in which the techniques of survival and pragmatic resistance to oppression are emphasized. The values that are presented in the trickster tales arise out of the struggle between two racially defined castes. The tales legitimate the struggle to defeat the master, or to rebuild the community in opposition to his control. However, the tales also plot the failure of resistance and the need always to continue the struggle. Dickson argues that black American slave tales, though based on struggle, did not envision the transformation of the slave system through that struggle: "the situation of slavery was taken as a given and defined traditional limits upon creation and variation within the genre."[43] The Caribbean tales likewise presuppose the Manichaean conflict inherent in the colonial situation. Hurbon makes the point that the king in Haitian Bouki and Malice tales is a metaphor of the social formation. The trickster, he argues, calls this formation into question and parodies it. But the contradiction remains.[44] There is a similarity between the king in the Haitian tales and the big monkeys in the tale "Annancy and Brother Tiger." The big monkeys, who chase away both Tiger and Anancy, are the ultimate guarantors of the social structure (colonial disorder).[45] In the trickster tales, the plantation system is ultimately taken as a given with the consequence that it is indirectly legitimated.

In this respect, there is a parallel with some of the trickster tales in the European folk tradition. Robert Darnton writes: "Tricksterism does not offer a recipe for revolution. It shows that the clever underdog may exploit some marginal advantage by playing on the vanity and stupidity of his superiors. But the trickster works within the

---

42. Dennis Forsythe has highlighted this, perhaps in an extreme way, in *Rastafari: For the Healing of the Nation* (Kingston, Jamaica: Zaika Publications, 1983), pp. 214–36.

43. Dickson, p. 423.

44. Laënnec Hurbon, *Culture et dictature en Haïti: l'imaginaire sous contrôle* (Paris: Harmattan, 1979), p. 175.

45. Jekyll, pp. 7–9.

system, turning its weak points to his advantage and therefore ultimately confirming it. Moreover, he may always meet someone
trickier than himself, even in the ranks of the rich and powerful."[46]
Darnton does not explore the possibility that the behavior of the
trickster is more than rampant Malthusian individualism, that a type
of behavior that may be approved in dealings with the overlord is
deemed unacceptable in internal intragroup relationships. Nevertheless, Darnton has correctly pointed to the limit in the trickster tale.
Not only the structure of the trickster narrative but also the aesthetic
techniques used in performance are factors in the indirect acceptance
of the system: the language, symbolism, and humor camouflage the
resistance of the colonized, thus failing to bring the conflict directly
into the open.

There is, paradoxically, a sense in which the trickster–slave does
always emerge as a winner, even though he or she does not always
defeat the opponent. The point that Dickson makes with regard to
the black American John and Old Master stories is applicable to Brer
Rabbit and Anancy tales as well: even in failure, John (the trickster)
got the better of Old Master because he defined the situation as one of
equals in conflict, being neither superior nor inferior. This implicit
statement of equality should not be confused with an explicit demand
for liberation. Dickson argues that the ultimate questions of freedom
and slavery were rarely addressed.[47]

The realism in the trickster tale, the emphasis upon survival under
particular conditions, can be understood in terms of the notion of
Greek tragedy as mythical narrative as opposed to liberating narrative. Tragedy solves the contradiction created through the break-
down of order by sacrificing the aspirations of particular characters or
groups to the law of a broader community or social order. Still, the
contradiction can never be eliminated. The particular always rises up
to enter into a struggle with the universal. It is the situation of slavery
(or postemancipation oppression) that ultimately triumphs in the
trickster tales. This apparent order at the narrative level, however,
assumes the disorder created by the master's oppression and by the
cunning resistance of the slave.

If tragedy is the "suffered contradiction," comedy is the "painless

---

46. Darnton, p. 46.
47. Dickson, pp. 429, 422.

contradiction."[48] Having articulated lived contradictions, the community can see the humor behind their absurdity. Anancy tales are performed and listened to with "delighted chuckles" and "convulsions of merriment."[49] The powerful are satirized, the weak who do not know their limits are laughed at, and human excesses are ridiculed. But even comedy assumes the reality of the contradiction. Harry Oster has identified the role of laughter in blunting the blades of conflict: humor allows one to return to work.[50] No wonder, then, that folklore was sometimes encouraged by the master as a means of getting more work out of the slave.[51]

The trickster narrative assumes the system, even as it sees the necessity of struggle within it. It can be considered a form of mythical narrative that brings meaning to the experience of the community; it is an ever-renewed creative opening to the vicissitudes of existence. It cannot, however, be considered a form of liberating narrative, for it does not rest on the fundamental imperative of mutual recognition and the implications of such recognition for social transformation. The tragic (comic) form of the trickster tale denies the human possibility, which alone can transform the colonizer-colonized relationship.

The fact that the trickster tale ultimately accepts the parameters of social disorder in the colonial system should not be allowed to obscure the very real resistance to colonialism and oppression that is its essential historical function. Furthermore, the trickster's resistance should not be seen in isolation from other more direct or rebellious ways of resistance. Ultimately, the slave trickster is a rebel and his or her rebelliousness may erupt into the type of action that overtly challenges the system of oppression. Underlying the trickster's approach to reality is the wider cultural vision that patterns of religion, such as vaudou, exemplify: a cultural cosmos that orders the entire natural and social world of the colonized in reaction to the colonizer and that

48. Søren Kierkegaard, *Concluding Unscientific Postscript,* trans. David F. Swenson and Walter Lowrie (Princeton: Princeton University Press, 1968), p. 459.

49. Jekyll, p. 1.

50. Harry Oster, "Negro Humour: John and Old Marster," in *Mother Wit from the Laughing Barrel: Readings in the Interpretation of Afro-American Folklore,* ed. Alan Dundes (Englewood Cliffs, N.J.: Prentice-Hall, 1973), p. 558. It is not catharsis, as Oster suggests, but the tragic-comic acceptance of the contradiction that precludes fundamental change.

51. Roger Bastide, *African Civilizations in the New World,* trans. Peter Green (New York: Torchbook–Harper & Row, 1971), p. 172.

manifests the extent of the resistance of the colonized and its transformation into overt rebellion.

Although it is rooted in slave society and the postemancipation period, the trickster tale is still an important form in neocolonial Caribbean society. To the extent that a black bourgeoisie has replaced the white master and satisfied itself with an intermediary role, it is this class that both faces the trickster's attack and itself plays the role of trickster. Storytellers have responded to the increasing influence of American and European cultural forms and to modern technology by adapting and creolizing these forms. Louise Bennett performs Anancy tales to large audiences in person using sound equipment, issues recordings of the tales, and writes books about Anancy. In Bennett's works the stories remain traditional. Writers like Andrew Salkey introduce contemporary motifs and themes such as liberation, political betrayal, sexual equality, and nuclear war, though retaining Anancy's ambiguous character. Trevor Rhone has gone further to dramatize the pervasiveness of the trickster in the Jamaican tourist industry.[52]

In the contemporary period, the trickster's ambiguities have been called into question both by those who would fight their oppression more openly and by those who claim that the trickster's behavior is harmful to the national effort. Levine argues that black American trickster heroes have largely been replaced in the twentieth century by the black hero who directly confronts authority without resorting to cunning and guile.[53] The ghetto gunslinger hero indicates a similar tendency in the Caribbean. Rhygin (Ivan) of *The Harder They Come* is the classic example.[54] The new type of hero fights for justice in a romantic way, however. His story represents a wish fulfillment destined to clash with a brutal reality. In contrast to the ghetto hero is the "new man" building the "new" society. Rex Nettleford argues

52. Louise Bennett, *Anancy and Miss Lou* (Kingston, Jamaica: Sangster's Book Stores, 1979; Andrew Salkey, *Anancy's Score* (London: Bogle-L'Ouverture Publications, 1973). Trevor Rhone, *Smile Orange,* in *Old Story Time and Other Plays* (Harlow, Essex: Longman, 1981). See also Phoebe Chang's "Dis Women's Work," in *Focus 1983: An Anthology of Contemporary Jamaican Writing,* ed. Mervyn Morris (Kingston: Caribbean Authors Publishing, 1983), pp. 96–98, in which Anancy learns about housework.

53. Levine, pp. 384–85.

54. Michael Thelwell, *The Harder They Come* (New York: Grove Press, 1980). See also the film by Trevor Rhone and Perry Henzell.

that the "elusive cunning" and sabotage characteristic of the Anancy syndrome, though important historically as a survival mechanism, does not contribute to the struggle for national development today. What is needed is a new creative imagination and social practice born out of the strengths of the old. Nettleford is well aware of the risk that this new ethic entails: to the extent that men and women in the Caribbean are still not in control of their own labor, they become the servants of a neocolonial elite even as they attempt to build the new society.[55]

To a large extent, forms of popular culture such as music and film have begun to take the place of the folktale in the Caribbean. The calypso keeps alive the sense of struggle in the trickster tale and, along with reggae, takes that struggle one decisive step further by demanding social and political transformation. Some artists have turned to popular poetry, drama, and literature and have used them as means of struggle. In contrast, popular music and films imported from the United States often emasculate resistance. The challenge is to understand the trickster's struggle and the social totality circumscribing the limits of that struggle. The task is to realize that decisive leap for which Fanon calls: in the revolutionary moment, Fanon states, the storyteller "presides over a real invocation" in which a new historical movement and a new type of person are "revealed" (*WE*, p. 241; *DT*, p. 170).

55. Rex Nettleford, *Cultural Action and Social Change: The Case of Jamaica; An Essay in Caribbean Cultural Identity* (Ottawa: International Development Research Centre, 1979; Kingston: Institute of Jamaica, 1978), pp. 196–97, 215–16; see also "Jamaican Song and Story and the Theater" in Jekyll, p. xiv.

Chapter 5

The Quest for Identity: Negritude

Mulish reason, you will not stop me from casting [*lancer absurde*] on the waters at the mercy of the currents of my thirst
your form, deformed islands
your end, my defiance

> AIMÉ CÉSAIRE, *Cahier d'un retour au pays natal/Notebook of a Return to the Native Land*

Culture is more and more cut off from actuality. It takes refuge in a passionately glowing hearth and opens up concrete paths for itself with difficulty; still, these paths are the only ones capable of procuring for it the attributes of fertility, homogeneity, and density.

> FRANTZ FANON, *Les damnés de la terre* (my translation)

AIMÉ CÉSAIRE, Martinican poet and politician, published the first edition of *Cahier d'un retour au pays natal* (*Notebook of a Return to the Native Land*) in a Paris journal in 1939. A poetic statement of what it meant to be black in a colonial world, the poem was one of the major works of the Negritude movement in Paris and would significantly influence later Caribbean writing. Like many students in the 1930s, Césaire was influenced politically by the communist movement and culturally by surrealism. However, he was particularly interested in issues of black culture and identity and collaborated with Léon-Gontran Damas from Guyana, Léopold Senghor from Senegal, and others, on a newspaper entitled *L'Etudiant Noir*. According to Césaire, he and the other students felt that some of their black communist friends were "abstract Communists." Marxism had to be complemented and particularized in terms of the specificity of black history and culture.[1] Negritude as an aesthetic movement and ideology arose out of this project. Césaire would later define it as "the awareness of being black, the simple acknowledgement of a fact which implies the acceptance of it, a taking charge of one's destiny as a black man, of one's history and culture."[2]

Césaire's *Cahier* is an artistic attempt to resolve the tension between a communist ideology and lived black experience. It interweaves the Marxist call for liberation with reflection on colonial conditions, particularly those that Césaire himself had experienced in Martinique. In addition, it portrays aspects of African culture and its recreation in the Americas and positively reevaluates what it means to be black. Finding himself in Paris engaged in the process of assimilating European culture, Césaire, like other black intellectuals, reacted to his situation by trying to recover in poetry that lost part of his cultural inheritance.[3]

Whereas the culture of resistance characteristic of the folk tradition is created by the slave or colonized peasant out of lived experience, negritude is the product of a black intellectual elite confronting their separation and exile from this lived experience. Negritude represents a struggle for identity rather than for survival (the trickster tale) or for social change (vaudou religion). Through negritude, intellectuals draw on the experiences and struggles of the colonized and use them to make sense of themselves. At the same time, they legitimate themselves in the eyes of the oppressed. From the point of view of liberating narrative, negritude goes beyond the trickster tale and vaudou religion by posing the problem of total social transformation and human liberation. It moves from the experience of the particular to the universal, sometimes expressing the universal in Marxist terms. The problem is that this call for liberation is coupled with romantic and mythical claims that prompt Fanon and others following him to consider it a narcissistic deformation of the history of colonized

---

1. René Depestre, "An Interview with Aimé Césaire," in trans. Maro Riofrancos in *Discourse on Colonialism,* by Aimé Césaire (New York: Monthly Review, 1972), pp. 69–70. See also Thomas A. Hale, "Les Ecrits d'Aimé Césaire: Bibliographie Commentée," Etudes Françaises, 14 (October 1978), 221–24.

2. Quoted by Lilyan Kesteloot (from her 1959 interview with Césaire), in *Black Writers in French: A Literary History of Négritude,* trans. Ellen Conroy Kennedy (Philadelphia: Temple University Press, 1974), p. 105.

3. See the summary of this period in A. James Arnold, *Modernism and Negritude: The Poetry and Poetics of Aimé Césaire* (Cambridge: Harvard University Press, 1981), pp. 8–10.

blacks.[4] Césaire's negritude goes beyond simple narcissism, but it ultimately fails to resolve the contradiction between mythical and liberating narrative.

Fanon addresses the issue of negritude in considerable detail in his work. His discussion provides an incisive overview of negritude and puts us in a better position to understand Césaire's *Cahier* as an expression of negritude. Fanon was greatly influenced by the Negritude movement and by Césaire, in particular. He attended Lycée Schoelcher in Martinique while Césaire taught there, and he supported Césaire's bid for political office in the 1945 elections.[5] In 1947 Fanon went to France to study medicine. A year later, Sartre's *Orphée noir* (*Black Orpheus*) appeared as the introduction to Senghor's anthology of black writing. Though sympathetic to its goal of self-recovery, Fanon ultimately condemns negritude for providing a tool with which a dependent bourgeoisie can manipulate the people of an emerging nation; the intellectual spokesperson has only an exterior relationship to his or her people (*WE*, pp. 222, 233–35; *DT*, pp. 153, 163–65).

Negritude developed in reaction to the ideology of European colonialism and the process of internalization that it encouraged. The Europeans who established slaveholding plantation societies in the Caribbean insisted on the cultural and biological superiority of whites. The African and creole slaves on the plantation repudiated European culture through the creation of a creole culture of resistance, one that erupted into rebellion and revolution. From the beginning of the colonial period, however, the colonizer disrupted the culture of the colonized and delegated authority and privileges to those who accepted the white myths, accommodated the colonizers, and worked within the plantation system. The master, Fanon says, allowed such slaves "to eat at his table" (*BS*, p. 219; *PN*, p. 178). Coloreds on the slave plantation, the classic mulatto offspring of the white bookkeeper or overseer and one of his female slaves, were often the beneficiaries; their complexion indicated their connection to white civilization. Pragmatic resistance was transformed into internalization to the extent that the colonized began to believe that the European culture that held

---

4. *BS*, p. 45; *PN*, p. 36; Wole Soyinka, "And after the Narcissist?" *African Forum*, 1 (Spring 1970), 53–64.

5. Irene L. Gendzier, *Frantz Fanon: A Critical Study* (London: Wildwood House, 1973), pp. 14–15; Hale p. 418.

together the colonial plantation system was superior to African-based cultural forms. The second chapter of Fanon's *Black Skin, White Masks* provides the classic analysis of the process of internalization. Fanon describes and diagnoses the sociopsychological process by means of which an inferiority complex is created and, consequently, a drive for cultural and biological whitening ("lactification"). The coloreds and, later, blacks who became trapped in this process formed an elite among the colonized that would become a dependent bourgeoisie.

The basic contradiction in the process of internalization lay in the impossibility of assimilation, no matter how well European culture was internalized: skin color determined social status. This contradiction always threatened to pull apart the process of internalization and transform it into a tragedy of despair. A tragic conception of the world could be forestalled, however, if the individual was able to refind him or herself through immersion in the life and culture of subordinate, colonized classes. The Negritude literary movement was one such attempt to affirm African or black culture and demonstrate its existence to the colonizer.

In the early twentieth century, Europe experienced a period of socioeconomic disruption, political upheaval, and cultural disarray that made European ideals appear questionable and opened spaces for movements such as Negritude. The labor movement, the Russian Revolution, and anticolonial movements posed alternatives to Western bourgeois hegemony. European intellectuals explored the significance for human experience of "unconscious" psychological processes and "primitive" cultural systems. Others carried out research on complex non-European civilizations. Maurice de Lafosse and Léo Frobenius showed that unique West African civilizations were as developed as their European counterparts. Black elites began to realize that no matter how much they strived to belong to the European ruling class, they were denied equality. In response, some attempted to recreate an authentic black culture that would be the basis of a black identity. The Harlem Renaissance in the United States, the Negrista movement in Cuba, and the movement centered on *La Révue Indigène* in Haiti sought to recover black cultural values and, as such, were precursors of the Negritude movement.[6]

6. Kesteloot, *Black Writers,* pp. 93–96; David Nicholls, *From Dessalines to Duvalier: Race, Colour and National Independence in Haiti* (Cambridge: Cambridge University Press, 1979), pp. 142–43, 164, and Rhonda Cobham, "The Background," in *West Indian Literature,* ed. Bruce King (London: Macmillan, 1979), p. 14.

Fanon analyzes negritude in a sustained dialogue with Sartre's *Anti-Semite and Jew* and *Black Orpheus*. He argues that Sartre arrives at the key to understanding racism and responses to it such as negritude: the anti-Semite *"makes"* the Jew. The racist, Fanon comments, *"creates his inferior"* (*BS*, p. 93; *PN*, p. 75). The condition of the colonized is determined by racial oppression. The black person is treated as though he or she were a mere object, a thing; he or she "has no ontological resistance in the eyes of the white man" (*BS*, p. 110; *PN*, p. 89).

In *Anti-Semite and Jew*, Sartre states that anti-Semitism reduces the Jew to a thinglike state, "a stone," in which the individual is deprived of the possibility of participating in history. Forced into a situation of inauthenticity, the Jew allows him or herself "to be poisoned by the stereotype" and lives in constant fear that his or her actions will correspond to it. An attempt may be made to overcome inferiority by becoming a "missionary of the universal." However, the Jew remains a Jew: he or she is not allowed to assimilate. The Jew may continue in a flight into bad faith by denying his or her Jewish background or may simply abdicate responsibility altogether and accept misfortune as though it were fated. Some Jews may temper acceptance of fate with the exaltation of their own community and race. Sartre argues that there is no true Jewish community. What exists has been created by the anti-Semite. The Jewish community has been deprived of history and remembers only a long martyrdom and a long passivity: "its twenty centuries of dispersion and political impotence forbid its having a *historic past*." Unable to take pride in any specifically Jewish collective work, civilization, or even religion, Jews "must indeed end up by exalting racial qualities."[7]

Sartre's characterization of Jewish history is extreme. By reducing Jewish history to "passivity" and "martyrdom," he loses the tradition of resistance through which the Jewish community preserved itself through thousands of years of oppression. Still, there is some truth in Sartre's argument. Anti-Semitism, he says, cannot be understood in terms of normal ontological relationships to the other. A specific political dimension—the dimension of racial domination—must be taken into account: "the Jew has a personality like the rest of us, and on top of that he is Jewish. . . . The Jew is overdetermined."[8] As an

---

7. Jean-Paul Sartre, *Anti-Semite and Jew*, trans. George J. Becker (New York: Schocken, 1965), pp. 108, 95, 113, 66, 85. Cited in *BS*, pp. 115, 118; *PN*, pp. 93, 95.
8. Sartre, *Anti-Semite*, p. 79.

integral part of a total system of oppression, racial domination deprives specific human beings of their ontological relation to others in history. The Jew is caught in a social and political structure and is therefore forced to react to oppression. What Sartre fails to highlight, however, is that the challenge of Jewish history has been to transform reaction, as resentment, into liberating action.

Sartre analyzes colonial racism and responses to it in *Black Orpheus*. Like the Jew, the black person is racially oppressed. By virtue of certain physical traits he or she is considered to be a mentally and socially inferior being and is deprived of humanity. Reduced to a state of "particularism," the colonized is deprived of his or her role in universal history. But whereas the Jew may escape racism by virtue of the lack of distinguishing physical traits, the black person cannot escape his or her body. Assimilation is impossible. He or she is driven to confront his or her being as a member of a particular race in opposition to another race. Thus, argues Sartre, negritude, as the racial consciousness of the black person, has to manifest itself in the form of "antiracist racism."[9] Like the Jew, the black person is trapped in a total system of oppression to which he or she is forced to react.

In opposition to his dismissal of the authenticity of Jewish culture, Sartre finds in the racial consciousness of the black person the manifestation of a strong living culture. Damned by the white colonizer, the black person can fall back on his or her own living culture and community. According to Sartre, negritude is characterized objectively by the oral tradition of Africa—customs, arts, songs, tales, dances. Subjectively, it is characterized by an Orphic descent into the self, a plunge "under the superficial crust of reality." Negritude reflects the desire binding human beings to each other and to nature in a form of sensual pantheism. As the "being-in-the-world of the Negro," it confronts white culture with a nontechnical relationship to the universe.[10] The tale of suffering under colonial domination becomes part of the experience of negritude. The black person has

9. Jean-Paul Sartre, *Black Orpheus*, trans. S. W. Allen (Paris: Présence Africaine, 1976), p. 15. Sartre's "Orphée noir," introduction to *Anthologie de la nouvelle poésie nègre et malgache*, by L. S. Senghor (Paris: Presses Universitaires de France, 1948), is also found in Jean-Paul Sartre, *Situations*, 3 (Paris: Gallimard, 1949). Along with Allen's translation, there is a translation by Arthur Gillette ("Black Orpheus," *Strand*, 5, no. 4 [1960] and 6, no. 1 [1960]). Both translations must be used with caution.

10. Sartre, *Black Orpheus* (Allen translation), pp. 34, 41.

known servitude and knows that he or she is the innocent victim of the white colonizer. Attacked, like the Jew, by virtue of his or her racial being, the black person comes to a consciousness of his or her existence as a *black* person. The Jew becomes an antiracist racist because he or she lacks a historical community and must fall back on the anti-Semite's notion of race. The black has a distinct historical community on which to fall back. However, he or she likewise becomes an antiracist racist because he or she must respond to racial victimization by the colonizer.

In both *Anti-Semite and Jew* and *Black Orpheus*, Sartre addresses the problem of moving beyond this Manichaean drama. A distinction is made in *Anti-Semite and Jew* between two solutions to the problem of racial oppression: the moral choice of authenticity and the revolutionary change in the structure of society. "Jewish authenticity," Sartre writes, "consists in choosing oneself *as Jew*—that is, in realizing one's Jewish condition. The authentic Jew abandons the myth of the universal man; he knows himself and wills himself into history as a historic and damned creature; he ceases to run away from himself and to be ashamed of his own kind. . . . He chooses his brothers and his peers; they are the other Jews. . . . The authentic Jew *makes himself a Jew*. . . .In this isolation to which he has consented, he becomes again a man, a whole man, with the metaphysical horizons that go with the condition of man."[11] However, the moral choice of authenticity is not really a solution "because the situation which he has to lay claim to and to live in is quite simply that of a martyr." Others still regard him or her as a particular type of being, a Jew, and limit his or her possibilities. Since anti-Semitism is "a mythical, bourgeois representation of the class struggle," states Sartre, "it could not exist in a classless society." The situation in which the Jew finds him or herself alienated must be changed. Sartre suggests some concrete ways of beginning to change the situation: anti-Semitism must be eliminated through education, information and law; Jews must be respected; a militant league against anti-Semitism should be formed. Sartre says that none of these activities has any direct bearing on the class struggle, however. Neither the authentic Jew who acknowledges his or her situation, nor the authentic non-Jew who participates in these concrete activities can really do anything. They are martyrs, it seems,

11. Sartre, *Anti-Semite,* pp. 136–38.

tragic heroes doomed to wait for the class struggle to resolve itself before they can be free.[12]

The problem with *Anti-Semite and Jew* is that Sartre fails to resolve the contradiction between the concrete person authentically participating in a living community and the external social dialectic, the social totality, that determines the situation in which that person finds him or herself. Sartre states that everyone should have citizenship rights in a country because of participation in that country. But they should have these rights "*as* Jews, Negroes, or Arabs—that is, as concrete persons." This would facilitate not only the choice of authenticity on the part of that person but also, bit by bit, assimilation.[13] How one makes the leap from concrete person to assimilated citizen, indeed, why the authentic person should even want to make such a choice, Sartre does not explain. Grounded as it is in the idea of universal history, an abstract dialectic of class struggle, it is the Sartrean analysis in *Anti-Semite and Jew* that makes the Jew a martyr and a tragic hero.

Black Orpheus is a more sophisticated work than *Anti-Semite and Jew* because it attempts to work through the dualism of concrete person and universal history in terms of a living culture. However, just as the concrete, authentic person is annihilated in *Anti-Semite and Jew*, the living community in *Black Orpheus* is destined to make itself vanish out of existence. Unable to deny his or her choice, Sartre says, the black person is "driven to the wall of authenticity [*acculé à l'authenticité*]: insulted, enslaved, he pulls himself up [*se redresse*], picks up the word 'nigger' that has been thrown at him like a stone, and claims his due as a Negro [*noir*; that is, black], before the white man, proudly."[14] This moment of anti-racist racism, however, is merely a moment of negativity that will ultimately lead to the abolition of racial distinctions altogether, Sartre continues. The recognition of the culture and dignity of the black race is a necessary part of the cultural response to oppression because one is oppressed as a race by another race. Thus, negritude was a necessary moment for the self-under-

---

12. Sartre, *Anti-Semite*, pp. 91, 149–52. Albert Memmi's analysis of colonial conflict likewise fails to reconcile the external necessity of revolution with concrete action. See *The Colonizer and the Colonized*, trans. Howard Greenfeld (Boston: Beacon Press, 1965), pp. 151–52.

13. Sartre, *Anti-Semite*, pp. 146–47.

14. Sartre, *Situations*, 3, p. 237; *Black Orpheus* (Gillette translation), p. 5. Allen's translation (p. 15) is inaccurate here.

standing of the black person. However, argues Sartre, negritude recognizes that it is not an essence but a historical phenomenon, a becoming. Understanding his or her own suffering, the black person understands the suffering of human beings in general; in seeking liberation, he or she seeks the liberation of all persons. As it enters upon universal history, negritude must destroy itself.

In one of the most significant and influential passages in the history of negritude, Sartre completely eliminates the cultural background that he had analyzed so sympathetically:

> At once the subjective, existential, ethnic idea of *négritude* "passes," as Hegel puts it, into the objective, positive, exact idea of *proletariat*. . . . And, undoubtedly it is no coincidence that the most ardent poets of negritude are at the same time militant Marxists.
>
> But that does not prevent the idea of race from mingling [*se recoupe*] with that of class: The first is concrete and particular, the second is universal and abstract; the one stems from what Jaspers calls understanding [*compréhension*] and the other from intellection; the first is the result of a psychobiological syncretism and the second is a methodical construction based on experience. In fact, negritude appears as the minor term [*le temps faible*] of a dialectical progression: The theoretical and practical assertion of the supremacy of the white man is its thesis; the position of negritude as antithetical value is the moment of negativity. But this negative moment is insufficient by itself, and the Negroes [*noirs*, that is, blacks] who employ it know this very well; they know that it is intended to prepare the synthesis or realization of the human in a society without races. Thus negritude is the root of its own destruction, it is a transition [*passage*] and not a conclusion, a means and not an ultimate end.[15]

In *Anti-Semite and Jew*, Sartre ends with an unresolved dualism between lived experience and a necessitarian Marxist dialectic. Ultimately, the march of universal history will draw all into a common proletarian cultural experience devoid of the trappings of specific cultural backgrounds. A similar problem arises in *Black Orpheus*. The attempt to reconcile lived experience with universal history results in the sacrifice of cultural specificity. Sartre conflates that dimension of

---

15. Sartre, *Situations*, 3, pp. 279–80, cited in *BS*, p. 133 (*PN*, pp. 107–108). There are inaccuracies in the translations by Allen (pp. 59–60) and Gillette (pp. 17–18). Eric Sellin notes that the treatment of negritude as a necessary but "transitory" *prise de conscience* is also expressed by black socialists such as the Angolan Mário de Andrade ("*Négritude*: Status or Dynamics," *L'Esprit Créateur*, 10 [Fall 1970], 179–80).

negritude whose distinctive feature is its focus on racial claims, with the culture, indeed, *cultures*, of the colonized who are black. In Sartre's analysis, the deracialization of cultural claims, which for him is the ultimate intention of negritude, results in the loss of the concrete cultural uniqueness of particular groups of peoples.

Fanon's commentary on Sartre's passage indicates both the importance of the issues raised by Sartre and the extent to which Sartre's analysis is marred by its lack of clarity and tendency to reduce all cultural experience to a Marxist model of culture. Fanon makes Sartre's passage central to his discussion of the being-in-the-world of the black person. In a subjective and highly ambiguous dialogue with the Sartrean text, he shows how Sartre had both demystified negritude and created a new mythology. Sartre shattered the romantic illusions of an "immanent" black consciousness by showing that negritude was a form of antiracist racism, a minor term dependent on a major premise, colonial racism (*BS*, p. 135; *PN*, p. 109). Chinua Achebe says that antiracist racism can be an important antidote to white racism.[16] However, all racism, including antiracist racism, had to be transformed into universal human awareness. Like Sartre, Fanon realized the significance of deracializing cultural claims. Thus he comments: "The dialectic that brings necessity into the foundation of my freedom drives me out of myself. It shatters my unreflected position" (*BS*, p. 135; *PN*, p. 109). Elsewhere in *Black Skin, White Masks*, Fanon states that a black skin is not the depositary of "specific values"; there is no "Negro mission" (*BS*, pp. 227–28; *PN*, pp. 184–85). Indeed, he states that there are members of many different nations who are black. The black race cannot claim unity (*BS*, p. 173; *PN*, p. 139).

Fanon picks up this critique of negritude again and develops it in *The Wretched of the Earth*. Given the colonizer's racialization of thought, those colonized who decide to reaffirm their own culture do so at the level of the race as a whole. This unconditional affirmation, however, this emotional antithesis to the white person's insult, neglects "the historical character" of human beings. The conditions of blacks differ as the historical situation differs (*WE*, pp. 211–12, 216; *DT*, pp. 146–47, 149). The idea of black culture is a mere mystifica-

16. Cited in John Erickson, "Sartre's African Writings: Literature and Revolution," *L'Esprit Créateur*, 10 (Fall 1970), 196.

tion, a myth, to the extent that it does not encompass the necessity of the struggle for freedom under particular conditions of oppression. Negritude is the ideology of a dependent and oppressive national bourgeoisie that legitimates itself by claiming to represent the true culture of the masses.

Fanon calls this type of ideology "abstract populism." He uses the examples of Jacques Rabemananjara and Léopold Senghor to illustrate briefly some of the ways in which this process of mystification functions. Rabemananjara, he states, claims to be a representative of a free Madagascar and a proponent of African cultural unity. When Algeria began to liberate itself, however, Rabemananjara threw his support behind the French colonizers rather than behind a struggling African nation. Senghor, one of the greatest exponents of negritude and president of an independent Senegal, did likewise (WE, pp. 233–35; DT, pp. 163–65). The implication is not only that these proponents of black culture fail to contribute to the real cultural struggles of other colonized countries, but also that they fail to fulfill their responsibilities to further the authentic liberation of their own people. Popular cultural symbols are co-opted for the benefit of a new dictatorial ruling class. Although Fanon seems more sympathetic to negritude in *Black Skin, White Masks* than in *The Wretched of the Earth*, the two works are essentially compatible: both realize the necessity of deracializing cultural claims.

The problem with Sartre's analysis of negritude, Fanon indicates, is that it made the black person feel as though he or she had been robbed of his or her last chance. His or her Orphic descent into self and community had been reduced to relativity, to a term in the dialectic. "And so it is not I who make a meaning for myself, but it is the meaning that was already there, pre-existing, waiting for me" (BS, p. 134; PN, p. 109). Negritude was a form of cultural therapy for the black intellectual. Fanon realized that Sartre was losing the subjective moment so emphasized in the rest of *Black Orpheus*. Sartre, "who remained The Other," left the black person "damned": "Jean-Paul Sartre had forgotten that the Negro suffers in his body quite differently from the white man. Between the white man and me the connection was irrevocably one of transcendence" (BS, pp. 137–38; PN, pp. 111–12). In spite of all the historical differences, the black person shared with other blacks the historical experience of being treated as a Negro, as a particular type of inferior being (BS, p. 173; PN, p. 140).

Fanon sets himself the task of recapturing "L'expérience vécue du Noir," the lived experience of the black person.[17] It was necessary to pull together past and future in order to critically recognize the personal and social significance of black self-consciousness: "So I took up my negritude, and with tears in my eyes I put its machinery together again" (*BS*, p. 138; *PN*, p. 112).

Gendzier argues that this attempt by Fanon to rescue negritude is in conflict with Fanon's critique of negritude defined in racial terms. However, Kesteloot points out that Sartre, unlike Fanon, considered negritude "only from an angle of opposition to the white man, thus mistaking a part for the whole concept." Sartre was "too anxious to assimilate the conflict of races with class struggle."[18] According to Fanon, it was necessary to take up the struggle of negritude and go beyond it, to deracialize it. It is part of the experience of the black person to belong to a group of people that was and still is oppressed on the basis of race. The culture of this oppressed group took form in relation to this oppression. In spite of this common focus, however, black culture developed in the context of widely varying social and historical situations. To talk about black culture is to reduce to an abstract idea the specific cultural expressions that developed in response to unique conditions. If one is to put the machinery of negritude together again one can authentically do so only by moving away from a race analysis of culture to an analysis that starts from lived historical realities. Sartre had reduced the lived experience of a particular group of people to an a priori, closed narrative, a Marxist metanarrative based on the European experience. He had fallen victim to his own vision of an external dialectic, that is, to a form of alienation that he himself would later criticize in his *Critique of Dialectical Reason*.

17. The title of chapter 5 of *PN*, "L'expérience vécue du Noir," translated by Markman as "The Fact of Blackness" in *BS*. See Sartre's definition of *le vécu* as "the ensemble of the dialectical process of psychic life, in so far as this process is obscure to itself because it is a constant totalization, thus necessarily a totalization which cannot be conscious of what it is" (Jean-Paul Sartre, "Itinerary of a Thought," in *Between Existentialism and Marxism*, trans. John Mathews [New York: William Morrow, 1976] p. 41). Fanon's appreciation of the lived experience to which negritude appealed is ignored in Janheinz Jahn's criticism of Fanon. Jahn argues that Fanon failed to recognize that *indigenismo* and negritude were forms of protest and sources of spiritual strength (*A History of Neo-African Literature: Writing in Two Continents*, trans. Oliver Coburn and Ursula Lehrburger [London: Faber & Faber, 1968], pp. 278, 281–82).

18. Irene L. Gendzier, "Reflections on Fanon and the Jewish Question," *New Outlook*, 12 (January 1969), 17; Kesteloot, *Black Writers*, pp. 113–14.

"Understanding" had been reduced to "intellection" and quasi-sovereignty emasculated. By depriving the black person of his or her own choice of him or herself, Sartre was playing the role of the white master, the guarantor of history.[19]

The idea of negritude confuses the cultural awakening of black intellectuals with the differing cultural expressions of black people in general. This is particularly true of Sartre's conception of negritude. Fanon observes that negritude was the creation of the black bourgeoisie (*BS*, p. 224; *PN*, p. 182). Wole Soyinka, following Fanon, has commented that the majority of blacks never lost their culture in the way that the elite did and, therefore, never had to refind it. Soyinka argues that negritude may have been necessary for those colonized who had internalized the white myth of black inferiority. However, negritude became a narcissistic contemplation of a contrived self; it reaffirmed the Manichaeism of European racism by romanticizing Africa, glorifying intuition over reason, and proudly presenting itself as the antithesis of European culture. By reaffirming black experience, but in a European way, the elite legitimated their own leadership without truly representing their people. In the words of the Dahomean Stanislas Adotevi, negritude "is the black way of being white."[20] According to Wole Soyinka, Sartre accepted the Manichaean self-misunderstanding of the elite then proceeded "to drink it under the table" by saying that negritude would lead to its own transcendence in the universal.[21] Sartre had to annihilate negritude in order to avoid the problem of racism. In doing so, Sartre lost precisely that which was particular to the experience of black people, the

---

19. John Erickson states that Sartre is justified in speculating about a "natural process" that follows certain universal principles (p. 195). However, in making this statement, Erickson merely introduces the external dialectic and sacrifices living culture.

20. Quoted in Maximilien Laroche, *L'Image comme écho: Essais sur la littérature et la culture haïtiennes* (Montreal: Nouvelle Optique, 1978), p. 145; other writers who are critical of the romanticization of Africa, Yambo Ouologuem and Ezekiel Mphahlele, for example, are discussed in Sellin, pp. 177–78. See also Richard C. Clark, "Contrasting Views of 'Black' African Literature," *Review of National Literature* 2 (Fall 1971), special issue, *Black Africa* (New York: St. John's University Press, 1972), p. 248.

21. Wole Soyinka, *Myth, Literature, and the African World* (Cambridge: Cambridge University Press, 1976), pp. 126–35; "Drama and the Revolutionary Ideal," in *In Person: Achebe, Awoonor, and Soyinka,* ed. Karen L. Morell (Washington, D.C.: University of Washington Institute for Comparative and Foreign Area Studies, 1976), p. 101. See also "And after the Narcissist?" p. 53.

lived experience of blacks in different historical circumstances; only an ideal, communist culture remained. Fanon and Soyinka, in contrast, realized both the need for the elite to recover their historical being, in a nonnarcissistic way, and the historical reality of living, popular cultures, vital in the struggle against colonialism. Rather than transcending itself in the universal, popular culture could become the vehicle for historically specific expressions of the universal quest for liberation.

A student in Paris, Aimé Césaire belonged to the French-schooled intellectual elite who were trying to find their own unique identity through negritude. In his Caribbean homeland, African culture had been creolized. Through symbols such as the trickster, and through religious and other cultural practices, Afro-Caribbean culture remained a dynamic basis for the consolidation of identity, resistance, and rebellion. While Césaire's formal education pulled him away from this popular culture, his informal contact with African and West Indian students, and with various ethnographical works, afforded him the opportunity to recover African and West Indian culture and to use it in poetic creations addressing such problems as colonialism, racism, and the struggle for liberation. His *Cahier* is a rich and complex poetic attempt to recover African and Caribbean culture and to transcend their particularities in the expression of a universal quest for mutual recognition. It demonstrates how difficult it is to recover an authentic popular culture in a narrative of liberation, and it shows how this very project can become caught in the Sartrean dualism and the recreation of mythical narrative.

The *Cahier* is a poetic work with an overall narrative structure and underlying narrative substructures. The poem moves from description (*mimesis*) to mythical construct (*mythos*) in the process of creating a narrative about what it means to be a black person in the Caribbean. The colonial contradiction is the fundamental social and political contradiction in the poem. Two primary responses to this contradiction are presented, both related to ideological positions of the black elite: internalization of the white value system and immersion into black culture. Underlying these responses are two basic narrative resolutions: the white myth and the reaction to it, the black myth. The poem is complex, however: a romantic resolution of the colonial contradiction gives way to a tragic conception of negritude as the historical dimension in the poem calls romantic myths into question. In the final analysis, the poem is a unified work that the poet constructs in an attempt to reclaim his history and arouse his people into an act of self-creation. It concludes with a movement to the universal, to human recognition and brotherhood.

In contrast to the mythological and symbolic depiction of the sociopolitical contradiction in vaudou ritual and trickster stories, the *Cahier* opens in a mimetic mode with an explicit and vivid description of the living conditions in the Caribbean and of the suffering associated with them. The poem describes the "hungry" Antilles, "pitted with smallpox, . . . dynamited with alcohol," and moves to geographically more specific locations of social deprivation. Martinique, Césaire's island home, is "a desolate bedsore on the wound of the waters." Fort-de-France, its capital, suffers the inertia of its "eternally renewed cross." There is the hill infested with "malarial blood," the "bumpy road," and "the carcass of wood" called "our house." The community appears to be broken down into separate individuals, divided from each other, who constitute a "throng which does not pack, does not mix"; fearful, suicidal, corrupt, hypocritical, they are "clever at discovering the point of disencasement, of flight, of dodging." Or they dream; at Christmastime they create an illusory world to hide their suffering; they "live as in a dream," shout and sing as in a dream, only to arrive at "aborted dreams."[22]

The situation is one of social disorder in which people are marginalized and do not participate in the colonial order. The *Cahier* makes it clear that the source of the Martinican's suffering is the system of colonialism. People are "not connected with anything that is expressed, asserted, released [*se libère*]. . . . Neither with Josephine, Empress of the French, dreaming way up there above the nigger scum [*négraille*]. Nor with the liberator fixed in his white washed stone liberation. Nor with the conquistador. Nor with this contempt, with this freedom, with this audacity" (pp. 36–37). The presentation

22. Aimé Césaire, *Cahier d'un retour au pays natal* / *Notebook of a Return to the Native Land*, in *Aimé Césaire, The Collected Poetry*, trans. Clayton Eshleman and Annette Smith, biling. ed., (Berkeley and Los Angeles: University of California Press, 1983), pp. 35–43 (all page numbers in the text refer to this edition). A useful, earlier translation was made by Emile Synder (*Cahier d'un retour au pays natal* / *Return to my Native Land*, biling. ed. [Paris: Présence Africaine, 1971]). First written between 1935 and 1939, revisions were made in later editions to the *Cahier*, especially to the 1947 Bordas edition and the 1956 Présence Africaine edition (definitive edition). See Arnold, p. 147; Hale, pp. 224–29; and especially Lillian Pestre de Almeida, "Les Versions successives du *Cahier d'un retour au pays natal*," in M. a M. Ngal and Martin Steins, eds., *Césaire 70* (Paris: Editions Silex, 1984), pp. 123–40.

of the inert city is followed by a statement of the dehumanizing relationship of the colonizer to the colonized person. Césaire indicates the similarity in the condition of the European Jew to the non-European colonized, just as Sartre and Fanon would later do: his or her life worth little to the colonizer, the individual person becomes "a Kaffir-man, a Hindu-man-from-Calcutta, a Harlem-man-who-doesn't-vote, . . . a Jew-man, a pogrom-man" (pp. 42–43). The colonial situation is a situation of physical and spiritual death, as Césaire's friend Damas comments: "SINCE / how many of ME, ME, ME / have died / since they came this evening."[23]

By describing the colonized in racial terms, Césaire draws attention to the specificity of the colonial situation in Martinique: the preeminence of the racial factor over the economic.[24] He states in his essay *Discourse on Colonialism* (1950) that under colonialism there is "No human contact, but relations of domination and submission which turn the colonizing man into . . . a slave driver [*garde-chiourme*], and the indigenous man into an instrument of production." Like Fanon, he argues that colonization equals "thingification [*chosification*]." Colonization is both "based on contempt for the native and justified by that contempt." The colonizer eases his conscience by seeing the colonial subject as an animal, but in so doing he begins to transform himself into an animal. This is the "boomerang effect of colonization." Nazism, Césaire insists, was born out of this colonial relation.[25]

There is a sense of fatalism in the description of the colonial situation in the opening pages of the *Cahier*. Césaire overemphasizes the "thingification," atomization, degradation, and passivity of the colonized, to some extent entrapping himself in the colonizer's stereotypes. In this respect, there are similarities between the portrayal of the colonial situation in the *Cahier* and Jacques Roumain's depiction of the colonial legacy in *Masters of the Dew* (1943–44). Roumain's novel, written shortly after the first version of the *Cahier*, begins with

23. Léon-Gontran Damas, *Pigments* (Paris: Présence Africaine, 1962), p. 11; English translation in Edward A. Jones, *Voices of Negritude: The Expression of Black Experience in the Poetry of Senghor, Césaire, Damas* (Valley Forge, Pa.: Judson Press, 1971), p. 65.

24. See Bernard Zadi Zaourou, *Césaire entre deux cultures* (Dakar: Nouvelles Editions Africaines, 1978), pp. 61–64.

25. Aimé Césaire, *Discourse on Colonialism*, trans. Joan Pinkham (New York: Monthly Review, 1972), pp. 14–15, 20–21; *Discours sur le colonialisme*, 5th ed. (Paris: Présence Africaine, 1970), pp. 13–14, 17–19. See also *WE*, pp. 36–37, 111, 101; *DT*, pp. 6, 66, 58.

a depressed, divided, poverty-stricken Haitian community in the midst of a drought: "We're all going to die," says Délira, in desperation.[26] Both writers are trying to find ways in their respective plots of retrieving the history and culture of the colonized and orienting it toward liberating struggle. Even in these fatalistic portrayals, there appear glimpses of the struggle and hope that allowed the colonized to endure. "[D]etoured from its true cry" of hatred and revolt, the town is "mute" and "inert," writes Césaire in the *Cahier*; but the cry is present in its absence: "you feel it lives in it in some deep refuge and pride" (pp. 34–35). It is present in the old man's memory of the *coumbite*, the communal labor project, in the opening pages of the *Masters of the Dew*.[27]

The task of the poet in the *Cahier*, as first-person narrator, is to bring cultural order to social disorder: "My mouth shall be the mouth of those calamities which have no mouth, my voice the freedom of those who break down in the solitary confinement of despair" (pp. 44–45). Césaire uses language not just to describe but also to castigate. A cursory glance at the imagery used in the first section indicates that this "reality" is unreal. The poet's point of view, which is implicit from the beginning, is explicitly and poignantly stated near the end of the section: this rue Paille [Straw Road] is a "disgrace" (pp. 42–43). The task of identifying the historical situation and of exhorting the reader to define and orient him or herself to challenge colonialism is the task of the remainder of the poem. The poet must encode this disorder in a narrative form; he must tell a story that makes sense of the suffering, shows ways of coping with and transforming the situation, and challenges people to act. He immerses himself in his people and he makes his contribution to his people. Commenting on this aspect of the poem, Maryse Condé writes that the poet attempts to "take possession of the symbols and images relative to the past, give history a new light, and lead his people to take control of their lives [*à prendre vie*]."[28]

The white myth and the black myth are the two basic ideological

26. Jacques Roumain, *Masters of the Dew*, trans. Langston Hughes and Mercer Cook, Caribbean Writers Series, 12 (London: Heinemann, 1978), p. 23.

27. Roumain, *Masters*, pp. 25–30.

28. Maryse Condé, *Cahier d'un retour au pays natal—Césaire* (Paris: Hatier, 1978), p. 37. See also Abiola Irele, "Literature and Ideology in Martinique: René Maran, Aimé Césaire, Frantz Fanon," in *The African Experience in Literature and Ideology* (London: Heinemann, 1981), pp. 137–38; Arnold, p. 68.

patterns that inform the poet's orientation to himself and his community in the colonial situation. The black student in the colonial educational system learns the colonizer's values and internalizes the white myth. Internalization, the response of the elite to the colonial contradiction, is a primary focus in the poem. Césaire piercingly illustrates the consequences of internalization with the tram incident in the *Cahier*. A bent black man, reduced to undignified servility, is laughed at by female passengers. The poet himself is on the tram and, like an obsequious coward, he too offers a "complicitous smile" (pp. 62–63). Black men and women, particularly those who aspire to, or belong to, the ranks of the dependent bourgeoisie, can redeem themselves from an imposed racial inferiority complex to the extent that they can show that they are like the white colonizer and, as such, superior to other blacks. The poor black man on the tram is a real "nigger"; he is not like "us." The narrator's complicity is a way of carefully hiding from consciousness the fact that the situation of the man on the train has its origin in the system of colonial oppression.

Césaire illustrates the process of internalization elsewhere in the poem. He describes as "zebras" those among the colonized who try "to wash off their stripes in a dew of fresh milk." When this attempt fails, the person who believes in the myth of assimilation states to the European, "pay no attention to my black skin: the sun burned me" (pp. 78–79). To the extent that the colonized tries to assimilate by internalizing the values of the dominant class, he or she internalizes an ideology that justifies domination and exploitation on the basis of race. The colonized submits to the colonizer and does his or her utmost to defend the colonial or neocolonial system and his or her place in it.

Césaire sees through this white mythical order. In the *Cahier*, the narrator condemns himself, the person who smiled in complicity on the tram, for being mean and servile, and for cannibalizing his own race (pp. 64–65). As in Fanon's work, there is a hint that the rejection of assimilation may be prompted by direct contact with European discrimination and the consequent realization that the black person cannot assimilate in a racist society. The narrator states: "I would be a Jewman / a Kaffir-man" (pp. 42–43), suggesting that this is how European racism meets those who try to assimilate. One tries to be white but finds that one is still treated as an inferior because of one's racial background. Fanon argues that direct contact with European racist sailors was a major catalyst in the growth of negritude in Martinique during the Second World War (*AR*, p. 23; *RA*, pp. 27–28).

To escape the contradiction of assimilation, one can turn back to one's culture and history. The poet who would lead his people must encounter them in the depths of their being. At this level of analysis, the colonizer-colonized contradiction in the *Cahier* is resolved in terms of the black myth and some of its variants: the appeal to an African golden age; the idea of a black essence; the presentation of heroic black struggles. Césaire highlights the idea of an African golden age in his introduction, written in 1948, to a book on slavery and colonization by Victor Schoelcher, governor of the French islands at the time of emancipation. Césaire states that the African peoples whom the Europeans enslaved were, as individuals, superior to those who tortured them, that they were industrious, civilized people with beautiful religions and customs, knowledgeable in science and magnificently gifted in art. There existed a state of reciprocity in which individuals assisted each other. There was no need for coercion, since everyone freely accepted the discipline of the group. Césaire sums up African civilization in the following terms: "Order-Earnestness-Poetry and Freedom."[29] He expands on this theme in his *Discourse on Colonialism*, where he adds that the old African societies were communal, anticapitalist, democratic, and cooperative. Quoting Frobenius, he states, "Civilized to the marrow of their bones! The idea of the barbaric Negro is a European invention."[30]

In the *Cahier* there is a lyrical appeal to a beautiful and harmonious precolonial era that characterizes the romantic aspect of the idea of Africa in the poem. The poet as healer, the poet who has become rooted like a tree, who has become "a Congo resounding with forests and rivers" (pp. 50–51), utters a sacred invocation:

> voum rooh oh
> that the promised times may return
> and the bird who knew my name

29. Césaire, introduction to *Esclavage et colonisation,* by Victor Schoelcher (Paris: Presses Universitaires de France, 1948), p. 7; quoted in *BS*, pp. 130–31; *PN*, pp. 105–106.

30. Césaire, *Discourse*, pp. 23–24, 32; *Discours*, pp. 20–21, 31. However, without explaining the inconsistencies, Césaire also states here that some African societies were feudal, tyrannical, and unequal.

> and the woman who had a thousand names
> names of fountain sun and tears
> and her hair of minnows
> and her steps my climates
> and her eyes my seasons
> and the days without injury
> and the nights without offense
> and the stars my confidence
> and the wind my connivance. [Pp. 52–55]

It is here that Césaire's poetry takes on the mystical quality of Senghor's. Senghor liked Césaire's reference to the rustling Congo; he has his own version:

> Oho! Congo oho! I move the voices of the *koras* of
>   Koyaté to make your great name their rhythm
> Over the waters and rivers, over all I remember (the ink
>   of the scribe remains nothing).[31]

This vision of an African golden age is an attempt to recover a lost mythical past that could be a source of dignity and racial pride, that is, black identity. The poet's vision of Africa provides an image of cultural order that resolves the contradictions of racism and colonialism and lifts the colonized out of the situation of sociopolitical disorder. The colonizer's denial of history and culture to the colonized is challenged by the poet's invocation. The stereotypes legitimating colonialism are called into question. However, the vision of Africa remains romantic, even narcissistic. Whereas the storyteller knows that Anancy is of African origin even though creolized in the Caribbean, and whereas the serviteur knows that the loa reside in Africa, the intellectual invents and lays claim to his or her own utopian African source.[32]

Closely interwoven with the myth of Africa is the idea of negritude as an essence: coming from Africa, the black person has some fundamental characteristics that guide his or her way of existing in the world.

> Eia for the royal Cailcedra!
> Eia for those who have never invented anything

31. Leópold Sédar Senghor, *Liberté I: Négritude et humanisme* (Paris: Seuil, 1964), p. 141; Jones, p. 37.

32. See Frederick I. Case, "Négritude and Utopianism," *African Literature Today*, 7 (1975), 72–74.

for those who never explored anything
for those who never conquered anything

but yield, captivated, to the essence of all things

. . . . .

spark of the sacred fire of the world
flesh of the world's flesh pulsating with the very motion of the world!
Tepid dawn of ancestral virtues

Blood! Blood! All our blood aroused by the male heart of the sun

. . . . .

Eia! perfect circle of the world, enclosed concordance! [Pp. 68–69]

Though this passage uses irony to dismiss a number of racial stereotypes, it is primarily an evocation of a black physical and spiritual
essence. The Cailcedra is a Senegalese tree that in Dogon mythology
has protective, medicinal virtues. M. a M. Ngal argues that Césaire
uses the tree as a symbol to capture the mythical, sacred time of the
ancestors, the time of innocence, vital force, and harmony.[33] These
ancestral virtues are the essential characteristics of the black person,
who has an immediate and intuitive, nonrational grasp of the world
in all its profoundness, richness, and fecundity. He or she encounters
in a harmonious and creative way the social and natural world and
exists in spiritual contact with the essence of the universe. There is no
stronger appeal to a mythical black essence to be found in the
Cahier. "Blood! Blood! . . . Birth! Ecstasy of becoming!" is Fanon's
ironic comment on this passage (*BS*, p. 125; *PN*, p. 100).

Césaire contrasts this close concordance with the discordance of the
white world. Instead of having a sacred and creative relationship with
the world, white civilization is destructive: "hear its blue steel rigidity
pierce the mystic flesh." White civilization is fatigued and cracking,
"its deceptive victories tout its defeats" (pp. 68–69).

Critics have argued that Césaire is concerned with an honest assess-
ment of the difference and originality of the black way of experiencing the world rather than with the romantic promotion of irrational-
ism or surrealism. He has returned to the tradition of the African
poet-sorcerer (healer) who creates and produces things by means of

33. M. a M. Ngal, *Aimé Césaire: Un homme à la recherche d'une patrie* (Dakar:
Nouvelles Editions Africaines, 1975), pp. 153–54.

the power of the word (*Nommo*). Through invocation and incantation, rather than narration or description, he commands and transforms the world. Césaire, they say, acknowledges the inferiority of the African understanding of technology in comparison with the European but also recognizes the real spiritual values of his people.[34] The problem is that these critics accept the resentment and racialization of culture characteristic of such passages: on the one hand is European technical knowledge; on the other, the black intuitive grasp of the world. We are not far from the reactive posture of Sartre's antiracist racism. This is a mythical and dualistic depiction of complex cultures with complex histories and very real problems. Caught in the drama of colonialism, mythical narrative reconstructs the romantic story of black experience. The spiritual transformation that the Cailcedra tree offers the poet-healer may restore psychological equilibrium, but it is far from being a solution to the problems of Africa or the Caribbean.[35]

In its most extreme form, this mythical depiction of the specificity of the black way of experiencing the world takes on racist overtones in the works of negritude writers. This is particularly true of Senghor: although an eloquent propounder of humanism, Senghor argues that emotion is the domain of the black person and cites the racial theories of Gobineau and others in support of his argument.[36] Some of Senghor's ideas parallel those of the Haitian ethnological movement of the early twentieth century. J. C. Dorsainvil, who influenced the racial theories and black nationalist ideology of François Duvalier, talked of the "special physiognomy" of different ethnic groups and of the intuitive, sentimental, "affective logic" of African people.[37] Duvalier himself began his literary career with the Haitian group of poets, Les Griots. He helped shape a Haitian form of negritude that insisted on the influence of the biology of a racial group on its psychology and collective behavior through "the laws of ancestral

---

34. See Janheinz Jahn, *Muntu: An Outline of Neo-African Culture,* trans. Marjorie Grene (New York: Faber & Faber, 1961), pp. 135–55; Marcien Towa, *Poésie de la négritude: Approche structuraliste* (Sherbrooke, Quebec: Naaman, 1983), pp. 167–68, 250–55; Kesteloot, *Black Writers,* pp. 170–71.

35. Ngal, pp. 154–55.

36. See Senghor, pp. 136, 141, and Towa, pp. 276–77.

37. Quoted in Nicholls, pp. 152–53.

heredity." When Duvalier came to power, negritude became part of the ideology legitimating his dictatorial regime.[38]

There is some evidence, as Arnold argues, that even Césaire may have gone to the extreme of linking the black experience to biology. Contemporaneous with the early version of the *Cahier* is the introduction to a piece by Frobenius in *Tropiques*, presumably written by Césaire. The introduction states: "But there flows in our veins a blood which demands of us an original attitude toward life . . . we must respond, the poet more than any other, to the special dynamic of our complex biological reality."[39] At several points in the *Cahier*, however, Césaire explicitly denies that there can be a connection between racial biology and culture (pp. 76–77). Elsewhere, he has distinguished his version of negritude from the Haitian version: he states that while his version rests on critique, the Haitian version rests on notions of biological determinism that legitimate a black neo-colonial dictatorship.[40]

The black myth also underlies aspects of the *Cahier's* presentation of the epic struggle of black heroes against oppression. There stands out the example of Haiti, "where negritude rose for the first time and stated that it believed in its humanity." The depiction of the struggle against colonialism reveals some of the tragic limits to the romantic presentation of the black myth. The Haitian rebel commander Toussaint L'Ouverture fought with his people against the French only to be outmaneuvered by Napoleon and end his days in "a little cell in the Jura." Blood, death, "stymied" and "ignominious revolts"; this is the tragic drama of resistance and oppression in the colonial world (pp. 46–49, 58–59). In contrast to the harmony of the African golden age is the drama of conflict between master and slave, colonizer and colonized, the history of successes, but also of defeats. Here the poem begins to capture the complexity of lived reality, but the epic grandeur of the black commander, of revolt, and of revolutionary strug-

38. Nicholls, pp. 163–64, 169, 191–93, 210–11, 237; see also Michael J. Dash, *Literature and Ideology in Haiti, 1915–1961* (Totowa, N.J.: Barnes & Noble, 1981), pp. 113–15.

39. Aimé Césaire, introduction to "Que signifie pour nous l'Afrique?" by Léo Frobenius, *Tropiques,* no. 5 (April 1942); issue reprinted Paris: Jean Michel Place, 1978, p. 62 (my translation); Arnold, pp. 37–38.

40. See Lilyan Kesteloot, *Aimé Césaire, l'homme et l'oeuvre* (Paris: Présence Africaine, 1973), p. 236.

gle keeps the black myth alive. Toussaint is the tragic hero who dares defy the colonial order. Even in his defeat he is successful, for he remains a symbol of defiance. As mythical narrative, the tragic drama of anticolonial struggle marks the possibility of a new uprising and a new birth, but it also warns of new defeats, in an endless struggle.

It is not in the *Cahier* but in a later work, *The Tragedy of King Christophe* (1963), that Césaire presents the fullness and awesomeness of the tragic character of the Haitian Revolution. With the strength, pride, and determination of the African divine king, Shango, Henri Christophe raised himself from the status of cook to become a leading general under Toussaint and Dessalines, and from there to become leader of independent Haiti itself. King Christophe had a vision of a powerful and free Haitian nation, equal in strength, glory, and "civilization" to France and the rest of Europe. But Christophe, too, is trapped in the colonial system. In his very attempt to bring his vision into being, he resorts to the behavior of the colonizer: the fortress that will defy Napoleon is built by means of forced labor. "I ask too much of men? But not enough of black men. . . . From the bottom of the pit we cry out, from the bottom of the pit we cry out for air, light, the sun. And if we're going to climb out, don't you see that we need feet which support firmly [*le pied qui s'arcboute*], tense muscles, clenched teeth, and cool clear heads—ah yes, heads! And that's why I have to ask more of blacks than of other people, more work [*plus de travail*], more faith, more enthusiasm, a step, another step, and still another, and never a step backward."[41] Christophe struggles for Haitian glory in the play, and he does so out of step with the Haitian people. Peasants are not even allowed to practice their own religion. Caught between his dream and reality, Christophe distrusts the capacity of his people to transform themselves. The nation cannot keep up with the labor required to build the citadel, the soldiers rebel, and Shango's own weapon, lightning, sets ablaze the ammunition in the fortress. Baron Samedi, Lord of Death, stands witness at the end of the play to the death of Christophe's dream.

With Christophe, the tragic presentation of the black myth reaches

---

41. Aimé Césaire, *The Tragedy of King Christophe,* trans. Ralph Manheim (New York: Grove Press, 1970), pp. 41–42 (*La Tragédie du roi Christophe* [Paris: Présence Africaine, 1970], p. 59); my revisions to the translation when French original is indicated. Cf. Alejo Carpentier's treatment of the Haitian Revolution and its aftermath in *The Kingdom of This World,* trans. Harriet de Onís (London: Victor Gollancz, 1967), pp. 92–97.

a new level of social critique. Césaire's Christophe is the model not only of the neocolonial Haitian dictator but also of the new leaders in the recently independent African and Caribbean countries. Christophe is conscious of his dignity as a black man, but he remains trapped by the white myth and the need of the black bourgeoisie and elite to prove themselves in front of the white world. Deromanticized, the black myth lives on in *The Tragedy of King Christophe*. Like the Yoruba king Shango before him, Christophe destroys himself.[42] This is the nemesis of him who reenslaved his people and in a Shangolike manner dared defy Shango himself. The sacrifice of the black population to the glorious cause of black dignity (Kierkegaard's ethical) turns into its opposite and it is Christophe who is sacrificed for his people. This is mythical narrative in its tragic moment: the everlasting struggle between the particular and the universal. But Shango was reborn a divinity, and King Christophe left a living legacy for Haiti of tragic pride and struggle.[43]

The *Cahier* also deals with the struggle for survival of the ordinary person who is not a rebel leader, general, or king. Life in the Caribbean did not consist of one heroic adventure after another. The romantic image of Africa and its black essence, and even the heroic image of rebel slaves, can be contrasted with the tragic drama of endurance and survival under slavery and colonialism: "I may as well confess that we were at all times pretty mediocre dishwashers, shoeblacks without ambition, at best conscientious sorcerers and the only unquestionable record that we broke was that of endurance under the chicote [slave whip]" (pp. 60–61). Enslaved in the Americas, black people were no longer kings and princes; dehumanized by white Europeans, they had been forced into a drama of survival.[44] But the whip did not totally dehumanize its victim. Césaire emphasizes the ability of the black person to simply "stay alive" and endure the "white death" of colonialism (pp. 46–47, 54–55). To survive, the colonized adopted strategies of pragmatic resistance: playing with the typical racial and colonial stereotypes, Césaire states that the colonized "as-

42. See Condé, *Cahier*, p. 69, and Frederick I. Case, "Sango oba ko so: Les vodoun dans *La Tragédie du roi Christophe*," *Cahiers Césairiens*, no. 2 (Autumn 1975), pp. 9–24.

43. Laroche, *L'Image*, pp. 104–106. Laroche argues that this tragic process involves a learning experience and should therefore not be confused with the fatalistic terms of Greek tragedy. However, the progression toward an impossible ideal is nothing but the recurrence of Greek tragedy.

44. Cf. Arnold, pp. 156, 158–59, and Kesteloot, *Black Writers*, pp. 167–68.

sassinated God" with his or her laziness, words, gestures, and obscene songs and "exhausted the missionaries' patience" (pp. 52–53). Beyond the colonizer's image of the colonized is the human trickster who subverts the very system within which he is trapped.

The poem identifies a number of character types who are sufferers, their lives deformed by the colonial situation. Sitting on a tram is a "nigger [*nègre*]"; his "negritude discoloured as a result of untiring tawing" (pp. 62–63). His wretched situation has forced him down, has molded and deformed him, and others laugh at him. He tragically endures colonial oppression, and it is through this very endurance that he affirms his humanity. As Condé points out, just to live, just to survive, was already a victory for the Antillean.[45] Similar in many respects is the "good nigger [*bon nègre*]," who has not only felt the power of the whip but has had "stuffed into his poor brain that a fatality impossible to trap weighed on him" (pp. 78–79). Yet, he too has discovered a way to survive.

The poem sometimes presents the "nigger," the "nigger scum," the "good nigger," as though they have been forced to accept their fate as creatures of the colonizer. However, not only did slaves survive their destiny under the master's control, many also wrested what little space and power they could for themselves. The "good nigger" and the "nigger scum" are aspects of Quashee's personality; so too is that cunning that may deceive the master or frustrate him. The "good nigger" behaves *as though* he or she has accepted the colonizer's values and view of the social order in order to facilitate survival under colonialism. But lurking beneath the image of the "good nigger" is the subversive rabbit, the disrespectful spider. Likewise, the "nigger scum" may be fully in control of the trickster's dagger. Underneath the stereotyped appearance often hides the otherness and subtle defiance of pragmatic resistance. Even Harriet Beecher Stowe's Uncle Tom, the archetypal "good nigger," can be distinguished from the slave who has accepted all by his sense of integrity and otherness.[46]

The *Cahier* is unified as a poetic act to the extent that it pulls together the differing responses to colonialism and reconciles its diverging narrative strategies. Through its focus on the struggle for liberation, it is intended to be a liberating act in which a text is created

45. Condé, *Cahier*, p. 49.
46. Harriet Beecher Stowe, *Uncle Tom's Cabin, or Life among the Lowly* (Harmondsworth: Penguin, 1981), pp. 90–91.

to encounter history and engage its readers in the struggle for mutual recognition. Using the example of the Rebel in *Et les chiens se taisaient,* Arnold has shown how Césaire's tragic hero is a life-giving symbol of struggle and resistance: "the tragedy is that of the slave who will not submit to bless the order and the morality of the master." The Rebel accepts death as his destiny. "It is the collectivity," argues Arnold, "that is represented as renewed, reborn as a result of the sacrifice."[47] The tragic "blood" of the *Cahier* is the sacrificial blood of martyred slaves who have refused to submit to the colonizer's moral order. Their refusal makes possible a new life for the community. At the climax of the *Cahier,* the poet recovers the epic struggle of his people in order to initiate anew this resurgence. The poet is a foetus entering the world: "I am forcing the great waters that girdle me with blood" (pp. 56–57). As healer he takes responsibility for his country: "your form, deformed islands / your end, my defiance" (pp. 74–75). As leader, he convokes his people for action, guiding them as he would a canoe surging forward to the climactic moment when he can say: "And we are standing now, my country and I, hair in the wind, my hand puny in its enormous fist" (pp. 76–77). The poet envisions the "nigger scum" standing:

> standing in the hold
> standing in the cabins
> standing on deck
> standing in the wind
> standing under the sun
> standing in the blood
>
> > standing
> > and
> > free [pp. 80–81]

This is the apocalyptic moment, "The End of the world," whose necessity is announced earlier in the poem (pp. 54–55). The *Cahier's* culminating section, it contains the final formulation of negritude in the poem: "the old *négritude* progressively cadavers itself [*se cadavérise*]" (pp. 78–79). The "good nigger" and the "nigger scum" are standing up. The once passive, atomized crowd is replaced by the group that assumes its destiny. The black person does not take his or

47. Arnold, pp. 115–17, 124; Aimé Césaire, *Et les chiens se taisaient,* in *Les Armes miraculeuses* (Paris: Gallimard, 1970), pp. 144–52.

her situation as a given. In the tradition of resistance and struggle, a new negritude is born, and the black myth discloses itself in a new drama of the black person in the Caribbean.

The entry into this new era is at the same time a leap into universal "brotherhood." This is the moment in the poem that marks the radical but unfulfilled possibility of a leap from mythical to liberating narrative, from colonial drama to historical struggle. The poet who has prayed that he be preserved from all hatred (pp. 70–71) repudiates any notion of racial determinism: negritude can no longer be taken as "a cephalic index, or plasma, or soma"; "and no race has a monopoly on beauty, on intelligence, on strength / and there is room for everyone at the convocation of conquest" (pp. 76–77).[48] In a statement of love, with the spirit of peace, the poet embraces his readers and the people of his homeland, the colonized embrace the colonizer, and purities mingle into "multi-colored purities" (pp. 82–83). Colonialism disappears, racism vanishes, the perfect circle is restored, and the myth of negritude reaches a new, romantic climax. The poet is the magical being, the tragic hero purged and reborn, who makes possible the resolution of the initial contradiction and the conquest of good over evil. He is like Manuel in Roumain's *Masters of the Dew*, Manuel, the selfless, black, proletarian savior, who miraculously locates the spring that will transform "the wretched of the earth" into the "general assembly of the masters of the dew."[49]

This vision of final unity is informed by a utopian vision of communist society. The *Cahier* leaves this vision implicit, open to a number of utopian possibilities, but *Discourse on Colonialism* is more direct. The struggle of the colonized slides into that of the proletariat in a vision of the communist transformation that will lead to a classless, raceless society. The new society, Césaire states, will not be a return to the past but, rather, "a society rich with all the productive power of modern times, warm with all the fraternity of olden days." He takes the Soviet Union (1950) as an example of the new society.[50] As Frederick Case argues, this appropriation of the Western myth of a

---

48. See also Kesteloot, *Aimé Césaire*, p 236, where Césaire states in an interview that his conception of negritude is not biological but cultural and historical.

49. Even before Fanon used as his title the words from "L'Internationale," the French workers' song by Eugène Pottier, Roumain had employed it in one of his poems; see *Ebony Wood / Bois d'ebène*, trans. Sidney Shapiro, biling. ed., (New York: Interworld Press, 1972), pp. 31, 45; Roumain, *Masters*, p. 75.

50. Césaire, *Discourse*, pp. 61, 31; *Discours*, pp. 64, 30.

future utopia, where universal harmony will reign, amounts to cultural assimilation into European thought patterns and leaves the black person still alienated.[51] The reality of anguished, historical struggle becomes lost in the harmonious closure of a mythical narrative structure.

Arnold maintains that the final movement in the poem should be understood in terms of the Hegelian dialectic: a synthesis or sublation (*aufheben*) takes place in which a new, revolutionary consciousness is achieved.[52] Understanding the epic history of one's people, one joins other peoples in a movement to the universal. It seems, however, that Césaire has conflated the problematic of the external dialectic (synthesis; birth, death, and rebirth) with the fundamentally different problematic of reciprocal recognition (the dialectic of freedom). In both Greek tragic drama and Greek epic, a heroic movement of death and rebirth, of endurance and struggle, can be traced; recognition is represented as a utopian point outside of history. The *Cahier* has both epic and tragic aspects and it culminates at a point outside of history. The Hegelian dialectic differs from this in a decisive way: it introduces the idea of freedom as the foundation of the human, as necessity and imperative. The *Cahier* also has elements of this notion of freedom. The Hegelian dimension is subordinated, however, to an external dialectic: the movement of death and rebirth, culminating in a moment of recognition outside of history, the utopian world of universal "brotherhood."

We are back to the dualism that Sartre had discerned in negritude: "anti-racist racism" versus the struggle of the proletariat. Unlike Sartre, who "negates" the black experience, however, Césaire does not repudiate the black myth in its entirety: it remains present as the "black hole" of origins (pp. 84–85). Nor does he entirely accept the myth of communist society. Instead, a new utopian myth dominates, a new myth of the End, and the reconciliation of the black myth and the white myth is never worked through. The poem appears to solve our problem in the dove's flight into the heavens (pp. 84–85), but it is just there that our problem really begins. It is the reader who must

51. Case, "Négritude and Utopianism," pp. 72–74. In order to save Césaire's poetics, Arnold (pp. 164–68, 178) plays down the utopian element in *Cahier* but recognizes its prominence in *Discourse*. Cf. Towa, pp. 250–55; Kesteloot, *Black Writers*, pp. 170–71.

52. Arnold, pp. 164–65.

take up the struggle for recognition and reconcile the black and the white myths in an entry into a concrete history of struggle and conflict, but also of hope and possibility.

Césaire has stated that the writer "writes in the absolute," whereas the politician "works in the relative."[53] Césaire's negritude demonstrates this dualism of the absolute, understood as the state of perfection or harmony, and the relative, the condition of everyday life and reality. If politics is relative and art absolute, then it is not possible to incorporate a liberating political project into an artistic work. Césaire's *Cahier* goes beyond a race-based notion of negritude to build a vision of human community. It goes beyond the impasse of the black communists who sacrificed the specificity of black colonial experience. Yet, rooted in a mythic past at once romantic and tragic, and gazing on a utopian future, its ultimate vision remains absolute. In light of Césaire's tasks as mayor of Fort-de-France and communist deputy for central Martinique in the French National Assembly (elected 1945), his negritude takes on an ideological dimension, legitimating his leadership role in Martinican politics.

In 1956 Césaire's affiliation would change in a significant way: he withdrew from the French Communist party and founded the socialist-oriented Martinican Progressive party (Parti progressiste martiniquais). In his letter to Maurice Thorez, French Communist party leader, he expressed outrage at the party's refusal to condemn Stalinist dictatorial practices and the associated "state capitalism" that exploited a new class of workers. He criticized the party for its failure to understand the specificity of the struggle of colonized peoples and for its assimilationist and utopian policies. Césaire denied that he was renouncing Marxism or communism: what was required was a universal (socialism) that allowed for particularity; it was time for Martinique "to invent" its own way on the basis of its African heritage.[54] Implicitly, this renunciation of the French Communist party and its assimilationist policies was also a self-critique. In 1946 Césaire had cosponsored a bill transforming the Caribbean colonies into departments. Yet Césaire never completely renounced his assimilationist propensity: in his continuing capacity as mayor and deputy, he supported the French government's policy of limited autonomy for the

53. Quoted in Kesteloot, *Aimé Césaire,* p. 228.

54. Aimé Césaire, "Lettre à Maurice Thorez" (Paris: Présence Africaine, 1956), pp. 6, 12–15. See also Hale, pp. 365–70.

island, rather than outright independence. He was criticized by fellow Martinicans, including Fanon, for continuing to accommodate himself to French colonialism in his role as dependent politician.[55]

The positive dimension of negritude is that it makes possible a cultural recovery that restores to the black person some of the dignity and humanity usurped by the colonizer's stereotypes. As C. L. R. James puts it, salvation for the Caribbean lay in Africa, in bringing what Africa had to offer into the common rendezvous of humanity.[56] The return to Africa resulted in an awareness that colonial ideology had denied the black elite. However, negritude became the means through which a black elite could create a new black myth, antithetical to the white myth, for their own self-understanding and legitimation.[57] Edouard Glissant, Césaire's fellow writer from Martinique, opposes negritude to *antillanité,* calling for a movement from poetic desire to reality: in the Caribbean, the artistic work must take the national experience of the West Indies (les Antilles) as its center, rather than Africa. Césaire recognizes the importance of dealing with the Caribbean specificity but denies that there is any opposition between negritude and antillanité.[58] The *Cahier* goes beyond the mythic presentation of Africa to deal with the Caribbean. It also goes beyond the question of black identity to deal with the level of the universally human. However, bound by its own starting point, it remains caught in the white myth. Despite its innovative form, the *Cahier's* grand style and brilliant eloquence in its use of the French language helped to ensure that such was the case.

Fanon, too, recognized the role of negritude in the recovery of the

55. *AR,* p. 168; *RA,* p. 170. Another Martinican writer influenced by Césaire, Auguste Macouba, depicts Césaire as the absent mayor (he is in Paris as deputy) in *Eia! Man-Maille là!* (Paris: Pierre Jean Oswald, 1968); when he does appear to demobilize students rioting against racial discrimination, he is described by other characters as bourgeois dirt (*salaud*); his party shows no support for the students (pp. 57, 76, 78). In his interview with Kesteloot in 1971, Césaire says that it was his party that first proclaimed Martinique as a nation distinct from France. Yet he avoids taking a decisive position on the question of Martinican independence (Kesteloot, *Aimé Césaire,* pp. 229–30). For the historical background, see Arnold, pp. 14–15, 169–73; Hale, pp. 370–84.

56. C. L. R. James, *The Black Jacobins: Toussaint L'Ouverture and the San Domingo Revolution,* 2d ed. (New York: Vintage–Random House, 1963), pp. 399, 401.

57. See Frederick I. Case, "Aimé Césaire et l'occident chrétien, *L'Esprit Créateur,* 10 (1970), 256, and "Négritude and Utopianism," pp. 70, 72–74.

58. Beverley Ormerod, "Beyond *Négritude:* Some Aspects of the Work of Edouard Glissant," *Savacou,* nos. 11–12 (September 1975), p. 40; and Condé, *Cahier,* pp. 67, 75.

intellectual, but he emphasized, in contrast, the importance of culture as it was concretely expressed in the struggle for liberation. Beyond the mythical constructions of the poet are the everyday popular struggles of his or her people. This is the underside of negritude, the living culture of the colonized, in which the authentic poet-healer can situate him or herself, and out of which a liberating message can be articulated. Only through a total spiritual transformation in which the colonized recognize their situation and take responsibility for the sociopolitical totality can there be a new beginning. West Indian writers would go beyond a racialized notion of culture to a notion of a liberated creole culture. Likewise, they would go beyond a universalist notion of social harmony imported from the metropolis to a notion of struggle defined indigenously, democratically, and historically. The mythical absolutes separated from a politics of the relative would be replaced by an absolute, liberation, defined relatively within the context of Caribbean creole culture. The work of the narrative of liberation, this is the new historical point of departure.

Chapter 6

The Liberation of Narrative: George Lamming and Derek Walcott

It is necessary to take up again the pathways of history, that history of man damned by men, and call forth, render possible, the meeting of one's people and other men.

FRANTZ FANON, *Les damnés de la terre* (my translation)

This corpse, dead as he may be, cannot be allowed to go free; for unawareness is the basic characteristic of the slave. Awareness is a minimum condition for attaining freedom.

GEORGE LAMMING, *The Pleasures of Exile*

GEORGE LAMMING published *In the Castle of My Skin* in 1953, in London. The year before, Fanon's *Peau noire, masques blancs* had appeared in Paris. Both books were expressions of a growing awareness of what it meant to be colonized, and both were calls to action. The black consciousness of the Negritude and similar movements had posed questions of cultural identity and sociopolitical practice to which Lamming and Fanon were responding. Lamming, like Fanon, was at the 1956 conference of black writers in Paris. There, Césaire had insistently argued the basic tenet of negritude: the continuing existence of a single "Negro-African civilization" in Africa and throughout the black diaspora. Fanon, in contrast, analyzed the process through which this "overvaluation" of traditional culture is transformed in the creation of a liberating *national* culture. Lamming, like Fanon, pointed out the fallacy of reducing oneself and one's world to a racial definition that the colonial other has created, and he called for the writer to accept his or her human responsibility as an individual in a particular social situation.[1] Lamming, a Barbadian, drew on the lived experience and culture of the West Indian community, on religious symbolism and the oral tradition. Situated in the creole tradition, yet not bound by it, he rearticulated the history of the community in the colonial and neocolonial contexts and addressed the question of liberation. Derek Walcott began publishing poetry and plays in the late 1940s in St. Lucia. His *Dream on Monkey Mountain* (1967) dealt with the problem of black identity, presented a critique of negritude, and reconstructed the lived experience of the Caribbean community from the point of view of the problem of liberation. Lamming and Walcott were part of a wider national movement that situated itself in the history of the Caribbean and demanded political independence and social justice: the Rastafarian, the calypsonian, the poet, novelist, and dramatist, all entered a new realm of awareness and, as spokespersons of the community, articulated various aspects of the narrative of liberation.

The works of Lamming and Walcott[2] are contemporaneous with those of Fanon in a way in which vaudou mythology, the trickster tale, and negritude are not. These cultural patterns were already given symbolic structures that Fanon could analyze and criticize from the point of view of the struggle for national liberation. Fanon also identified types of liberating symbolic structures that were in the process of being created and recreated, structures that influenced him and that he would influence. Lamming's novels and Walcott's plays responded to the same types of problems as Fanon's works and raised the same types of issues that were raised by him. Though it is unlikely that their early works influenced Fanon's work directly, there is no

1. Aimé Césaire, "Culture et colonisation," especially pp. 190–93, 200–202; Frantz Fanon, "Racisme et culture," pp. 130–32 (also in *AR,* pp. 42–44; *RA,* pp. 43–45); George Lamming, "The Negro Writer and His World," pp. 320–21, 323–25; all in *Présence Africaine,* n.s., nos. 8–10 (June–November 1956).

2. My analysis will focus on the following of their many published works: George Lamming, *In the Castle of My Skin* (New York: Collier-Macmillan, 1970), cited in the text as *Castle,* and *Season of Adventure* (London: Michael Joseph, 1960), cited as *Season;* Derek Walcott, *Dream on Monkey Mountain* in *Dream on Monkey Mountain and Other Plays* (New York: Farrar, Straus & Giroux, 1970), cited as *Dream, Ti-Jean and His Brothers* in *Dream on Monkey Mountain and Other Plays,* cited as *Ti-Jean,* and *Pantomime* in *Remembrance and Pantomime: Two Plays* (New York: Farrar, Straus & Giroux, 1980), cited as *Pantomime.*

doubt that Fanon influenced their later works: he gave them some of the analytical tools that would allow them to go further in the direction in which they were already proceeding.

Fanon's texts analyze the drama of colonialism and encode a narrative of liberation in sociopolitical terms. In addition, they analyze both the cultural forms that lend meaning to this drama and those that demand its total transformation. Religious mythology and ritual, the trickster narrative, and negritude are mythical structures bound into the drama of colonialism. The leap to history, the revolutionary consciousness of colonial and neocolonial sociopolitical systems and the possibilities for their transformation, is the point of departure for a culture of liberation.

History is not a sequence of "empirical" events nor an "objective" and impersonal force nor a drama of enforced roles. Unlike the ordering of myth, true history demands that one step out of the drama of life in order to render human activity meaningful in terms of a movement to mutual recognition. History is the ordering of events in such a way that a story is told that becomes the basis for a revolutionized understanding of the social world. History presupposes a *prise de conscience*, a leap to consciousness, and a willingness to be a new person. Categories of political, social, and economic change become historically significant when brought into relation with traditional mythical patterns and transformed in terms of the imperative of liberation. Narrative as a political, social, and cultural event becomes humanly meaningful when grounded in the necessity of freedom and communicated in terms that are comprehensible to the people addressed.

According to Fanon, "consciousness must be helped" (*WE*, p. 304; *DT*, p. 224). The humanizing imperative of liberating narrative is the key to a new critical self-understanding: "It is necessary to take up again the pathways of history, that history of man damned by men, and call forth, render possible, the meeting of one's people and other men (*DT*, p. 215, my translation; see *WE*, p. 293). This is the task of all culture in the new nation, both the culture that arises out of the oral tradition of the colonized and the culture that began as the borrowed art of the colonizer.

The leap to consciousness occurs in the revolutionary moment. The call to battle is made. Fanon argues that traditional symbolic patterns are transformed and made part of the struggle. The storyteller, for example, gives a new creative range to his or her imagination. Characters and actions are remodeled as the storyteller, together with his or her public, responds to a developing situation; in an act of "invocation," a new person is "revealed" (*WE*, p. 241; *DT*, p. 170). This process is typical of other popular arts as they begin to express the reality and necessity of the formative nation. Faces in woodwork, which had become inexpressive, now come to life and sketch an action. Ceramics and pottery, dancing, singing, and religious ritual begin to express "the same upward-springing trend. . . . Everything works together to awaken the sensibility of the colonized and to make unreal and inacceptable the contemplative attitude, or the acceptance of defeat. . . . His world comes to lose its accursed character" (*WE*, pp. 243–44; *DT*, p. 172). Assimilation or immersion, accommodation or resistance, these are no longer the tragic options of the colonized.

In the sphere of written literature, argues Fanon, assimilationist, immersionist, and tragic writing are replaced by "a fighting literature, a revolutionary literature and a national literature." The writer joins the nation, becomes "an awakener of the people," and will "shake the people" (*WE*, pp. 222–23; *DT*, p. 154).[3] Literature becomes part of the struggle of a specific community against colonialism and its neocolonial perpetuation. What is decisive about this form of communication is its grounding in the imperative of liberation in a historically specific context. The colonized take total responsibility for themselves. National literature, argues Fanon, is "a literature of combat because it takes charge, because it is will temporalized [*volonté temporalisée*]" (*DT*, p. 169, my translation; see *WE*, p. 240).

Fanon's work is a narrative in this sense, and it demands that all narrative be evaluated from the point of view of a cosmogonic leap into history. The form of consciousness that ultimately manifests itself in Fanon's work is liberating national consciousness, committed to transforming relations of oppression and to initiating a process of internationalism. Fanon states that "universality resides in this decision to take charge of the reciprocal relativism of different cultures, once the colonial status is irreversibly excluded" (*RA*, p. 45, my translation; see *AR*, p. 44). Two formerly opposed cultures are now able to face and enrich each other (*RA*, p. 45, my translation; see *AR*, p. 44). Reciprocal relativism is a critical relativism that rests on the

3. Ayi Kwei Armah invokes Fanon's significance as an "awakener" in "Frantz Fanon: The Awakener," *Negro Digest*, 18 (October 1969), 4–9, 29–43.

absolute demand for human recognition. The paradoxical significance of Fanon's work is its demand that all Third World culture, in
fact, all culture, however different, manifest liberating consciousness.

National culture is the medium for the expression of national consciousness. National culture is the symbolic form that develops out of
the tradition of resistance to colonialism at the point when that resistance is transformed into the struggle for authentic national liberation. National culture gives meaning to the process of liberation. It
sustains the sociopolitical struggle and the economic change through
which the community liberates itself and establishes its human dignity. National culture is not given as a finite symbolic structure in the
way that nationalism is. It remains eternally open to the process of
human liberation, to the constraints that threaten to terminate that
process, and to the horizons of the given across which liberation must
be achieved.

Lamming and Walcott are among the writers of the former British
Caribbean colonies who have most successfully contributed to the
formation of a West Indian national culture, Lamming in his novels,
Walcott in his drama. Their works are part of a broader literary (and
cultural) movement that ushered in political independence in the
1960s. As in the case of negritude writers like Césaire, many of the
poets, dramatists, and novelists of the English-speaking Caribbean
had moved away from their peasant and working class roots. The
purpose of a colonial education was to relegate lived history to the
obscurity of the "bush." Racial prejudice might drive one to seek to
attain the white ideal, but then came the "harsh awakening"
expressed in one of Walcott's early poems: "And the day you suddenly realized that / You were black, and that meant / Quite a few
things. . . ."[4] The Caribbean writer began to subvert Prospero's language into a tool for exploring Caliban's history.

Like negritude, this indigenous literature in the British Caribbean
was a response to a number of international developments: the social
transformation brought about by the Russian and, later, Cuban revo-
lutions; economic depression and social unrest, particularly in the
period between the European wars; and the growing quest for self-
determination, beginning in places such as Ireland, India, and Egypt
in the immediate postwar period and spreading throughout the colo-

4. Quoted in Errol Hill, "The Emergence of a National Drama in the West Indies,"
Caribbean Quarterly, 18 (December 1972), 33.

nial world. In the Caribbean, nationalist-oriented labor movements arose in the 1930s and initiated a momentum that would eventually lead to independence in many West Indian colonies. This nationalist movement was accompanied by a cultural reawakening among the intellectuals and a renewed respect among the popular classes for things African or "Ethiopian." European intellectual trends were also influential: socialist realism and Marxism, the concern for the "unconscious," the "primitive," and the non-European. So, too, were black movements such as the Harlem Renaissance and Negritude.[5]

The literature of the English-speaking Caribbean in the twentieth century is oriented toward sociopolitical relevance and cultural authenticity. Its focus is the ordinary person, the colonized peasant and worker, the fisherman, charcoal burner, and slum dweller. This focus has led to an increasing emphasis on a creole form that captures the rhythm, vocabulary, and syntax of island "dialect" as well as other indigenous aesthetic forms: proverbs, oral poetry, storytelling, song, music, dance, and drama. In spite of the thrust toward the redemption of the oppressed under colonialism and neocolonialism, however, much of the writing of the English Caribbean is a mythical form of romance, tragedy, or comedy, lacking any imperative of liberation. The white myth, characteristic of the literature of the colonizer and the literature of assimilation, has largely been repudiated. It is often replaced by a version of the black myth, characterized by a romanticization of the language and culture of the race, or folk.[6] These works lend themselves to appropriation by the new black dependent bourgeoisie and may legitimate neocolonialism in the way that negritude does.

The white or black mythical structures sometimes give way to an equally mythical form of social "realism" that is tragic in Kierkegaard's sense of Greek tragedy. The oppressed are so powerless, so destined to defeat when they try to assume power, that no incisive critique can envision new horizons: the sociopolitical contradiction is fated to remain eternally. "De harder dey come . . . / is de harder dey

---

5. An excellent summary of the background to West Indian literature is provided in Rhonda Cobham's article, "The Background," in *West Indian Literature,* ed. Bruce King (London: Macmillan, 1979), pp. 9–29. For a discussion of the European situation see Raymond J. Sontag, *A Broken World: 1919–1939* (New York: Harper Torchbooks, 1972), especially pp. 4–15, 90–96.

6. See, for example, Bruce St. John's "Kites," in *Caribbean Anthology I,* ed. Bruce St. John (Bridgetown, Barbados: Cedar Press, 1981), pp. 48–50.

fall," sings Ivan (Jimmy Cliff) in *The Harder They Come*.[7] Lamming comments that Walcott's "Ruins of a Great House" makes "despair a darling of the senses, an idol of the intellect."[8] One of Walcott's later poems vividly demonstrates this despair:

> safe and conservative, 'fraid to take side,
> they say that Rodney commit suicide,
> is the same voices that, in the slave ship,
> smile at their brothers, "Boy, is just the whip,"
> . . . . .
> when Spoiler see all this, ain't he must bawl,
> "area of darkness," with V. S. Nightfall?[9]

Modern tragic narrative in the English-speaking Caribbean, typified by V. S. Naipaul, goes beyond Greek tragedy to condemn the repressive law of the sociopolitical order in the name of a higher humanity. However, humanity has become just another hopeless dream. Creative, historical possibility is absent from the narrative. There can be no new beginning. From the point of view of the colonized the message is the same as that of Greek tragedy: "Now all is lost."[10] The irony of tragic narrative is that, although sympathetic to the oppressed, it ultimately legitimates the myths of the ruling classes.

The challenge of liberating narrative is to transform the sociopolitical totality so that lived history becomes open possibility. This is the challenge of Lamming's novels. It is also the imperative of Walcott's drama. (Much of Walcott's poetry remains tragic.) The death of the white master-mistress is the point of departure, the complex symbol that marks the end of the drama of colonialism and the beginning either of neocolonialism or of a new West Indian history. There are remarkable structural parallels between Lamming's *In the Castle of My Skin* (1953) and Fanon's *The Wretched of the Earth* (1961), especially in the portrayal of the drama of colonialism. (Some of these parallels are shared with Césaire's *Cahier* [1939–1956].) Lamming and Fanon present a detailed, spatial metaphor in order to capture the

7. Michael Thelwell, *The Harder They Come* (New York: Grove Press, 1980), p. 281.

8. George Lamming, "Caribbean Literature: The Black Rock of Africa," *Africa Forum*, 1 (Spring 1966), 41.

9. Walcott, *The Fortunate Traveller* (London: Faber & Faber, 1982), pp. 56, 58.

10. Søren Kierkegaard, *Fear and Trembling*, in *Fear and Trembling and Sickness Unto Death*, trans. Walter Lowrie (Princeton: Princeton University Press, 1968), p. 45.

typical nature of the colonial situation. In contrast, Walcott leaves the spatial metaphor implicit and emphasizes instead the experiential and temporal relationships between the colonizer and the colonized.

The spatial metaphor of colonialism is presented very early in *In the Castle of My Skin* and with poetic force:

> An estate where fields of sugar cane had once crept like an open secret across the land had been converted into a village. . . . To the east where the land rose gently to a hill, there was a large brick building surrounded by a wood and a high stone wall that bore bits of bottle along the top. The landlords lived there amidst the trees within the wall. Below and around it the land spread out into a flat unbroken monotony of small houses and white marl roads. From any point of the land one could see on a clear day the large brick house hoisted on the hill. When the weather wasn't too warm, tea was served on the wide, flat roof. [*Castle*, p. 19]

In the eyes of the villagers, the landlord's house is large, strong, and fortified; they perceive it to be a "castle" (*Castle*, pp. 23, 188). In contrast, the village houses are small, wooden structures "raised jauntily on groundsels of limestone." The landlord's house can withstand the flood that occurs at the beginning of the novel because it is firmly hoisted. The village houses, in contrast, are precariously hoisted and become swamped: Mr. Foster is seen "sailing down the river," perched on his roof. Lamming mentions the poverty and "stench of raw living" that characterizes the village, but he avoids a degrading social realism (*Castle*, pp. 2–6).

The spatial metaphor encodes the primary contradiction between the colonizer and the colonized. On the hill live the persons in authority, below them those forced into subservience. The colonizer is white, the colonized black. The landlords are "the Great"; the villagers are "low-down nigger people" (*Castle*, pp. 20–22). The spatial metaphor represents both the political fact of domination on the basis of race and the social fact of caste (class) division also on the basis of race. The dominated caste is also an exploited caste. The colonized pay rent and perform cheap labor (in the landlord's house, on his grounds, or in his enterprises in the city). In between the colonizer and the colonized is an intermediary class. It is represented in the novel by characters such as the overseer, the teacher, and the policeman. This is the group that will become the dependent national bourgeoisie identified by Fanon.

The racial ideology that sustains and legitimates the colonial system in the novel is buttressed by the religious and educational systems. The landlord advises his tenants to pray, thereby implying that their lot has been chosen by God (*Castle*, p. 28). The school teaches the children of the tenants to be good subjects in "the great design," the British Empire (*Castle*, p. 330). The colonized can overcome their "nigger" status to the extent that they are able to imitate the white people and build Little England in Barbados. Mrs. Foster, who has lost her house to the flood, swallows this myth: she gratefully accepts the sixty cents and cup of tea that the landlord gives her (*Castle*, p. 28).

The colonial conflict may be displaced onto relationships between the colonized themselves because the black overseer and members of his class do the landlord's dirty work. Mrs. Foster is grateful to the landlord but calls the overseer a "bad-minded black son-of-a-bitch" (*Castle*, p. 29). The relationship between the overseer and the villager is one of mutual enmity and distrust, each representing for the other "an image of the enemy" (*Castle*, p. 20). The workers on strike realize the true nature of the colonial drama as they wait in ambush, knives ready, for the landlord. This is the Manichaean colonial world that Fanon would later describe in terms of enmity, violence, and recipro- cal exclusivity in *The Wretched of the Earth*. Whether in the form of little boys taunting a white man with fowl droppings on his suit (*Castle*, pp. 13–14) or in the form of direct confrontation between the colonizer (or his agent) and the colonized, the "seeds of revolt" are present in the colonial situation from the beginning. Lamming's Caliban is a rebel.[11]

Castle traces the origin and development of the tragic misadven- ture of neocolonialism typical of the Caribbean. The period in which *Castle* is set, the 1930s and 1940s, was a period of transformation for the colonial plantation system. A labor movement emerged, and

11. Ambroise Kom, "*In the Castle of My Skin*: George Lamming and the Colonial Caribbean," *World Literature Written in English*, 18 (November 1979), 411. For Lam- ming's reflections on Caliban, see George Lamming, *The Pleasures of Exile* (London: Michael Joseph, 1960), p. 98. Kom, along with critics such as Ngugi and Paquet, conflates a specifically colonial relation, based on race, with the European feudal or semifeudal relation. See Kom, pp. 408–409; Ngugi Wa Thiong'O (James Ngugi), *Homecoming: Essays on African and Caribbean Literature, Culture, and Politics* (New York: Lawrence Hill, 1973), pp. 114–15; Sandra Pouchet Paquet, *The Novels of George Lamming* (London: Heinemann, 1982), pp. 13–17.

there were strikes and riots. A new dependent bourgeoisie began to assume positions of influence in this movement as well as in the civil service and professions. Political parties, linked to the labor movement, were established and began to work toward the independence that would eventually arrive in the 1960s.

In the novel, the rise of Slime symbolizes the rise of the dependent bourgeoisie. Formerly a village teacher, Slime organizes the Penny Bank (a mutual-aid society), becomes a labor leader, and wins a seat in a general election. The workers go on strike against the landlord, who owns the shipping company, and the strike turns to violence. As a result of the riots, the landlord's traditional hold on his villagers and workers is broken. A new bourgeoisie, characterized by Slime, has gained a socioeconomic and political foothold. The Penny Bank buys the village land, but not on behalf of the people. Such is the tragic irony of the dependent bourgeoisie. Critics have pointed out the link to Fanon's neocolonial bourgeoisie.[12]

The novel ends with a new spatial metaphor that is essentially a repetition with differences of the original colonial model. The landlord's house remains on the hill, the trees cut down, as both a relic of the colonial period and a reminder of its lingering influence. The white landlord still dwells there, but there is an expectation that someday his old overseer will take up residence in the house. Some of the black and colored middle class have moved into formerly white colonial enclaves. Others have purchased the choice plots in the village and will erect on them solid houses that will appear sumptuous beside the village huts. Two final images symbolize the new spatial order in which the villagers have lost their only security, their house and their rented plot: the image of the shoemaker's house lifted from its groundsel—"suddenly there was a crash from within. . . . The shoemaker's shop became a bundle of wood heaped on stones"—and the image of the old man, Pa, homeless, forced to take up residence in an almshouse for the destitute (*Castle*, pp. 337, 340).

Neocolonial society is the focus of Lamming's later work *Season of Adventure* (1960). In this novel, the spatial metaphor consists of the huts of the Forest Reserve on the one hand and the mansions of the dependent bourgeoisie on the other. The descriptive, mimetic style of *Castle* is much less in evidence given the rich symbolic texture of

---

12. Ian H. Munro, "The Theme of Exile in George Lamming's *In the Castle of My Skin*," *World Literature Written in English*, 20 (November 1971), 54; Kom, pp. 413–15.

Season. (The book uses aspects of several islands rather than focusing on one in particular.)[13] However, the spatial depiction of neocolonialism is there in all its vividness: on the one hand, the village of the Drum Boys in the valley—"a squalid village of communal huts encrusted in this forest"—on the other hand, Lady Carol Baden-Semper's huge plantation in the Maraval hills, "the finest example of colonial architecture in San Cristobal" (*Season*, pp. 52, 69).

The national bourgeoisie in the novel consists mainly of an elite, often of mixed blood. Their professions, economic intersts, and illicit dealings have brought them wealth. Their involvement in politics and law enforcement gives them control over the society. They have adopted the values of the colonizer: the lighter the skin, the better; the quest for European culture, and the conspicuous consumption they associate with it, is their supreme goal. Through their Eurocentricity they can justify their status and power. There is some attempt to legitimate themselves in the eyes of the ordinary black citizen through the encouragement of such local black culture as the steel band (at Vice-President Raymond's party). But in general, this is a minor theme. Like Fanon, who was writing at the same time, Lamming emphasizes the corruption of this intermediary class: "they were *there*, simply *there*, a self-propelled circus of talking animals deprived of their original voices: a frozen weight that could not stir without the touch of money" (*Season*, p. 246). Dependent on the colonial economic legacy, on men such as Sir Patrick Bloomfield, hereditary governor of the local sugar syndicate, they cannot compete with new American investors like Jim Aswell, king of Coca-Cola. In his essay "The West Indian People," Lamming uses some lines from one of Walcott's poems to depict some members of this class: "I watch the best minds root like dogs / For scraps of favour."[14]

The Manichaean hatred, which separated the villagers from the overseer in *Castle*, divides the people of Forest Reserve from this elite; the colonial drama continues in the neocolonial period: "I live for the day I see those bastards burn," says the musician Crim at the vice-president's party (*Season*, p. 144). When Raymond is assassinated by another musician, Powell, the police descend on the helpless village,

13. See the discussion of this difference between *Castle* and *Season* in Gloria Yarde, "George Lamming: The Historical Imagination," *Literary Half-Yearly*, 11 (July 1970), 41–43.

14. George Lamming, "The West Indian People," *New World Quarterly*, no. 2 (Crop Time 1966), p. 68.

armed with bayonets, under the command of the commissioner of police, Piggot, a man "committed to revenge, sure of the torture his enemy would have to endure" (*Season*, p. 264).

Lamming has written that the title of *In the Castle of My Skin* is taken from a poem by Walcott in which the poet states in rage: "You in the castle of your skin, I among the swineherd." The landlord's house is his castle. In Lamming's novel as in Walcott's poem, the castle symbolizes domination on the basis of skin color. The task of Lamming's novel, therefore, is to restore the castle to its rightful place. This does not mean moving from the village to the castle, as it does for the dependent bourgeoisie. It means recognition by the villager of his own heritage and dignity. Pa loses his house and is forced to move to the almshouse. However, he does not lose his sense of himself and his people. "And the meaning of Papa's departure," Lamming states in *The Pleasures of Exile*, "is the story of *In the Castle of My Skin.* . . . Papa could never possibly see himself among swine. Nor could the village. So I thought it was correct, and even necessary to appropriate that image in order to restore the castle where it belonged."[15] There is a movement in *Castle* from outer to inner experience, from space to time, to the history of the struggle of the colonizer against the colonized, the struggle to preserve "the you that's hidden somewhere in the castle of your skin" (*Castle*, pp. 291–92). This movement is central to all Lamming's work; Fola's quest in *Season* is a remarkable attempt to recover the hidden you in the fullness of its historical ambiguity.

The history of the struggle for dignity, and the assumption of this history by the colonized, is also the key to Walcott's drama. Both Lamming and Walcott are concerned with the transformation of the colonizer-colonized dualism in a struggle for recognition, a liberating encounter with history. At the heart of the spatial metaphor is the colonizer-colonized relation. The Prospero-Caliban relation is a persistent theme in Lamming's collection of essays, *The Pleasures of Exile*.[16] It is the essential relation that binds together the Manichaean opposites.

The Prospero–Caliban relationship is built on violence. The other is the enemy, who must be dominated (the colonizer's position) or eliminated (the position of the colonized). Violence may be latent and

15. Lamming, *Pleasures of Exile*, p. 228.
16. Lamming, *Pleasure of Exile*, especially pp. 95–117.

covered up; it may be turned in on oneself or one's community; it may be sublimated into various forms of covert resistance; it may erupt into vengeful violence and rebellion. In *Dream on Monkey Mountain*, Makak, the charcoal burner, slays the corporal, his jailer; Makak's friend, Moustique, is beaten to death by a crowd of his own people when he is revealed as a false messiah. In *Season of Adventure* Crim, a musician, quietly slips glass into the vice-president's pocket, a prelude to the vice-president's assassination by another musician, Powell.

The dockworkers' strike, the rioting, and the ambush of the landlord are significant events in *Castle*, related to the rise of the new bourgeoisie. Through his organizing activities, both in the village and among workers, Slime is able to build his political base. He is able to manipulate the spontaneous violence erupting among the people by directing it against the enemy (the shipping company) or by thwarting its direction (when the landlord is about to be attacked). The landlord's ambush is a momentous event in the novel:

> The landlord stood. He had reached the corner where the roads made four. He stood quiet as though he had seen his death or his escape. The men were puzzled. They couldn't understand why he had stopped. They came out into the streets, and now he saw them. The enemy was there, and they advanced quietly, confidently. . . . They argued as they advanced quiet and cautious like boys baiting crabs. The landlord walked away and as the men stepped nearer, Mr. Slime turned the corner. He waited at the corner where the roads made four and then walked towards the men. He had seen the landlord and the landlord had seen him. The men weren't sure now what they could do. [*Castle*, p. 229]

The men do not attack the landlord. With the appearance of Slime a new factor is introduced. The men waiver. Slime himself is unsure of his own position and power. When the men fail to carry out their action, he is relieved and thanks them. Now his power is assured in relation to both the landlord and the men: the landlord must reckon with him as leader of the people; the people must reckon with him as new master. The men give up their own mastery of the situation. Their final action contrasts sharply with that of Fanon's colonized, who eliminate the colonizer. The men in *Castle* are on the threshold of that leap or risk of life that according to Fanon (following Hegel) would be the condition for their assumption of their humanity. By not taking that risk, and by giving in to Slime, the men reassume their traditional colonial position in a neocolonial world. Commenting on the novel in his introduction to the 1983 edition, Lamming states that the status of independence had preserved the colonial legacy, the withdrawal of Britain making way for the "new colonial orchestration" of the Americans.[17]

Writing about another of his novels, *Water with Berries*, Lamming states that Teeton breaks away from the colonizer's hold by killing the white landlady. Likewise, he states, the rape of the former controller's daughter by the islanders in the novel is a way of exorcising the colonizer's control. Lamming continues: "I believe that it is against all experience that a history which held men together in that [colonial] way can come to an end in a cordial manner. . . . That horror and that brutality have a price, which has to be paid by the man who inflicted it—just as the man who suffered it has to find a way of exorcising that demon. It seems to me that there is almost a therapeutic need for a certain kind of violence in the breaking. There cannot be a parting of the ways. There has to be a smashing."[18] This is the language of catharsis. In using it, Lamming runs the risk of trapping himself in a justification of vengeful violence, or, to put it in Nietzsche's terms, resentment. Does Lamming mean that the act of violence when directed against the colonizer or his or her image, the dependent black bourgeoisie, is in itself liberating?

In *Season* Powell represents the negative side of the counterviolence of the colonized. Powell assassinates the vice-president and desperately tries to kill Fola, stepdaughter of the commissioner of police. Whereas the rioters in *Castle* fail to kill the landlord, Powell succeeds in committing the ultimate act of violence. If we place this act in relation to Powell's personal ideology, we might be tempted to conclude that Powell is a hero working for the liberation of his people. In a brilliant statement, approvingly quoted by C. L. R. James, Powell announces that human beings are existentially free and, therefore, must act to preserve that freedom when it is constrained in so-

17. George Lamming, introduction to *In the Castle of My Skin* (New York: Schocken, 1983), p. xiv.

18. George E. Kent, "A Conversation with George Lamming," *Black World*, 22 (March 1973), 91. See also the more guarded comments in Ian Munro and Reinhard Sander, eds., *Kas-Kas: Interviews with Three Caribbean Writers in Texas: George Lamming, C. L. R. James, Wilson Harris* (Austin: African and Afro-American Research Institute, University of Texas, 1972), pp. 14–15.

ciopolitical experience: "Free is how you is from the start, an' when it look different you got to move, just move, an' when you movin' say that is a natural freedom make you move." Powell argues that independence has been given rather than taken through active struggle, and, therefore, dependency is perpetuated (*Season*, pp. 17–18).[19]

Powell, however, is trapped in the colonial drama. The idea that he can liberate himself and his society through eliminating one term in the opposition is a bitter romance based on resentment. The novel makes this perfectly clear. He has an insane drive to kill not only Raymond but also Fola, not realizing the liberating implications of Fola's quest for her own heritage. He blindly follows the Manichaean laws of colonialism: "it too late for me to learn what rules you have for murderin' me. So is me go murder first" (*Season*, p. 328). Powell's resentment is an attempt to resolve his own deep internal conflict: he wants to go to school, to be educated like the members of the professional class. His sociopolitical situation is the limit to this possibility (*Season*, pp. 343–49), and he reacts with violent resentment to this impossibility. Powell's insanity is a neocolonial version of the "rage for whiteness that does drive niggers mad" (the corporal's diagnosis of Makak's condition in *Dream*, p. 228). Representing the moral and spiritual decay of poverty and oppression,[20] his mental disorder can also be compared to that of Lovelace's Bolo in *The Wine of Astonishment*, and to those of some of the patients Fanon analyzes in his discussions of colonial war and mental disorder. Reactive and self-destructive, Powell's violence is not in itself liberating.

What the comparison of *Castle* and *Season* reveals is that it is not anticolonial violence per se that is liberating but, rather, the assumption of one's own destiny with all the risks that that entails. This process involves a leap of consciousness and must therefore be clearly distinguished from the process of catharsis. In *Season* it is not to Powell that we look for a liberating encounter with history but to characters such as Chiki, Baako, Gort, and, most decisively, Fola.

The author's note, which Lamming dramatically inserts into the text toward the end of *Season*, highlights the symbolic and cultural transformation by means of which the act of violence becomes the

19. See C. L. R. James, "From Toussaint L'Ouverture to Fidel Castro," in *The Black Jacobins: Toussaint L'Ouverture and the San Domingo Revolution*, 2d ed. (New York: Vintage–Random House, 1963), p. 413.

20. Paquet, p. 67.

source of a liberating, historical consciousness. The artist faces in a heightened way the challenge and responsibility that ultimately grips the colonized in general. The author of the author's note (who should be seen as a construct rather than as our author, George Lamming) states that he is Powell's "brother." He is the assassin's brother. The author received a public scholarship and was able to move into the professional class. Powell was unable to win admission to this class and developed a deep resentment toward it. In the changing colonial order it was possible for a select few to move up in the social hierarchy; most could not. The implication, though deliberately left ambiguous, is that it was the author's duty to understand and act toward the transformation of this oppressive neocolonial situation. He states: "I shall go beyond my grave in the knowledge that I am responsible for what happened to my brother" (*Season*, p. 332).

The idea that the author has a particular responsibility to his or her brother is the key to other relationships in the text. Chiki is also Powell's brother and, therefore, has a special responsibility to him. Moreover, Chiki, like the author, is an artist. It is the artist's duty to accept responsibility, not merely for his or her biological brother, but for his or her fellow human beings in a particular historical situation, for all his or her sisters and brothers. This is the point of Baako's criticism of Chiki in the novel. Chiki is the educated artist who has returned to his community. He shares much of Powell's resentment of the dependent bourgeoisie. Baako is an old school friend of Chiki's, a medical doctor and leading science academic at the university, who belongs to the ranks of the local bourgeoisie. Baako is critical of Chiki for not taking an active role in the process of liberation. "Leaves blossom and die and blossom again, but the tree remains, because it cannot choose to be other than that tree. But if politics is the art of the possible, then your work should be an attempt to show the individual situation illuminated by all the possibilities which keep pushing it always towards a destiny, a destiny which remains open" (*Season*, p. 324). From Baako's point of view, Chiki is satisfied merely to survive in a rotten situation. He is content to adhere to a form of pragmatic resistance to the oppressor. In contrast, Baako demands that art realize its liberating potential at the widest social and political levels. For Baako, national consciousness oriented to actual rather than to formal independence is the truthful expression of culture. He fears that the crowd is about to break out into reactive

violence. (Powell's action is an example.) This hatred must be channeled creatively and transformed.[21]

Baako knows the meaning of Powell's act, he knows that it is an
attempt to assume the burden of one's history, but he also knows that
that attempt can turn into spontaneous, resentful violence. Catharsis
does not provide liberating meaning. To avoid Powell's tragedy,
Baako calls for a "leap" to responsibility, a leap that parallels the
author's realization of his responsibility for Powell (*Season*, pp. 324–
26). The novel actually comes to an apocalyptic climax with Baako
and the Drum Boys making this leap. Gort has dared to rally all the
musicians with their banned instruments in a grand parade through
the streets of San Cristobal. The tanks and guns of the bourgeoisie are
there, but they do not fire. Baako finds himself elected to power on
the strength of the drums. He announces his respect for democracy
and the language of the people; he states that the new nation is in a
state of emergency: the problem of a derivative bourgeoisie and of an
illiterate population must be overcome; the real problems of development must be addressed (*Season*, pp. 362–63). Baako articulates the
challenge of the author's demand that one take responsibility for one's
"brother," now understood as any fellow member in one's community.

Paquet argues that Baako has authorial approval.[22] Lamming,
however, is far too subtle to create a simple, flawless character.
Baako's role in the novel is to present the problematic of national
liberation and to illustrate all the risks and ambiguities that it entails.
However, Baako is an entrenched member of the derivative bourgeois class that he so strongly criticizes. There is the risk that Baako
the leader will turn out to be a sinister and authoritarian technocrat.
Lamming builds this possibility into Baako's personality and politics.
Baako speaks from an arrogant position above the "mob" (*Season*, p.
361). He respects democracy and debate, he states, but the emergency
is such that he will crush the opposition if it opposes for the sake of
opposing to the detriment of the nation. After Baako has been elected, the drums become "nervous and insecure" (*Season*, p. 365). It is

21. Paquet states that the name Sir Kofi James-Williams Baako is a composite of
Kofi Baako, a nationalist member of Nkrumah's cabinet; C. L. R. James, Trinidadian
historian and social theorist; and Eric Williams, Trinidadian historian and politician
(p. 80).

22. Paquet, pp. 80–81.

Chiki, ironically, who is able to reestablish contact with the community and guide Fola in her own self-discovery, though he ultimately fails to fulfill Baako's imperative. Baako's weakness lies in his separation from his cultural heritage and mooring.

The author of the author's note says that he has failed in the task of accepting responsibility for his brother Powell. If the author of the author's note has failed, however, George Lamming as author of *Season of Adventure* has succeeded in writing a novel that is for him an act of responsibility toward his brothers and sisters, his fellow persons. As Paquet correctly emphasizes, Lamming's novels "are intended as political acts," as "subversive, liberating and restorative."[23] The future is open; the imperative is to recover the past in a movement toward a freely chosen future in which the liberation of the oppressed is the primary concern. This is a story that has no end, a process in which persons constantly recreate their history. The author fulfills the imperative with which Baako confronts the artist Chiki, taking Chiki's work beyond its own failure.

The imperative of a leap to responsibility is similar to Kierkegaard's demand that the knight of faith accept responsibility for self in a recognition of the other. Lamming's understanding of the leap is influenced by Fanon, Sartre, Marx, and Hegel, among others, but it remains fundamentally Kierkegaardian. In the article "The West Indian People" Lamming mentions the tragedy of the West Indian middle class and their need for redemption. Separated from their own flesh, they are the other side of Powell's tragedy: "They have been pleased to trespass within the orbit of power; but to seize that power itself is a matter of *fear and trembling*" (my emphasis). Following Wilson Harris, Lamming makes his wager: *either* one says, "The pasture green, but they got me tied on a short rope" (the tragic), *or* one says, "Now is the time to make a new born stand . . . even if we fall on our knees and creep to anchor ourselves before we get up" (the liberating). These are Kierkegaard's terms and this is the dilemma with which Kierkegaard confronts us. We are challenged to accept the latter position, a position that Lamming, following Kierkegaard, calls "a stern and melancholy declaration of faith."[24]

This line of thought is pursued in another of Lamming's articles, "The Negro Writer and His World." Lamming states that the writer

23. Paquet, p. 4.
24. Lamming, "The West Indian People," pp. 68, 73–74.

has a triple responsibility in his writing: to his own inner self (Lamming specifically mentions Kierkegaard here); to his social world, which is essentially based on racial domination; to the world of human beings at its widest level. The author must challenge the reader to recognize and communicate his or her own freedom, in relation to the social and political totality, as the freedom of others.[25] This is the position of the author in the author's note. When Janet Butler comments that Lamming talks about freedom "not as a political goal but as an existential condition," she imposes her own dualistic mode of thought on Lamming's work.[26] She fails to recognize the imperative of liberating narrative that Lamming makes central to his work: the recognition of one's own freedom necessarily implies the recognition of the freedom of the other and the responsibility to actualize that freedom in history.

Lamming's link to Kierkegaard goes beyond the level of content to include the level of form as well. He uses the unorthodox technique of an author's note inserted into the text in order to emphasize Baako's call for a revolutionary leap. In a typically Kierkegaardian style of authorial distancing, Lamming separates himself as a person from the author of the novel, who is a fictive construct based on our reading of the novel. Another act of authorial distancing takes place in one of Lamming's lectures in which he comments on this author's note as though the author were someone other than himself. He states: "the author invents a shock tactic of intervention, entering in . . . to say that Powell of the book was in fact his half-brother by a different mother."[27] Lamming is using tactics of guerrilla writing to make his point about the recognition of responsibility. Who is this author? Is it the fictive author of *Season* or is it Lamming? It is both, but ultimately it is also ourselves, the readers, who, by accepting responsibility for ourselves in a liberating relationship to others—all must accept responsibility—authorize the text and become the authors (authorities) of the social and political drama of life.

This act of authorial distancing extends to the basic form of all of Lamming's novels. The novels are acts of indirect communication in Kierkegaard's sense. They communicate the necessity of freedom in

---

25. George Lamming, "The Negro Writer and His World," *Présence Africaine,* n.s., nos. 8–10 (June–November 1956), 323–25.

26. Janet Butler, "The Existentialism of George Lamming: The Early Development of a Writer," *Caribbean Review,* 11 (Fall 1982), 15.

27. Lamming, "The West Indian People," p. 73.

an open-ended way. They bring us into history, the history of real human beings in real situations, with no romantic resolutions at their disposal. Thus *Season* ends *not* with the apocalyptic moment, the "heaven of music after judgement day" (*Season*, p. 357), but with the "nervous" awakening of the Second Republic, led by the popular leader Baako. The authorial imperative is stated in the last words of the novel, "the drums must guard the day" (*Season*, p. 367). The culture and art of the people must express the freedom of the people and ensure the preservation and enrichment of that freedom. This is an awesome imperative, one that Chiki, in despair, cannot realize, one with which Baako, in his determination, may come into conflict. The challenge is to reconcile Baako's political will with the cultural expression of Chiki and Gort in the creation of a national identity through which we assume complete responsibility for the "full economic possession of the House [Castle] in which we live."[28] The reader is confronted with a story that cannot be told, with the "lack" out of which history must be created. Lamming calls this type of ending "the open end" and states that it is typical of his novels.[29] Every ending is a new beginning, and it is essentially in the reader's hands that the new beginning lies.

Selwyn Cudjoe has faulted Lamming for recognizing but not sufficiently exploring "the therapeutic need for revolutionary violence" and for overemphasizing dialogue and reciprocity rather than conflict.[30] Cudjoe makes this claim, however, without examining in any systematic way Lamming's treatment of violence in specific cases such as that of the landlord in *Castle* or Powell in *Season*. Furthermore, Cudjoe does not analyze the latent violence and lack of reciprocity between overseer and villagers or between vice-president and Drum Boys. Lamming recognizes the reality of the drama of colonialism, but like Fanon he demands that its Manichaean terms be transformed in a liberating encounter with history. Lacking the courage and conviction to overthrow the landlord, the rioters succumb to neocolonialism. Powell fights the new authority out of resentment, also succumbing. Cudjoe fails to see that the issue is not violence as catharsis but the meaning of violence: meaning as the will to act, to

28. Lamming, "The West Indian People," p. 72. See also Lamming's comments on the responsibility of the politician and the artist in Munro and Sander, p. 12.

29. Kent, p. 88.

30. Selwyn, R. Cudjoe, *Resistance and Caribbean Literature* (Athens: Ohio University Press, 1980), pp. 183–84, 202, 216.

organize the struggle for recognition in a particular historical situation.

Walcott's works of drama are structured in a way similar to Lamming's novels. Characters are developed in relation to a fragmented Manichaean colonial or neocolonial world, and they face the challenge of understanding and transforming this situation. As in Lamming's novels, the relationship between colonizer and colonized is one of violence. Whereas Lamming focuses on actual violence and the process of understanding it, however, Walcott shifts the emphasis to the role of the symbolic itself, to a symbolic killing that makes possible regeneration.

In the play *Ti-Jean and His Brothers* (1958), Walcott uses the folktale form to explore the colonial tension. The spatial metaphor is evident but undeveloped: the poor inhabitants of a little "wood and thatch" house on a mountain are in conflict with the devil, who resides in "a hell of a big white house" overlooking the cane fields (*Ti-Jean*, pp. 88, 109). The planter is a devil. From the point of view of Ti-Jean and his family, the planter (the colonizer) is the evil enemy who eats from plates "painted golden" while the family (the colonized) starves (*Ti-Jean*, p. 91). The planter makes Ti-Jean work. Ti-Jean resists. Then he sets the planter's house and fields afire.

Walcott's other plays assume the spatial metaphor without depicting it. The playwright's major concern is the lived relationship between the colonizer and the colonized, that is, the process of action and reaction over time, the colonial drama. Makak (Monkey), the hero of *Dream on Monkey Mountain* (1967), lives in a shack on the mountain, away from the colonizer. He is an ugly charcoal burner, a member of the exploited peasantry. Like Ti-Jean, he finds himself in opposition to the colonizer and his agents. Makak is jailed for drunkenness and disorderly behavior: he had declared himself to be an African king, insulted a market inspector, and destroyed a shop.

The problems of violence and consciousness, and their symbolic treatment, are central to *Dream*. Makak dreams that he escapes his prison cell by stabbing his jailer, Corporal Lestrade. The corporal is a mulatto and symbolizes the colonized person who has internalized the values of the colonizer and become an instrument of colonization. Just as Powell shoots Raymond in violent anger in *Season*, Makak stabs Lestrade in a rage and exclaims: "God dead, and his law there bleeding. Christian, cannibal, I will drink blood" (*Dream*, p. 286). Makak's action is essentially based on vengeance. He is a cannibal, whether Christian or pagan, caught in the reactive syndrome of resentment. However, there is an ambiguity in his statement. Makak is the Christian who has killed God and drinks his blood for redemption. He faces the challenge of transforming this violent act into liberating consciousness. This is the challenge that Nietzsche's madman poses. It is the challenge that must be confronted by Fanon's guerrilla group, which has sealed its pact in blood.

In his dream, Makak pursues his vision of African redemption and succeeds in establishing himself as king in his African homeland. However, he is still under the influence of the colonizer. It was a white goddess who had appeared to him in a vision, told him that he was a king, and set him on his path to Africa; it was in reaction to the white world that he had sought to discover the dignity of his blackness. This white goddess, this whole white world, must be destroyed. In the dream, the dead corporal, dead to his whiteness, is miraculously reborn in the fullness of his blackness. He tells Makak what to do to the image of his longing: "Nun, virgin, Venus, you must violate, humiliate, destroy her; otherwise, humility will infect you" (*Dream*, pp. 318–19). The corporal insists that the beautiful white apparition is "the wife of the devil, the white witch . . . the confounder of blackness" (*Dream*, p. 319). She is the Manichaean other that must be eliminated.

For Corporal Lestrade the act of violence is essentially a vengeful reaction based on resentment; it is a form of antiracist racism whose object is to assert blackness in opposition to whiteness. When Makak kills the white goddess, however, the myths of blackness and whiteness are both destroyed, for the colonizer's myth (black is evil) is the source of the myth of the colonized (black is good). (Walcott is playing on the negritude theme, particularly Sartre's version of it.) Makak awakens from this illusory, mythical dreamworld. He remembers his name, Felix Hobain. He is no longer an animal, a shadow of colonial oppression. He rejects the white mask symbolizing the colonizer's dehumanization of the colonized. He is freed from his prison and returns to his home, "to the green beginning of this world," his feet firmly rooted on the "ground" (*Dream*, p. 326). He has made the leap to a liberating consciousness.

What is most significant here is that Makak comes to a consciousness of himself through a symbolic act, the dream, rather than through a real act of murder. In a profound grasp of this subtlety, Theodore Colson states that the white head must and must not be chopped off: "If it is not done in ritual, in dream, in art, in religion, spiritually, it *will* be done in actuality, or if it is not done it will hold us, as it has and does, in the most awful slavery."[31] For Walcott, the entry into history is essentially based on a particular type of symbolic communication that enables one to realize one's freedom. Walcott's play is thus a type of indirect communication in Kierkegaard's sense. When Makak states that he lives "in the dream of his people" (*Dream*, p. 326), Walcott reminds his audience that the dream of liberation is their dream, too, and the resolution to the dream can likewise be theirs.

Those critics who have interpreted the new beginning in tragic terms (the "prison" of life) or in romantic terms (the "never-never land") miss the significance of Makak's leap to history.[32] "And believe in me," says Makak. "Faith, faith! / Believe in yourselves" (*Dream*, p. 249). Makak's return to the beginning is a return to his actual and original situation in life. Now Makak is Adamic (to use Walcott's own term)[33] in the sense that he has been transformed by a new self-awareness and has the power to name a new world. He now knows his history and is free to choose his future possibilities. The "green beginning" with which *Dream* ends is the "open end" that Lamming calls for in the literary work of art. The audience or readers face the task of understanding themselves in relation to an open-ended narrative, of understanding the narrative in terms of themselves, and of beginning a new history.

Walcott's *Pantomime* (1978) also takes the colonizer-colonized relation as its central focus. Where Lamming uses the Prospero-Caliban archetype, Walcott develops his theme using the Crusoe-Friday paradigm. We are presented with the story of Harry Trewe, a white expatriate guesthouse owner, and Jackson Phillip, his black ex-calyp-

31. Theodore Colson, "Derek Walcott's Plays: Outrage and Compassion," *World Literature Written in English*, 12 (April 1973), 90.

32. Samuel Omo Asein, "Derek Walcott: The Man and His Ideas," *The Literary Half-Yearly* (Mysore), 17 (July 1976), 75. Carolyn Joy Cooper, "A Different Rage: An Analysis of the Works of Derek Walcott, 1948–76" (Ph.D. diss., University of Toronto, 1977), p. 198. Diana Lyn's sense of Eden as a place of mature creative activity is more accurate; see "The Concept of the Mulatto in Some Works of Derek Walcott," *Caribbean Quarterly*, 26 (March–June 1980), 62–63.

33. Derek Walcott, "The Muse of History: An Essay," in *Is Massa Day Dead? Black Moods in the Caribbean*, ed. Orde Coombs (New York: Anchor-Doubleday, 1974), pp. 3–6; see also Robert Hamner's discussion in "Mythological Aspects of Walcott's Drama," *Ariel*, 8 (July 1977), 56.

sonian factotum, in neocolonial Tobago, Crusoe's island. The plot revolves around the rehearsal of a pantomime of the Crusoe-Friday myth with which Harry plans to entertain his European and North American guests. Jackson is to be Friday. From the beginning a parallel is established between the myth and the Caribbean colonial context that it sustains and legitimates. Jackson recalls the history of this relationship: "For three hundred years I served you. Three hundred years I served you breakfast in . . . in my white jacket on a white veranda, boss, bwana, effendi, bacra, sahib . . . in that sun that never set on your empire I was your shadow, I did what you did, boss, bwana, effendi, bacra, sahib . . . that was my pantomime. Every movement you made, your shadow copied . . . and you smiled at me as a child does smile at his shadow's helpless obedience, boss, bwana, effendi, bacra, sahib, Mr. Crusoe" (*Pantomime*, p. 112).

The shadow may be in a relationship of dependence to the master and may look up to the master's culture as the ideal. However, the shadow's pantomime is not necessarily what it appears to be. Jackson has no illusions about Crusoe, his language, or his culture. He has appropriated and creolized it. He is the calypsonian satirist, the trickster, who has built and continues to build a creole culture as a form of resistance to Crusoe. Whereas Makak must cast out the internalized master, Jackson has already accomplished this task. He kills the parrot, which is in the habit of screeching "Heinegger," in full consciousness of the colonial situation that has been justified and determined by the idea of the "nigger." Jackson reaffirms that he is not a shadow; he is not Crusoe's Friday. Makak becomes conscious of his mythical illusions only after he has beheaded the white apparition. In contrast, Jackson's elimination of the parrot arises out of an already given historical consciousness. The killing of the parrot is a symbolic statement that the continuing objective domination of the colonized is unacceptable. Jackson's resistance is not based on resentment. He has entered into a struggle for recognition. That he himself recognizes the master is indicated by the way in which he helps the master to understand the sentiments of lost mastery that have begun to lead Harry to paralysis.

This should not beguile us into thinking that the process of colonialism and neocolonialism is a closed narrative with a happy ending. Jackson is engaged in an ongoing struggle. The killing of the parrot is also a symbol of the violence inherent in that situation, of the violence that may be necessary at any time to further the liberation process and preserve it from the aggressor. Lamming, more than Walcott, deals with the reality of this continual struggle and its implications at the widest sociopolitical levels. Yet, what is crucial for Lamming, as for Walcott, is the transformation of consciousness through symbolic communication. Likewise, though Walcott is primarily concerned with the realm of the symbolic, it is this very realm that puts one in a position to undertake the process of creatively transforming social reality. Jackson states that the story of Robinson Crusoe is history, the history of imperialism. Jackson has accepted the task of truthfully entering into this history in order to transform it. This is what Harry fears. The Crusoe-Friday pantomime might become art; that is, it might make people "think too much." "Art," says Harry, "is a kind of crime in this society" (*Pantomime*, p. 125). Art, as liberating communication, is the point of departure for liberating action.

In the works of both Lamming and Walcott, the leap to history is an expression of a West Indian national culture. Fanon argues that national culture is a symbolic structure that sustains national consciousness in the revolutionary and postrevolutionary struggle. Even though liberating narrative takes as its starting point the real sociopolitical dramas of the Caribbean, it runs the risks of misunderstanding its own foundation and of appealing only to an elite to the extent that it neglects to tell its story through or in relation to the already given mythical narratives of the Caribbean. Negritude sought to recover the culture of colonized blacks in reaction to the stereotypes of the white colonizers. National culture is action rather than reaction; it is the living expression of a historical community. Lamming and Walcott, like Césaire, recognize that the culture of the colonizer denies and represses the culture and history of the colonized. One task of the artist is to recover that which has been denied and repressed in his or her own self and community, without creating a new mythology. As Edward Brathwaite writes "the recognition of an ancestral relationship with the folk or aboriginal culture involves the artist and participant in a journey into the past and hinterland which is at the same time a movement of possession into the present and future."[34]

The liberating recovery of the past in a movement toward the future is a central thematic and structural feature of both *Dream on Monkey Mountain* and *Season of Adventure*. In *Dream*, Basil, the under-

---

34. Edward Brathwaite, "Timehri," in Coombs, *Is Massa Day Dead?* p. 42.

taker, is a manifestation of Baron Samedi, vaudou loa of death (the past) and rebirth (the future). Baron Samedi does not appear in *Season*, but an ancestral ceremony associated with him is central to the novel. This ceremony of the souls is a recovery of the past in a movement toward the future. Walcott and Lamming make Afro-Caribbean creole patterns central to their work. However, myths are not simply reinterpreted in order to lend meaning to a new situation; they are radically transformed in terms of liberating consciousness. National culture is created through the process of transforming Afro-Caribbean culture and mythical patterns into liberating narrative.[35]

The theme of cultural recovery, centered on Fola's quest in *Season* and Makak's journey in *Dream*, provides the authors with an opportunity to explore and integrate various aspects of Caribbean culture. Fola, the heroine of *Season*, is a young, female member of the dependent bourgeois class in search of her cultural origins. Fola's task is to overcome the sociopolitical contradiction of colonialism that has lingered into the neocolonial period: the conflict between an economically powerless bourgeoisie that has internalized the colonizer's values and assumed political control, and a rural peasantry and lumpen proletariat that uses its Afro-Caribbean heritage to resist oppression.

The situation in *Dream* is different even though Walcott is likewise trying to recover the Afro-Caribbean heritage. Walcott's hero, Makak, a charcoal burner in the mountains, is a member of the oppressed and exploited peasant–lumpen-proletarian class. His resistance to colonialism has largely been muted and repressed, and, like the dependent bourgeoisie, he has begun to internalize the colonizer's values. However, unlike the bourgeoisie, he lacks the consolation of social status. The tenuous reconciliation with self that the bourgeoisie can sometimes maintain drives Makak to a severe social neurosis, just as it drove Powell psychotic. The psychogenesis of Makak's disorder is primarily a socio-political phenomenon, and for this reason he can recover his full human integrity only by understanding and transforming his own history. Makak's conflict is more intense than the average member of the bourgeoisie; it is also more intense than that of the colonized person who is able to resist the colonizer by being

35. Walcott, in particular, has been accused of being Eurocentric. As Ramchand argues, this is because his plays, which are firmly rooted in the folk and popular traditions of the Caribbean, have been largely ignored. See Kenneth Ramchand, "The West Indies," in *Literatures of the World Written in English,* ed. Bruce King (Boston: Routledge & Kegan Paul, 1974), p. 203.

firmly rooted in his or her own Afro-Caribbean culture (Moustique or Gort, for example). Still, it is precisely this difference that gives Makak's triumph its ultimate significance. Caught between these two patterns of reaction to colonialism, between resistance and total acceptance, Makak ultimately opts to step out of both.

The cultural forms through which Makak and Fola recover their history are different. Fola begins to recover her past when she encounters a vaudou ritual in which the souls of the recently dead are recovered from the waters of the abyss (the ceremony of souls). The souls of the dead must spend a year and a day in the waters. Their families can then recover their souls, store them in earthen jars, and appeal to them for counsel. There is a reciprocal need between the family and the dead: the family wants the counsel and support of their dead; the dead want to be freed from the water. No reconciliation between the living and the newly dead is possible, however, until the living have made amends to the dead. Events of the past are related by the dead and where necessary the living must make their apologies to them. This accomplished, the body of a possessed hunsi provides the medium through which the dead person can leave the waters and return to the land of the living to take up residence in sacred jars. The houngan addresses both Legba (crossroad, communication) and Baron Samedi (crossroad, death, rebirth) during such a ceremony, though other loa such as Grand Bois also play a role.[36] Lamming witnessed one of these ceremonies in Haiti and made it central to his understanding of the relationship between the present and the past. He stresses that the ceremony is a form of dialogue with the dead in which the living are forced to reckon with their past and in return are provided with a source of guidance in the future.

In *Season of Adventure* the ceremony becomes the point of departure for what Chiki calls the "backward glance" (*Season*, p. 92). Like other members of the dependent bourgeoisie, Fola has repressed her cultural origins, the national culture of the people of San Cristobal. Her past is a dead past, like a corpse in need of resurrection. When she witnesses an actual ceremony, however, this repressed culture threatens to erupt in her as she finds herself virtually possessed by a spirit. This is the beginning of her encounter with her past. She is no longer an

---

36. Maya Deren, *The Voodoo Gods* (Frogmore, Herts.: Granada-Paladin, 1975), pp. 52–58, 249; see also Alfred Métraux, *Voodoo in Haiti*, trans. Hugo Charteris (New York: Schocken Books, 1972), pp. 258–63.

outsider witnessing the ceremony, like her white teacher and friend Charlot. She has become a participant. Lamming lifts the ceremony of the souls out of its ritual context to make of it a symbol of the need for reconciliation in Fola's life and in the life of the society as a whole. Fola is aware that her father, Piggot, superintendent of police, is only her adopted (impotent, corpselike) father, not her real father. Fola's search to recover her real father is her search to bring her cultural patrimony back to life. According to Lamming the wound that the past has inflicted can be healed only through a "continuing dialogue between the living and the dead."[37] Fola's backward glance opens her eyes to the possibilities that are in herself. She is the Fola whom people know, but she discovers that she is more than this. She is free to create herself out of her situation. She is Fola "*and other than,*" states the narrator. "This Fola had started on a history of needs whose details she alone would be able to distinguish: a season of adventure which no man in the republic could predict" (*Season*, p. 185).

Fola enlists the help of Chiki, the artist, to accompany her in what Chiki had himself called the "backward glance." Fola sees in her own bastardy the ugliness of Chiki's face and, in his gift of creativity, her own possibilities of rediscovering her past. However, as there are few clues on which to base the search for her father, Chiki declares that they must invent them. With the gift of the artist he creates an unknown face on his canvas. Fola never finds her biological father. The symbolic search for her cultural patrimony takes precedence over the literal search in the novel. This is highlighted when Fola declares to her distressed stepfather that it is her father who has killed the vice-president, Raymond. It is a lie cunningly conceived to protect the Forest Grove community from the terror of the police. Ramchand insightfully argues that this is the point at which Fola the corpse comes alive "as a dead coming to bear witness . . . a believer possessed by the gods."[38]

The police begin to base their search for the murderer on the portrait of Fola's father. Chiki's painting, however, is a composite of everyone and anyone in the nation. Everyone can be recognized in it, and by virtue of this, no one. The image is a symbol of the anguish of the colonized, one eye casting a backward glance, the other holding a

37. Kent, p. 94; see also Lamming, *Pleasures of Exile,* pp. 9–10, and "The West Indian People," pp. 64–65.

38. Kenneth Ramchand, *The West Indian Novel and Its Background* (London: Faber & Faber, 1970), p. 148.

triumphant glare of certainty. It is an image of the corpse calling for redress from the living, a past calling for recreation in a liberating future. The real father turns out to be not one, but two, the white bishop's son, followed by Chiki's own brother, both of whom raped Agness, Fola's mother. This is the colonial conflict, the black and the white, that are part of Fola and of her nation; it is the burden that the new republic must bear, a conflict that must be relieved and resolved if the building of the new republic is not to be a repetition of ancestral error.

Only by means of a backward glance can Fola and, like her, the members of her class reconcile themselves to their past in a liberating movement toward the future. The members of San Cristobal's national bourgeoisie are like the living who must reconcile themselves with the past and the dead. In another sense, however, they are like the dead who are trapped in their past. Fola sees her relatives and friends as being "decrepit skeletons . . . polluting the live air with wave upon wave of their corpse breathing." Like the dead in the ceremony of souls, they "could not leap beyond themselves, beyond the moment their own story had ended" (*Season*, pp. 246–47). By using this image of the corpse, Lamming emphasizes that the bourgeoisie have failed to make an entry into authentic history. Their history is a closed narrative without a future. Only through the type of leap to responsibility that Baako talks about can the dependent bourgeoisie liberate themselves. Fola realizes the importance of this "leap beyond" and its significance for being "alive" (*Season*, p. 247). The important point here is that the leap beyond is an essential part of the backward glance; a blackward glance that lost itself in a past-oriented closed narrative could not initiate that liberating leap to the future.

The understanding of the backward glance in terms of the leap beyond transforms Lamming's appropriation of Caribbean mythical narrative into liberating narrative. Lamming takes a particular ritual form, which is essentially Haitian in origin, as his starting point. This ritual form is a way of preserving the wisdom of the community through the memory of the ancestors; it also heals wounds in the community: those who have done wrong confess and make amends. A drama is acted out and the tension between the living and the dead is resolved in the plot. The drama is a form of mythical narrative because it brings order to social events without grounding them in the imperative of liberation. This mythical structure is supported by the core myths of the tradition, including the myth of Baron Samedi, loa of crossroads and cemeteries.

Lamming creatively transforms the ceremony. In the first place, he is less concerned with anthropological accuracy than with symbolic potential. The ceremony is transported from Haiti to the fictitious island of San Cristobal, symbol of the Caribbean as a whole. Furthermore, the drummers play Trinidadian steel pans, not the traditional Afro-Haitian drums. More important than this is the symbolic leap from vaudou ritual to the sociopolitical totality. The society as a whole, and the dependent bourgeoisie, in particular, must reconcile themselves with their past. However, this cannot be a mythical reconciliation. There is no question of restoring a harmonious order based on past tradition. The future is open; the imperative is to recover the past in a movement toward a freely chosen future in which liberation from oppression is the primary concern. This is a story that has no end, a process in which persons constantly recreate their history.

Makak's self-discovery occurs by means of a dream rather than a specific ritual. Though dreams are personal unconscious narratives, while rituals are communal, conscious dramas, there are certain similarities between the two forms. Dreams rely on narratively ordered symbols that resolve a sociopolitical conflict experienced by an individual. Rituals likewise rely on narratively structured symbols to resolve crises, but the crises are usually experienced by a number of people rather than a particular individual. In the case of *Season* and *Dream* the similarities are even greater because Lamming is concerned with the way the individual, Fola, experiences and resolves the sociopolitical conflict, while Walcott is concerned with the way a similar sociopolitical conflict is dealt with by an individual, Makak.

Dream on Monkey Mountain opens in a prison cell on a moonlit night. Makak is the colonized black person reduced to a marginalized existence, subjected to the stereotypes of the colonizer. Makak has internalized the colonizer's image of himself, but his psyche undergoes a profound struggle in the dream. The dream is his way of escaping the prison cell of colonialism. However, Walcott molds the imaginary dream form into a symbolic mode of realistic self-understanding.

Makak's dream is an extension of a colonially engendered neurosis associated with fits resembling possession. Whereas Lamming's Forest Grove community experiences its unity in the ceremony of the souls, Makak's fits are a personal odyssey into a world of human dignity. Alcohol, a mask of a white woman-devil, and the misty moonlight of early morning set the ceremonial context for Makak's personal vision of a divine apparition: "I feel I was God self, walking through cloud, in the heaven of my mind. . . . I see this woman singing, and my feet grow roots! . . . I behold this woman, the loveliest thing I see on this earth, floating towards me, just like the moon, like the moon walking along her own road. . . . She say I should not live so any more, here in the forest, frighten of people because I think I ugly. She say that I come from the family of lions and kings" (*Dream*, pp. 235–36). The dream in the jail cell allows Makak to fulfill the demands of his moon goddess by escaping his prison cell, healing the sick among his people, and triumphantly returning to Africa as the king that he is.

In his dream Makak casts a backward glance at his own Afro-Caribbean heritage and lives this heritage to its fullest. (There are echoes here of the Garvey and Rastafarian movements.) The healing episode in Makak's dream is a recollection of Afro-Caribbean ritual. At a crossroad in the moonlight, robed women sing and dance around a dying man as they try to exorcise the evil that has doomed him. Baron Samedi is present in the person of Basil the undertaker. Makak, the charcoal burner, becomes a possessed healer and invokes the spirit that will return the dying man to life, like a burning coal. Makak's prayer is revealing: "I see you all as trees, / like a twisted forest, / like trees without names, / a forest with no roots!" (*Dream*, p. 248). The act of healing the dying man symbolizes the process of restoring the community to itself through recollecting its past. In this respect it is similar to the ceremony of souls in Lamming's work. The man sweats, his fever is relieved, and he gets up to walk.

Makak reaches his apotheosis when his followers establish him as the omnipotent ruler of an African kingdom. In a scene in which a ritual context is again recollected, Makak sits in judgment, surrounded by his court and warriors. This religio-political event recalls the ritual basis of the Haitian Revolution, particularly the Bois Caïman ceremony, which would find its ultimate completion in the slaying of the plantation whites. In Walcott's play the drums beat, the dancers chant, and gods appear in their masks and costumes. Baron Samedi is present. Makak gives the order to eliminate all those in any way implicated in the rule of the white colonizer. In this vision of African redemption, Makak's backward glance is at the same time a movement forward. Makak moves back through the culture and history of his people. He also moves forward to an era of black redemption in which the ways of old are reestablished. However, this movement forward, this vision of cultural reconciliation, is not really a forward movement. It is merely a repetition of the past in the future. Makak, more corpse than king, begins to see himself as a "hollow God," a "phantom," a "shadow" (*Dream*, p. 311). He has become a zombie under the control of a sorcerer, Corporal Lestrade, and his divine master, Baron Samedi. Makak's goddess, the moon, his mask, all are one, all are the colonizers' image and must be destroyed. This is the point at which the tensions in Makak's dream force the dream to destroy itself. Makak beheads his goddess, he eliminates the white mask, but in so doing he must likewise destroy the black reaction to that mask, the black illusion that the mask itself has engendered. As in the case of a nightmare where the personal conflict underlying the dream is so strong that the person wakes up, so Makak's conflict forces him to awaken. But whereas the dreamer wakes up in order once again to repress the conflict, Makak awakens to a new beginning. The conflict has destroyed itself. The dream has engendered its own self-destruction. In this moment, Walcott transforms the backward glance into a leap beyond. The illusions of the masks, white or black, are destroyed and Makak returns to reality.

Walcott explicitly appeals to the myth of Baron Samedi to structure the incoherence of Makak's dream. Baron Samedi is present both at the healing ceremony and on the day of judgment. It is he who is taking the life of the dying man, and it is he who oversees the death of the white woman. But, as a healer and giver of life, it is Baron Samedi who also ensures that death is transformed into life. Through his power Makak is able to restore the dying man. Through him, the death of the white woman is transformed into the renewal of life for Makak. However, Walcott, like Lamming, goes beyond myth itself to transform the Afro-Haitian Baron Samedi into a new creative symbol for the Caribbean as a whole. Baron Samedi is as much an undertaker as he is a loa. Most important of all, he is made into more than a constantly recurring symbol of death and rebirth: he is now the symbol of liberation. The baron is death and life in tension, but he is also white and black in conflict. Ultimately, he is the death of the white colonial world *and* of the black world created in resistance to colonialism. He is the liberating rebirth of the human in the fullness of a history as future possibility. In his leap beyond, his own mythical origins are destroyed, and Caribbean history is born as liberating narrative.

Just as Lamming's novels and Walcott's plays recover and reshape the Afro-Caribbean religious tradition, they reclaim and recreate other elements of the creole tradition. Music, dance, song, storytelling, language—these are all aspects of the Afro-Caribbean tradition on which Walcott and Lamming draw. The trickster motif, like the use of religious ritual, is of particular interest because of the sociopolitical significance of the trickster symbol in resistance against colonialism. Moreover, the trickster possesses many of the playful and creative traits of the artist, whose task it is to recreate culture. Creolization, Walcott argues, consists of a process of "cunning assimilation." The Tiger's stripes imitate the grass of its surroundings, but the Tiger retains its awesome difference. The slave wrested God from the captor and gave God an African rhythm and African names; the slave adopted the master's culture but created something new out of it.[39] Walcott's tricksters are masters of pragmatic resistance, they subvert colonial culture, and they go further to transform the trickster symbol into a call for liberation.

The Joker of Seville is a creolized interpretation of Tirso de Molina's play and of the whole Don Juan tradition in Western culture. Walcott goes beyond the sexual anarchism of the Don Juan trickster to explore his liberating implications both for women repressed by their husbands and for the oppressed in society at large. Don Juan dies in Walcott's play, but unlike in Tirso de Molina's ethical (moralistic) version, the trickster's spirit lives on, purged and liberating. Don Juan is essentially a European trickster and is not our primary concern. However, this transformation of the trickster's ambivalence into liberating meaning is also characteristic of Walcott's Afro-Caribbean folk tricksters such as Ti-Jean and Moustique.

Ti-Jean and His Brothers is a dramatized folktale. The tale itself is possibly European in origin. Walcott creolizes it by creating Afro-Caribbean characters (some of them animal characters), by making the devil into a white planter, and by adding Afro-Caribbean language, song, music, and dance. To a large extent, Ti-Jean is a classical Afro-Caribbean trickster.[40] Whereas Gros-Jean fails to defeat the master with his strength, and whereas Mi-Jean fails to defeat the

39. Walcott, "Muse," pp. 7–13.
40. Albert Olu Ashaolu, "Allegory in *Ti-Jean and His Brothers*," *World Literature Written in English*, 18 (April 1977), 207; Lloyd Coke, "Walcott's Mad Innocents," *Savacou*, no. 5 (June 1971), p. 122; Robert Hamner, *Derek Walcott* (Boston: Twayne, 1981), p. 72.

master by using his intellect, Ti-Jean uses Anancy's cunning and common sense to become the victor. Ti-Jean handles the problem of the runaway goat by castrating it; he solves the problem of counting the canes by pretending to be a foreman and then ordering the workers to burn them; he escapes the chores of cleaning and cooking by preparing himself a curried goat meal, eating it, and then burning the plantation house down.

In Walcott's play, these acts of defiance move beyond mere shrewdness to become overtly rebellious. Furthermore, there is no attempt at symbolic camouflage in the form of the tale itself: the devil plainly is the master, the colonizer; Ti-Jean, the oppressed, the colonized. Walcott goes even further in his remolding of the trickster as represented by Ti-Jean. The ambivalence of the trickster symbol, its representation both of the processes of community building and of arbitrary individualism, is not an issue here. Ti-Jean acts in the interest of the community to overthrow the white planter. This is not to say that he is a romantic ethical hero or, as Carolyn Cooper argues, a wish-fulfilling, fairy-tale character.[41] He is an ordinary person who has to rely on his common sense and who experiences anger, fear, and sorrow at the loss of his two brothers and then his mother. Nor is he a tragic hero who merely accepts his lot and looks to salvation in his death. No, he affirms life even as he acknowledges the reality of struggle and death. His faith is in his song: "I go bring down, bring down Goliath" (*Ti-Jean*, p. 165). Ti-Jean is the Afro-Caribbean trickster whom Walcott has fused with David of the Judaeo-Christian tradition. The Bolom, child of the devil, strangled infant wandering endlessly in search of vengeance, aborted foetus preserved by its mother from enduring the wretchedness of colonialism, is witness to Ti-Jean's endurance and affirmation of life: the Bolom demands to be born so that it can undertake the struggle of creating a human world: "Ask him for my life / O God, I want all this / To happen to me!" (*Ti-Jean*, p. 163).

Moustique, the pesky insect, Makak's foil in *Dream on Monkey Mountain*, is another of Walcott's trickster figures.[42] Moustique, along with Tigre and Souris, Makak's associates in jail, are survivors rather than visionaries, and they look for ways of exploiting Makak's

---

41. Cooper, p. 181; Ashaolu may be correct in seeing an element of Toussaint L'Ouverture in Ti-Jean (Ashaolu, p. 206).

42. This has been commented on by Hamner ("Mythological Aspects," p. 50) and Coke (p. 123).

vision. In Makak's dream, Moustique deceives people in order to obtain the food, clothing, and money necessary for survival. Moustique first convinces a crowd that Makak can cure a dying man. To his surprise, his trick works: Makak heals the dying man. Moustique then decides that he himself will imitate Makak and he poses as a healer. He is revealed as an impostor and beaten to death.

Though Moustique is associated with a spider in Makak's dream, there is no indication that this spider is Anancy the trickster. However, the spider in *Dream* is closely associated with the crossroad, the moonlight, and the divine trickster Baron Samedi. The crossroad is the symbol in vaudou of the intersection of life and death, the human and the divine. In West Africa, the crossroad is the domain of the great African trickster Legba (Eshu). In Haiti it is also the domain of Baron Samedi. Baron Samedi is Lord of Death, but he is also a trickster, a great magician and healer, a symbol of fertility and of rebirth. He frequently works at night, in the moonlight. When a greedy Moustique appropriates Basil's top hat and coat (Baron Samedi's ritual clothing) at a crossroad in the moonlight, Basil warns him to beware of a white road with four legs. Moustique immediately thinks of a white spider with eggs that he has killed (*Dream*, pp. 252–53). Basil is again on the scene at a crossroad when Moustique impersonates Makak for worldly gain. The undertaker reveals Moustique's ruse by pointing out that Moustique is afraid of spiders whereas a great healer like Makak would not be afraid.

The spider in Makak's dream is also closely linked to the white goddess, the female apparition that is the ultimate driving force in Makak's dream of African redemption. When Makak has his vision, he has in his possession a mask of a white woman. Other aspects of the reality around him are drawn into the vision: the white mist, and "the web of the spider heavy with diamonds" (*Dream*, p. 226). Makak is uneasy when Moustique kills the spider because he senses a link between the spider and his vision. The death of the spider is a foreshadowing of the death of Makak's white apparition. It also foreshadows Moustique's death.

Moustique is like the trickster hero who satirizes those in authority. Pretending to be Makak, he has his followers dance around the market inspector singing a song about an imitative monkey. He humorously assaults the inspector with words saying that he hears a voice the color of milk, the voice of a milk inspector, an English voice; but the color of English is supposed to be white, which the inspector is not.

Moustique goes beyond the trickster's challenge to authority to envision a new society and time "when people will not need money, . . . when niggers everywhere could walk upright like men" (*Dream*, p. 254). However, he argues that one cannot feed oneself with dreams. Makak will have to sell his own African dream just for bread and shelter if he wants to avoid being a beggar. This conscious justification for exploiting one's own people introduces an element of the demonic into Moustique's character that is not present in the traditional trickster figure. (The traditional trickster hero does not have a vision of a liberated society, even though he himself is an implicit call for liberation.) Moustique's demonic consciousness ultimately becomes a vehicle of liberation, however. When he is exposed as an impostor by Basil, the undertaker (Baron Samedi), he in turn unveils the masks in his society: "God after God you change, promise after promise you believe, and you still covered with dirt; so why not believe me. All I have is this [*shows the mask*], black faces, white masks! I tried like you" (*Dream*, p. 271).

The mask is the mask of the white goddess that inspired Makak's vision. The mask symbol is also tied to the white moon that appears in the darkness, to the white crossroad that the moon lights up; to Baron Samedi, whose face in the play is half-white and half-black; and, ultimately, to the white spider with eggs. White is the symbol of the white myth. Moustique's direct reference to Fanon's *Black Skin, White Masks* is the playwright's challenge to the audience to transform the struggle for survival and the manipulation of myths into liberating action. Moustique kills the white spider. Moustique must be killed for manipulating the mask and vision of the white goddess so as to exploit his people. The white goddess, the ultimate symbol of the white myth, must be killed.

This unveiling of the white mask is the prelude to the regeneration and rebirth that can come out of the meeting of the black and the white at the crossroad. The trickster, Moustique, reveals the truth of the mask once he has been exposed by the even greater trickster, Baron Samedi. In the play, the agents of deception and death are transformed into agents of truth and rebirth. "If there's resurrection," sings the Ace of Death in Walcott's *The Joker of Seville*, "Death is the Joker."[43]

43. Derek Walcott, *"The Joker of Seville" and "O Babylon"!* (New York: Farrar, Straus & Giroux, 1978), p. 150.

The most revealing trickster hero in Walcott's dramatic works is Jackson, the black hotel worker and calypsonian in *Pantomime*. In his relationship to his English employer, Harry Trewe, Jackson plays on the Quashee stereotype: he resists with impunity. Having had a disagreement with his employer, who wants him to act in a Crusoe-Friday pantomime, Jackson teases Harry by engaging in what he jestingly calls "Creole acting." He fixes the roof, banging the hammer very noisily and violently as his master tries to rest; he loudly imitates a sea gull—a "black" sea gull—much to his master's chagrin; finally he improvises a calypso melody humoring Harry's idea of a Crusoe-Friday pantomime and culminating in the words: "But one day things bound to go in reverse, / with Crusoe the slave and Friday the boss" (*Pantomime*, pp. 130–32). Jackson has other tricks up his sleeve. He is gifted at playing language games to irritate his master: Mr. Trewe becomes "Robinson Trewe-so" and "Harry, boy"; "tragedy" is transformed into "tradegy"; sarcasm is his basic tone (*Pantomime*, pp. 133, 138–39, 154). With his words come his big exaggerated grin. Time, his master's time, when it is not whittled away with words, goes into other activities such as a precise and long toilet ritual.

This is the behavior of the trickster pushed to its limit, resistance with impunity. Harry knows this and calls his employee an Uncle Tom playing games, a "stage nigger" with "a smile in front and a dagger behind," a smile that itself becomes "the bloody dagger" (*Pantomime*, p. 140). Jackson knows it too; the smile, he admits, goes with the job. It is here that Jackson, like Walcott's other trickster heroes, breaks with the traditional trickster. Whereas the historical novelist like Orlando Patterson portrays the trickster in terms that are sociologically accurate, Walcott is more concerned to find new meaning in the trickster.[44] Jackson is conscious of the social and political totality that defines the master-servant relation, and he never identifies himself with the role he is playing. In the pantomime that Harry wants him to rehearse, he refuses to play the role of Friday, and he does not imprison himself in a mythical black Crusoe. Though he has chosen to play the social role of servant in a guesthouse, he knows that he is more than a servant, that he is a person, a free agent, who cannot be reduced to one particular role. To use Peter Berger's language, he is

---

44. Orlando Patterson, *Die the Long Day* (New York: Morrow, 1972), pp. 48, 70–72.

ecstatic: he is able to step out of socially defined roles and then reenter them without confusing self and role.[45]

Whereas the traditional trickster hero is determined to resist and challenge the master, to reveal his strengths and weaknesses, and perhaps even to eliminate and replace him, Jackson is concerned to arouse social and political awareness in a struggle for mutual recognition. Jackson says with complete self-consciousness: "You see, two of we both acting a role here we ain't really believe in, you know. I ent think you strong enough to give people orders, and I *know* I ain't the kind who like taking *them*. So both of we doesn't have to *improvise* so much as *exaggerate*. We faking, faking all the time. But, man to man, I mean . . . that could be something else. Right, Mr. Trewe?" (*Pantomime*, p. 138). Lamming makes a relevant observation about Prospero's "camouflage of inflation" and Caliban's "camouflage of self-evaporation." Though the first can easily be detected, the second, Lamming states, "contains an incalculable secret whose meaning stays absent until time and its own needs order an emergence."[46] Walcott's Jackson knows that it is time to order that emergence. He plays the Quashee role the way Hamlet plays madness. It is done consciously, with distance, in the interest of truth. Jackson's ultimate goal is not to deceive Harry but to cut through the illusions of racial domination and neocolonial exploitation.

Caribbean religious deities, binding the community together and instructing it, led rebels into conflict and war with the colonizer. In the face of defeat, trickster folk heroes such as Anancy enabled the colonized to distance themselves from the colonizer and to continue to envision transformations of the colonizer-colonized relationship. The trickster hero, however, was a symbol of the tragic ups and downs of slave and peasant existence; it did not explore the creation of fundamentally new, liberating sociopolitical structures. Walcott's trickster makes this fundamental leap: he is Hegel's slave, Caliban, Friday, fully aware of the totality of colonialism and neocolonialism, of the originality of differing traditions, and of history as possibility. Fola's quest for her patrimony and Makak's search for his cultural identity are efforts to reclaim a distorted past in a resurrection that moves toward a radically new future. Like the negritude poets and

45. Peter Berger, *Invitation to Sociology: A Humanistic Perspective* (New York: Anchor-Doubleday, 1963), p. 136.
46. Lamming, *Pleasures of Exile*, p. 166.

writers, Lamming and Walcott attempt in their works to recover the full heritage of their people and offer a liberating critique of colonial oppression and exploitation. In their symbolic approaches to the colonial situation in the Caribbean, however, Walcott and Lamming go beyond negritude by re-presenting a specifically Caribbean and West Indian history, using narrative forms and symbols indigenous to the Caribbean, though recreated anew. Indeed, their works are critical commentaries on the negritude theme.

Pa's dream in *Castle* contains, in part, a mythical recollection of Africa. However, the ancestor who appears in the dream warns that present history should not be confused with a mythical past: "So if you hear some young fool fretting about back to Africa, keep far from the invalid and don't force a passage to where you won't yet belong" (*Castle*, p. 234). In an essay entitled "Caribbean Literature: The Black Rock of Africa," Lamming praises the faith of the poet (E. M. Roach) "that the solidity of that black rock has bestowed some portion of itself, some diamond fragment from its seam, upon the heirs of those valiant and tormented ancestors." However, Lamming goes on to criticize any form of mythical black consciousness. Elsewhere, he rebukes the fanatic pride that sets up new walls, the "rhapsodic and uncritical embrace of Africa as a mother once stolen and now miraculously restored to our experience." He calls for a national West Indian consciousness built around the black rock that has been the main sustenance of West Indians, but forged as well out of India and Europe.[47]

In Lamming's *Castle*, Trumper returns from the United States with a consciousness of what it means both to be black and to be betrayed by blacks. He declares to an uncomprehending G. that his people are the Negro race. The look of the other that has fixed him as a "nigger" has taught him this. At the same time, he is very critical of what Slime and the new dependent bourgeoisie have done to the village. G. realizes that, compared with Trumper, he has a lot to learn about the social and political world, and as a result, he cannot help but admire Trumper. Moreover, G. is prone to experiences of nauseating anguish that, as Trumper points out, would not be experienced by a person who knows his people. The narrator states that Trumper "had found what he needed and there were no more problems to be

47. Lamming, "Caribbean Literature," pp. 40, 45, 49; introduction to *Castle*, p. xix.

worked out." He continues: "Henceforth his life would be straight, even, uncomplicated. He knew the race and he knew his people and he knew what that knowledge meant" (*Castle*, p. 335). G. is ignorant and has a lot of learning to do. Trumper knows what he knows and he can learn nothing new; he is in danger of becoming a "corpse."

Lloyd Brown and Wa Thiong'O Ngugi disregard this aspect of Trumper's presentation when they conclude that he has authorial approval.[48] As Ramchand points out, "warning signs" accompany the author's depiction of Trumper: his flashy clothes, his badge with stars and stripes, and his excessive certainty.[49] Nor does G. have authorial approval. In making this argument, Munro forces Lamming's novel into a tragic and unhistorical mold: because G. has rejected Trumper's alternative of political engagement, the novel, he states, ends without a vision of the future or commitment to change.[50] The tension between Trumper and G. is never resolved in the book. It is the reader who must struggle with the solution. The tension is an example of the open-endedness typical of the structure of Lamming's novels, and it puts in question the mythical closure characteristic of racially based consciousness.

There are elements of Trumper in two characters in *Season*: Powell and Baako. Powell's understanding of his race and class as an oppressed group is distorted by a dramatic resentment. Baako, who understands Powell's problem, offers a solution to the problem of colonial oppression, which is potentially elitist and technocratic. In contrast to Powell, Fola refinds her people in an authentic entry into history. Chiki, as a contrast to Baako, is ultimately unable to mobilize himself in the liberation process. Paradoxically, however, it is Chiki who leads Fola to self-discovery. The ceremony of souls is a symbol of a recovery of the past that is nonsentimental and that provides the community with the possibility of creating a new future. Whereas *Castle* leaves future possibilities implicit and unstated, *Season* explores alternatives, and issues the challenge of forming a liberating national culture that would be the basis of authentic independence

48. Ngugi, p. 125; Lloyd Brown, "The Crisis of Black Identity in the West Indian Novel," *Critique*, 11, no. 3 (1969), 98–100, 105; see also Kom, pp. 414–15; Paquet, p. 27; Butler, p. 39; Charles R. Larson, *The Novel in the Third World* (Washington, D.C.: Inscape, 1976), p. 123.

49. Ramchand, *An Introduction to the Study of West Indian Literature* (Sunbury-on-Thames, Middlesex: Thomas Nelson, 1976), pp. 54–56.

50. Munro, pp. 56, 58–59.

both at the individual and at the political level. Fola's quest is the quest of the dependent bourgeoisie for a liberating cultural identity.

The negritude theme and its critique are central to Walcott's *Dream*. Makak stabs his jailer, Corporal Lestrade, sets himself and his friends free, and heads for Africa. Baron Samedi appears to Lestrade and offers him only one alternative to death: conversion. "Now I feel better," says Lestrade, accepting the offer. "Now I see a new light. I sing the glories of Makak! The glories of my Race!" (*Dream*, p. 299). Under the influence of Baron Samedi, a dying Lestrade is reborn, converted from upholder of the white man's colonial law to enforcer of the laws of a mythical African civilization.

The play makes it very clear that this is a false reconciliation, a ceremony of souls capable of creating more corpses but not of liberating the living. Baron Samedi has shaped a new zombie, another shadow like Makak. This critique of a slavish black consciousness finds its fullest development in the death of the white goddess: when she is beheaded by shadows, the shadows disappear, for they were dependent on her light for their total being as reflections of that light. This is the point at which the leap to history occurs for Makak, the leap beyond Nietzsche's reactive slave ethics. Makak has overcome his awe of everything white, but, at the same time, he has learned, as Walcott himself puts it, "to shed the African longing, and to say that we are here."[51] Makak is the Caribbean peasant or working-class person who has completed the liberating journey of self-recovery.

A similarly critical appropriation of the return-to-Africa theme occurs in *Pantomime*. In the course of a Crusoe-Friday pantomime, roles are reversed and Jackson, the servant, mimes a black Crusoe: he rows his boat and is shipwrecked; he finds himself teaching his white servant an African language (*Pantomime*, pp. 114–15, 120). These scenes are reminiscent of scenes in Césaire's *Cahier* where the poet makes regal the canoe traversing the foaming waves, or utters the African word (*Cahier*, pp. 72–73, 52–53). However, Jackson is only too aware of the danger of becoming a "shadow" (*Pantomime*, p. 113). He knows that the assertion of an alternative, classical African Crusoe, dwelling in the golden age of Guinea, is a mythical reaction to the dominant white ideology and its traumatic impact. It does nothing to alter the fact that he is still a servant in a neocolonial world where blacks supposedly have power. There is a "pure black Afro-Arya-

51. Quoted in Lyn, p. 62.

nism," writes Walcott, according to which "only the unsoiled black is valid, and West Indianism is a taint." This "treason of the intellectuals" merely seeks an "escape to a special oblivion removed from the banalities of poverty and from the weight of a new industrial imperialism."[52]

The works of both Walcott and Lamming challenge racial consciousness, as myth, and call for a liberating West Indian consciousness. The trip through slavery back to Africa is one response to the racist look of the colonizer. This form of consciousness is merely a reaction to white racism, which, in affirming the difference of blacks, grants the initial premise of the colonial ideology. Therefore, the racial negation of race must open itself to history as the realization of human liberation in time. National consciousness is the ground for the realization of the nation as a political, social, and cultural totality through which the contradictions of race and class can be transformed in the context of an indigenous cultural base. However, the nation is not an ultimate totality for writers such as Walcott and Lamming. National consciousness is an aspect of historical consciousness. Should national consciousness become narcissistic nationalism, then it is the task of narrative to subvert it. It can be said of Lamming and Walcott that their work expresses the universal, but only if we understand the depth of Walcott's statement to Robert Hamner: "The more particular you get, the more universal you become."[53]

Commenting on Voltaire and Nietzsche, Walcott remarks: "It is necessary to invent a God who is dead."[54] If Caribbean culture is to be more than either assimilation of European culture or resentment for the past, it must create out of nothing, it must create its own history. This is the meaning of the trickster's transformation. Liberating culture is an open ending and a green beginning. Hamner correctly emphasizes that Walcott's vision of beginning with "nothing" is essentially creative and is grounded in the discovery of inner worth. However, Hamner concludes in dualistic and tragic terms that the revolutionary new discovery of an "authentic foundation" can be reconciled with "accommodation" to the environment.[55] By separat-

---

52. Walcott, "Muse," pp. 19–20.

53. Robert Hamner, "Conversation with Derek Walcott," *World Literature Written in English*, 16 (November 1977), 412.

54. Derek Walcott, "The Caribbean: Culture or Mimicry?" *Journal of Interamerican Studies and World Affairs*, 16 (February 1974), 12–13.

55. Hamner, *Derek Walcott*, pp. 89, 104–105.

ing the inner revolution from the process of outer transformation, the critic permits himself the luxury of gracefully stepping aside from the imperative of creating history out of nothing. In similar fashion, Gordon Rohlehr dualistically opposes Edward Brathwaite's emphasis on roots with Walcott's emphasis on the void. What Rohlehr fails to point out is that for Walcott the consciousness of history as absence, void, necessitates a leap to creativity and freedom in which the new must be created out of the old, that is, out of its very roots.[56]

"The future of West Indian militancy," states Walcott, "lies in art."[57] Liberating art, as the expression of historical consciousness, is the point of departure. Art is not opposed to politics. At their best, Walcott's works of art are demands that human dignity and freedom be recognized and realized. This is the only foundation on which an authentic politics can be built. Walcott barely examines the actual process of building in his works. That is our task. Lamming's vision is more directly political than Walcott's. He uses the novelistic form to explore the actual process of nation building. Yet, what remains fundamental in Lamming's work is not this process in itself but the leap to history of which it is a manifestation. For Lamming, the process is open, indeterminate, and art can, indeed, it must, bring us into this realm of indeterminacy.[58]

In a discussion of Prospero and Caliban reminiscent of Fanon, Lamming writes that Prospero gave Caliban a new language and used it to imprison him. Walcott makes the same point in his poem "Crusoe's Journal." Crusoe brings the word that will convert the colonized into "good Fridays who recite His praise." The gift of language is but the beginning of the forced internalization of the

56. Gordon Rohlehr, "Man's Spiritual Search in the Caribbean through Literature," in *Troubling of the Waters,* ed. Idris Hamid (San Fernando, Trinidad: Rahaman Printery, 1973), pp. 197, 204.

57. Derek Walcott, "What the Twilight Says: An Overture," in *Dream,* p. 18.

58. The skeptic looking for confirmation that politics is possible within the scope of Walcott's vision should consider the following comment by Walcott: "I think some form of socialism, evolved from our own political history, is the only hope for the archipelago" ("Meanings," *Savacou,* no. 2, [September 1970], p. 50). Selden Rodman quotes Walcott as saying that the only way to deal with imperialist exploitation in Trinidad is to nationalize the oil companies. Walcott also says that he is not a Marxist but that he is sympathetic to some of Fidel Castro's policies ("Derek Walcott," *Tongues of Fallen Angels* [New York: New Directions, 1974], p. 243.) More than Walcott, Lamming has involved himself in the everyday politics of the Caribbean. This can be seen in his numerous articles in newspapers such as *Caribbean Contact* and in his relationships with the labor movement in Barbados (Paquet, pp. 9–10).

culture of the colonizer. Lamming argues, however, that with the gift of language comes the risk that Caliban, like Adam, will use that language to become aware of his difference, that is, of the sinfulness that is the mark of his freedom. Provided that this "extraordinary departure" does not occur, Caliban belongs to Prospero. The dialectic that is given to the sinner to allow him or her to emerge from nature is not given to Caliban. Caliban can be a man, but not a person.[59] What Lamming means by an "extraordinary departure" is the grasp of the dialectic that would allow Caliban to make the liberating leap to history. This is why both Walcott and Lamming say that Caribbean men and women, like Adam, must name the world anew.

Commenting on Lamming, Janheinz Jahn situates this departure in the realm of culture. Caliban uses Prospero's language to recognize his own culture, and to break out of the prison of Prospero's language. Jahn argues that it is negritude that makes possible this "extraordinary departure."[60] However, Caliban did not have to wait for the negritude of the intellectuals to initiate the process of breaking out. It was a part of Caliban's religion, it was related in stories, legends, and songs; there was a culture of resistance from the beginning. Nevertheless, Caliban's culture often recovered the past in terms of mythical narrative. It was necessary for culture to encode the leap to history as a political act, as the slaying of the colonizer. Through the symbolism of this extraordinary departure, a leap to consciousness can be made. We can create out of nothing only if we have created nothing, to put it in Walcott's terms, and to slay the colonizer is to create nothing. This is the essence of liberating narrative and with it we are back to Fanon.

Charlot is Fola's teacher in *Season*, and it is he who introduces her to the ceremony of souls. He is a man of French, Jewish, and Chinese origin, who was born in West Africa but educated in England. He is a colonizer with a difference. He sees in his England only a tragic corpse locked incestuously to its past, all action turned into pantomime (*Season*, pp. 36–38). Harry, the guesthouse owner in Walcott's *Pantomime*, is also a colonizer with a difference. He is the melan-

59. Lamming, *Pleasures*, pp. 109–11; Kent, pp. 88–89; Derek Walcott, *The Castaway and Other Poems* (London: Jonathan Cape, 1969), p. 51; *BS*, pp. 17–40; *PN*, pp. 35–52.

60. Janheinz Jahn, *A History of Neo-African Literature: Writing in Two Continents*, trans. Oliver Coburn and Ursula Lehrburger (London: Faber & Faber, 1968) pp. 240–42.

cholic and lonely Crusoe whose son has died and whose wife has divorced him (*Pantomime*, pp. 158–64). He has not been able to leave his corpse behind in England: the attempt to play Crusoe is an attempt to conceal his own inferiority complex, loneliness, and impotence. Charlot and Harry are Crusoes with a difference because they have begun to crack out of their entombment. It is Friday who has made this possible. As the houngan calls up the dead through whom the living can be reconciled to themselves, and in the same way that the psychoanalyst retrieves the repressed past so that healing becomes possible, the colonized bring a history into being in which the colonizers too must find themselves. Man must live, says Jackson; it is Friday's "naked footprint" that is the mark of Crusoe's "salvation" (*Pantomime*, p. 164). The point of this metaphor is at once simple and complex. It is a Hegelian demand for mutual recognition. Prospero is afraid of Caliban, writes Lamming, because Prospero's encounter with Caliban is largely a self-encounter. Jahn is correct, therefore, in saying that Caliban's liberation gives Prospero "the chance of turning from a tyrant into a humane person."[61]

61. Lamming, *Pleasures*, p. 15 (see also p. 156); Jahn, *Neo-African Literature*, p. 242.

Epilogue

I am not a prisoner of history. I should not seek there
for the meaning of my destiny.
I should constantly remind myself that the real *leap*
consists in introducing invention into existence.

FRANTZ FANON, *Black Skin, White Masks*

INHABITED by Arawaks and Caribs; conquered, settled, and exploited by Europeans; worked and remolded by Africans, Indians,
Chinese, and others, the Caribbean has been witness to the drama of
colonialism, one of the major tragedies of the modern world. The
culture of the Caribbean, the creole discourse shaped out of Africa,
Europe, and Asia, recreates the history of struggle against colonialism
and issues the call for liberation. An explosive quest burst forth out of
the region—in Haiti, Jamaica, Cuba, Grenada, and elsewhere—a
quest to retrieve the dream of the modern world for political liberty,
social justice, and mutual recognition.

The works of Fanon, Lamming, Walcott, and others are at the
forefront of a long awakening. They draw from a popular tradition of
resistance that still lives in religion and language, tales, music, song,
poetry, and drama. Telling a story in which all human beings can find
themselves, Caribbean culture recreates the past, from the situation of
the present, with a view to the future. Its challenge is to destroy myth
without killing meaning, and this means creating art out of fantasy. A
culture is formed that is national because it understands its own history, human because it is part of the universal quest for recognition,
creative because it is a work without an end.

The process of creolization took shape in response to the colonial
drama and the colonizer-colonized relation. Creole culture enabled
peoples disrupted by the slave trade to recreate themselves, to dis-

tance themselves from those who tried to control their minds, to rebel, and to resist with cunning. Haitian vaudou contributed to the explosion of Saint Domingue plantation society and the destruction of its ruling class. The Haitian Revolution was the first of the great anticolonial struggles of the modern world. Fanon captured its spirit and its contradictions, albeit in a new time and guise, in *The Wretched of the Earth*. Where the colonizer's violence succeeded in shackling anticolonial violence, creole culture gave birth to an ongoing process of struggle through pragmatic resistance. Religion unified the community and gave the oppressed a sense of control over their destinies and of hope for the future. The tiny spider of the folktale, Anancy the trickster, symbolized the cunning and other patterns of behavior that were necessary for protection and survival on the plantation.

The loa fought for their followers, and the spider taught lessons to the community, but both loa and spider testified to the interpretation of reality as a tragic encounter. Could not the loa work for the enemy, or the spider represent the ways of the master? Vaudou entered the Haitian Revolution not only in the service of the slave but also as an armament of the master. It was not until the twentieth century, however, that the new neocolonial white, colored, or black master, the dependent bourgeoisie, learned to enter into the discourse of creole religion and popular culture and to draw from it the power to coerce people into accommodating a repressive regime. While the Duvalier regimes redeployed popular culture and invented a brand of negritude that would legitimate their own power, Césaire and other black writers espoused a humanistic negritude that would repair the damage that colonialism had done to the psyche of the black middle class and elite. Negritude helped heal the intellectual, but it also distorted the history of the Caribbean, coupling a mythical, racialized interpretation of human beings with a false universalism. The process of creolization that grew from below and the racial recovery inaugurated from above were both structured in the mode of mythical narrative and expressed the tragic drama of a dualistic, Manichaean world.

Fanon, Walcott, Lamming. These three writers are only a few of the spokespersons of new creative processes and open possibilities in the Caribbean. Building on the process of creolization, the leap to history was made and has to be ever remade. The movement to a liberating historical consciousness, generalized in Hegel's slave-servant, expresses the call for human emancipation, justice, independence, and liberation, in a particular historical context and culture.

This movement was present in the Haitian Revolution, but there it was to be repressed. It was present in the Afro-Christian religious movement that culminated in the Baptist War (1831), Jamaica's largest slave revolt. The movement to history manifested itself in social movements later in the nineteenth century, in the labor movement of the twentieth century, in the quest for an independent federation, in independence itself, and in the continual struggle against neocolonialism in the Caribbean today. Liberating historical consciousness is present in aspects of the Rastafarian movement, in some contemporary calypsoes, tales, poems, plays, novels, and other literary works. This is the history of liberating narrative in which Walcott, Lamming, and Fanon can be situated, from which they drew inspiration, and to which they have contributed.

The colonial social and political system did not radically change with emancipation. The colonizer and the allies of colonialism constantly generated new myths as new forms of oppression reared their heads. One myth that was introduced in the postemancipation period, and that is all too existent today, is the myth of a black history divorced from that of East Indian, Chinese, and other nationalities brought into plantation colonies to replace slave labor and keep wages low. These oppressed and exploited groups likewise had to confront colonialism, face the problem of cultural delegitimation, and recreate their own culture. In the neocolonial context, a racialized myth of black history is used in some areas to legitimate the continual disenfranchisement of specific ethnic groups. Like the Duvalier negritude myth, this myth legitimates a neocolonial dictatorship repressing not only East Indians but also blacks and others. The narrative of liberation is also the story of the struggle of the East Indian against the colonial and neocolonial systems, the story of the transformation of East Indian cultural systems in terms of the Caribbean, in ways that would inaugurate a leap to history. Creolized, Indo-Caribbean culture remains an important area of inquiry.

The Caribbean quest for its own identity, its own humanity, is a constant struggle that is sustained by the continual development of a symbolic discourse characteristic of the Caribbean and expressive of the meaning of existence in the Caribbean. Grasping the relationship of the human to history, it demands a new response from the world outside the Caribbean.

Selected Bibliography

Abrahams, Roger D. *The Man-of-Words in the West Indies: Performance and the Emergence of Creole Culture*. Baltimore: Johns Hopkins University Press, 1983.
———. *Positively Black*. Englewood Cliffs, N.J.: Prentice-Hall, 1970.
Arendt, Hannah. *On Violence*. New York: Harvest–Harcourt Brace Jovanovich 1969.
Armah, Ayi Kwei. "Frantz Fanon: The Awakener." *Negro Digest*, 18 (October 1969), 4–9, 29–43.
Arnold, A. James. *Modernism and Negritude: The Poetry and Poetics of Aimé Césaire*. Cambridge: Harvard University Press, 1981.
Asein, Samuel Omo. "Derek Walcott: The Man and His Ideas." *The Literary Half-Yearly*, 17 (July 1976), 59–79.
Ashaolu, Albert Olu. "Allegory in *Ti-Jean and His Brothers*." *World Literature Written in English*, 18 (April 1977), 203–11.
Auerbach, Erich. *Mimesis: The Representation of Reality in Western Literature*. Trans. Willard Trask. New York: Anchor-Doubleday, 1957.
Azoulay, J. "Contribution à l'étude de la socialthérapie dans un service d'aliénés musulmans." Thèse de médecine, Algiers, 1954.
Barker, W. H., and Cecilia Sinclair. *West African Folk-Tales*. London: George G. Harrap, 1919.
Barrett, Leonard. "African Religion in the Americas: The 'Islands in Between.'" In *African Religions: A Symposium*, ed. Newell S. Booth, Jr., pp. 183–215. New York: NOK Publishers, 1977.
———. *The Sun and the Drum: African Roots in Jamaican Folk Tradition*. Kingston, Jamaica: Sangster's Book Stores, 1977.
Bastide, Roger. *African Civilizations in the New World*. Trans. Peter Green. New York: Torchbook–Harper & Row, 1971.

Rémy Bastien. "Vodoun and Politics in Haiti." In *Religion and Politics in Haiti,* by Harold Courlander and Rémy Bastien, pp. 39–68. ICR Studies, 1. Washington, D.C.: Institute for Cross-Cultural Research, 1966.

Beckwith, Martha Warren. *Jamaica Anansi Stories.* 1924. Rpt. New York: Kraus Reprint, 1976.

Bennett, Louise. *Anancy and Miss Lou.* Kingston, Jamaica: Sangster's Book Stores, 1979.

Berger, Peter. *Invitation to Sociology: A Humanistic Perspective.* New York: Anchor-Doubleday, 1963.

Brathwaite, Edward. *The Arrivants: A New World Trilogy.* London: Oxford University Press, 1973.

——. *The Development of Creole Society in Jamaica: 1770–1820.* Oxford: Clarendon Press, 1971.

——. "Timehri." In *Is Massa Day Dead? Black Moods in the Caribbean,* ed. Orde Coombs, pp. 29–45. New York: Anchor-Doubleday, 1974.

Brown, Lloyd. "The Crisis of Black Identity in the West Indian Novel." *Critique,* 11, no. 3 (1969), 97–112.

Burke, Edmund. "Frantz Fanon's *The Wretched of the Earth.*" *Daedalus,* 105 (Winter 1976), 127–35.

Butler, Janet. "The Existentialism of George Lamming: The Early Development of a Writer." *Caribbean Review,* 11, (Fall 1982), 15, 38–39.

Candell, Art. "Zombies Are for Real." *Caribbean and West Indian Chronicle,* August–September, 1984, p. 13.

Carpentier, Alejo. *The Kingdom of This World,* trans. Harriet de Onís. London: Victor Gollancz, 1967.

Case, Frederick I. "Aimé Césaire et l'occident chrétien." *L'Esprit Créateur,* 10 (1970), 242–56.

——. "Négritude and Utopianism." *African Literature Today,* 7 (1975), 65–75.

——. "Sango oba ko so: Les vodoun dans *La Tragédie du Roi Christophe.*" *Cahiers Césairiens,* 2 (Autumn 1975), 9–24.

Cassidy, Frederic G. *Jamaica Talk: Three Hundred Years of the English Language in Jamaica.* 2d ed. London: Macmillan, 1971.

Caute, David. *Fanon.* London: Fontana-Collins, 1970.

Césaire, Aimé. *Cahier d'un retour au pays natal / Notebook of a Return to the Native Land.* In *Aimé Césaire, The Collected Poetry,* trans. Clayton Eshleman and Annette Smith, biling. ed. pp. 32–85. Berkeley and Los Angeles: University of California Press, 1983. (See also *Return to My Native Land,* trans. Emile Snyder, biling. ed. Paris: Présence Africaine, 1971.)

——. "Culture et colonisation." *Présence Africaine,* n.s., nos. 8–10 (June–November 1956), 190–205.

——. *Discourse on Colonialism.* Trans. Joan Pinkham. New York: Monthly Review, 1972. (*Discours sur le colonialisme.* 5th ed. Paris: Présence Africaine, 1970.)

——. *Et les chiens se taisaient.* In *Les Armes miraculeuses.* Paris: Gallimard, 1970.

——. Introduction to *Esclavage et colonization,* by Victor Schoelcher. Paris: Presses Universitaires de France, 1948.

——. Introduction to "Que signifie pour nous l'Afrique?" by Léo Frobenius. *Tropiques,* no. 5 (April 1942). Rpt. Paris: Jean Michel Place, 1978, p. 63.

——. "Lettre à Maurice Thorez." Paris: Présence Africaine, 1956.

——. *The Tragedy of King Christophe*. Trans. Ralph Manheim. New York: Grove Press, 1970. (*La Tragédie du roi Christophe*. Paris: Présence Africaine, 1970.)

Chang, Phoebe. "Dis Women's Work." *Focus 1983: An Anthology of Contemporary Jamaican Writing*, ed. Mervyn Morris, pp. 96–98. Kingston: Caribbean Authors Publishing Co., 1983.

Chatelain, Heli. *Folk-tales of Angola*. 1894. Rpt. New York: Kraus Reprint, 1969.

Chiodi, Pietro. *Sartre and Marxism*. Sussex: Harvest Press, 1976.

Clark, Richard C. "Contrasting Views of 'Black' African Literature." *Review of National Literature*, 2 (Fall 1971). Special issue, *Black Africa*, pp. 243–53. New York: St. John's University Press, 1972.

Cobham, Rhonda. "The Background." In *West Indian Literature*, ed. Bruce King, pp. 9–29. London: Macmillan, 1979.

Coke, Lloyd. "Walcott's Mad Innocents." *Savacou*, no. 5 (June 1971), pp. 121–24.

Colson, Theodore. "Derek Walcott's Plays: Outrage and Compassion." *World Literature Written in English*, 12 (April 1973), 80–96.

Condé, Maryse. *Cahier d'un retour au pays natal—Césaire*. Paris: Hatier, 1978

——. *La Civilisation du bossale: Réflexions sur la littérature orale de la Guadeloupe et de la Martinique*. Paris: Harmattan, 1978.

Cooper, Carolyn Joy. "A Different Rage: An Analysis of the Works of Derek Walcott, 1948–1976." Ph.D. diss., University of Toronto, 1977.

Coser, Lewis. *Continuities in the Study of Social Conflict*. New York: Free Press; London: Collier-Macmillan, 1967.

Courlander, Harold. *The Drum and the Hoe: Life and Lore of the Haitian People*. Berkeley and Los Angeles: University of California Press, 1960.

——. *Haiti Singing*. 1939. Rpt. New York: Cooper Square, 1973.

——. *Religion and Politics in Haiti*. ICR Studies, 1. Washington, D.C.: Institute for Cross-Cultural Research, 1966.

——. *A Treasury of African Folklore: The Oral Literature, Traditions, Myths, Legends, Epics, Tales, Recollections, Wisdom, Sayings, and Humor of Africa*. New York: Crown Publishers, 1975.

——. "Vodoun in Haitian Culture." In *Religion and Politics in Haiti*, by Harold Courlander and Rémy Bastien, pp. 1–26. ICR Studies, 1. Washington, D.C.: Institute for Cross-Cultural Research, 1966.

Craton, Michael, ed. *Roots and Branches: Current Directions in Slave Studies*. Historical Reflections, Directions Series, no. 1. Toronto: Pergamon Press, 1979.

Cudjoe, Selwyn R. *Resistance and Caribbean Literature*. Athens: Ohio University Press, 1980.

Damas, Léon-Gontran. *Pigments*. Paris: Présence Africaine, 1962.

Darnton, Robert. "The Meaning of Mother Goose." *New York Review of Books*, February 2, 1984.

Dash, Michael J. *Literature and Ideology in Haiti, 1915–1961*. Totowa, N.J.: Barnes & Noble, 1981.

Davis, Russell H. "Kierkegaard and Community." *Union Seminary Quarterly Review*, 36 (Summer 1981), 205–22.

De Beauvoir, Simone. *Force of Circumstance.* Trans. Richard Howard. New York: Putnam's, 1965.

Depestre, René. "An Interview with Aimé Césaire." Trans. Maro Riofrancos. In Aimé Césaire, *Discourse on Colonialism.* New York: Monthly Review, 1972.

Deren, Maya. *The Voodoo Gods.* Frogmore, Herts: Granada-Paladin, 1975.

Desan, Wilfrid. *The Marxism of Jean-Paul Sartre.* New York: Doubleday, 1965.

Dickson, Bruce D. "The 'John and Old Master' Stories and the World of Slavery: A Study in Folktales and History." *Phylon,* 35 (Winter 1974), 418–29.

Dobbin, Jay D. "The Jombee Dance: Friendship and Ritual in Montserrat." *Caribbean Review,* 10 (Fall 1981), 28–31, 51.

Doke, Clement M. *Lamba Folk-lore.* 1927. Rpt. New York: Kraus Reprint, 1976.

D'Oyley, Enid F. *Animal Fables and Other Tales Retold.* Toronto: Williams-Wallace International, 1982.

Dundes, Alan, ed. *Mother Wit from the Laughing Barrel: Readings in the Interpretation of Afro-American Folklore.* Englewood Cliffs, N.J.: Prentice-Hall, 1973.

Ellis, A. B. *The Yoruba Speaking Peoples of the Slave Coast of West Africa.* 1894. Rpt. Oosterhout, Netherlands: Anthropological Publications, 1970.

Erickson, John. "Sartre's African Writings: Literature and Revolution." *L'Esprit Créateur,* 10 (Fall 1970), 182–96.

Fanon, Frantz. "Altérations mentales, modifications charactérielles, troubles psychiques et déficit intellectuel dans l'hérédo-dégénération spino-cérébelleuse: A propos d'un cas de maladie de Friedreich avec délire de possession." Thèse de médecine, Lyons, 1951. Rpt. *L'Information Psychiatrique,* 51 (December 1975), 1079–90.

——. *Black Skin, White Masks.* Trans. Charles Lam Markmann. New York: Grove Press, 1967. (*Peau noire, masques blancs.* Paris: Points-Editions du Seuil, 1971.)

——. *A Dying Colonialism.* Trans. Haakon Chevalier. New York: Grove Press, 1967. (*Sociologie d'une révolution.* Paris: François Maspero, 1978.)

——. "L'Hospitalization de jour en psychiatrie: Valeur et limites; 1: Introduction générale." *La Tunisie Médicale,* 37 (December 1959), 689–91, 693–94, 696–97, 699–712. Rpt. *L'Information Psychiatrique,* 51 (December 1975), 1117–21.

——. *Toward the African Revolution: Political Essays.* Trans. Haakon Chevalier. New York: Grove Press, 1969. (*Pour la révolution africaine: Ecrits politiques.* Paris: François Maspero, 1964.)

——. *The Wretched of the Earth.* Trans. Constance Farrington. New York: Grove Press, 1968. (*Les Damnés de la terre.* Paris: François Maspero, 1961.)

Fanon, Frantz, and S. Asselah. "Le Phénomène de l'agitation en milieu psychiatrique: Considérations générales—signification psychopathologique," *Maroc Médical,* 36 (January 1957), 21–24.

Fanon, Frantz, and J. Azoulay. "La Socialthérapie dans un service d'hommes musulmans: Difficultés méthodologiques." *L'Information Psychiatrique,* 30 (October–November 1954), pp. 349–61. Rpt. *L'Information Psychiatrique,* 51 (December 1975), 1095–106.

Fanon, Frantz, and C. Geronimi. "L'Hospitalisation de jour en psychiatrie." *La Tunisie médicale,* 37 (December 1959), 689–732. Rpt. *L'Information Psychiatrique,* 51 (December 1975), 1121–30.

——. "Le T.A.T. chez les femmes musulmanes: Sociologie de la perception et de l'imagination." *Congrès des médecins aliénistes et neurologistes de France et des pays de langue française,* 54th session, Bordeaux, August 30–September 4, 1956, pp. 364–368.

Fanon, Frantz, and R. Lacaton, "Conduites d'aveu en Afrique du Nord." *Congrès des médecins aliénistes et neurologistes de France et des pays de langue française,* 53d session, Nice, September 5–11, 1955, pp. 657–60. Rpt. *L'Information Psychiatrique,* 51 (December 1975), 1115–16.

Fanon, Frantz, and François Sanchez. "Attitude du musulman maghrébin devant la folie." *Revue Pratique de Psychologie de la Vie Sociale et d'Hygiéne Mentale,* no. 1 (1956), 24–27.

Fanon, Frantz, and François Tosquelles. "Indications de la thérapeutique de Bini dans le cadre des thérapeutiques institutionelles." *Congrès des médecins aliénistes et neurologistes de France et des pays de langue française,"* 51st session, Pau, July 20–26, 1953, pp. 545–52.

——. "Sur quelques cas traités par la méthode de Bini." *Congrès des médecins aliénistes et neurologistes de France et des pays de langue française,* 51st session, Pau, July 20–16, 1953, pp. 539–44. Rpt. *L'Information Psychiatrique,* 51 (December 1975), 1091–93.

——. "Sur un essai de réadaptation chez une malade avec épilepsie morphéique et troubles de charactère grave." *Congrès des médecins aliénistes et neurologistes de France et des pays de langue française,* 51st session, Pau, July 20–26, 1953, pp. 363–68.

Fontenot, Chester J. *Frantz Fanon: Language as the God Gone Astray in the Flesh.* University of Nebraska Studies, n.s., no. 60. Lincoln: University of Nebraska Press, 1979.

Forster, Peter. "Empiricism and Imperialism: A Review of the New Left Critique of Social Anthropology." In *Anthropology and the Colonial Encounter,* ed. Asad Talal, pp. 23–38. London: Ithaca Press, 1973.

Forsythe, Dennis. *Rastafari: For the Healing of the Nation.* Kingston, Jamaica: Zaika Publications, 1983.

Frye, Northrop. *Fables of Identity: Studies in Poetic Mythology.* New York: Harvest–Harcourt Brace Jovanovich, 1963.

Gadamer, Hans-Georg. *Truth and Method.* Trans. Garrett Barden and John Cumming. New York: Continuum-Seabury, 1975.

Geggus, David. "Slave Resistance Studies and the Saint Domingue Slave Revolt: Some Preliminary Considerations." Occasional Papers Series, no. 4. Latin American and Caribbean Center of Florida International University, Winter 1983.

Geismar, Peter. *Fanon.* New York: Dial Press, 1971.

Gendzier, Irene L. *Frantz Fanon: A Critical Study.* London: Wildwood House, 1973.

——. "Reflections on Fanon and the Jewish Question." *New Outlook,* 12 (January 1969), 13–20.

Genovese, Eugene. *From Rebellion to Revolution: Afro-American Slave Revolts in the Making of the Modern World.* Baton Rouge: Louisiana State University Press, 1979.

Goveia, Elsa V. *Slave Society in the British Leeward Islands at the End of the Eighteenth Century.* New Haven: Yale University Press, 1965.

Greimas, A. J., and F. Rastier. "The Interaction of Semiotic Constraints." *Yale French Studies*, no. 4 (1968), 86–105.

Habermas, Jürgen. *Knowledge and Human Interests.* Trans. Jeremy J. Shapiro. Boston: Beacon Press, 1971.

Hale, Thomas A. *Les Ecrits d'Aimé Césaire: bibliographie commentée. Etudes Françaises*, 14, (October 1978), 215–516.

Hamner, Robert. "Conversation with Derek Walcott." *World Literature Written in English*, 16 (November 1977), 409–20.

——. *Derek Walcott.* Boston: Twayne, 1981.

——. "Mythological Aspects of Derek Walcott's Drama." *Ariel*, 8 (July 1977), 35–58.

Hansen, Emmanuel. *Frantz Fanon: Social and Political Thought.* Columbus: Ohio State University Press, 1977.

Haring, Lee. "A Characteristic African Folktale Pattern." In *African Folklore.* Ed. Richard M. Dorson, pp. 165–79. Bloomington: Indiana University Press, 1972.

Hedrick, Basil C., and Cezarija A. Letson. *Once Was a Time, a Very Good Time: An Inquiry into the Folklore of the Bahamas.* Museum of Anthropology Miscellaneous Series, no. 38. [Greeley, Colo.:] University of Northern Colorado, 1975.

Hegel, G. W. F. *Logic.* Trans. William Wallace. Part I of *Encyclopaedia of the Philosophical Sciences.* Oxford: Oxford University Press, 1975.

——. *Phenomenology of Spirit.* Trans. A. V. Miller. Oxford: Oxford University Press, 1977.

——. *Philosophy of Mind.* Trans. William Wallace and A. V. Miller. Part 3 of *Encyclopaedia of the Philosophical Sciences.* Oxford: Oxford University Press, 1971.

Herskovits, Melville J. *Life in a Haitian Valley.* New York: Anchor-Doubleday, 1971.

Herskovits, Melville J., and Frances S. Herskovits. *Dahomean Narrative: A Cross-Cultural Analysis.* Northwestern University African Studies, no. 1. Evanston, Ill.: Northwestern University Press, 1958.

——. *Suriname Folk-lore.* New York: Columbia University Press, 1936.

Hill, Errol. "The Emergence of a National Drama in the West Indies." *Caribbean Quarterly*, 18 (December 1972), 9–40.

Hollenbach, Paul W. "Jesus, Demoniacs, and Public Authorities: A Socio-Historical Study." *Journal of the American Academy of Religion*, 49 (December 1981), 567–88.

Hurbon, Laënnec. *Culture et dictature en Haïti: L'imaginaire sous contrôle.* Paris: Harmattan, 1979.

——. *Dieu dans le vaudou haïtien.* Paris: Payot, 1972.

Hurbon, Laënnec, and Dany Bebel-Gisler. *Cultures et pouvoir dans la Caraïbe: Langue créole, vaudou, sectes religieuses en Guadeloupe et en Haïti.* Paris: Harmattan, 1975.

Irele, Abiola. *The African Experience in Literature and Ideology.* London: Heinemann, 1981.

Jahn, Janheinz. *A History of Neo-African Literature: Writing in Two Continents.* Trans. Oliver Coburn and Ursula Lehrburger. London: Faber & Faber, 1968.

——. *Muntu: An Outline of Neo-African Culture.* Trans. Marjorie Grene. New York: Faber & Faber, 1961.

James, C. L. R. *The Black Jacobins: Toussaint L'Ouverture and the San Domingo Revolution.* 2d ed. New York: Vintage–Random House, 1963.

Jameson, Fredric. *Marxism and Form: Twentieth-Century Dialectical Theories of Literature.* Princeton: Princeton University Press, 1971.

——. *The Political Unconscious: Narrative as a Socially Symbolic Act.* Ithaca: Cornell University Press, 1981.

——. *The Prison House of Language: A Critical Account of Structuralism and Russian Formalism.* Princeton: Princeton University Press, 1972.

——. "Three Methods in Sartre's Literary Criticism." In *Modern French Criticism: From Proust and Valéry to Structuralism,* ed. John K. Simon, pp. 193–227. Chicago: University of Chicago Press, 1972.

JanMohamed, Abdul R. "The Economy of Manichean Allegory: The Function of Racial Difference in Colonialist Literature." In *"Race," Writing, and Difference,* ed. Henry Louis Gates, Jr., pp. 78–106. Chicago: University of Chicago Press, 1986.

——. *Manichean Aesthetics: The Politics of Literature in Colonial Africa.* Amherst: University of Massachusetts Press, 1983.

Jardel, Jean-Pierre. *Le Conte créole.* Montreal: Centre de recherches caraïbes de l'Université de Montréal, 1977.

Jekyll, Walter, ed. *Jamaican Song and Story: Annancy Stories, Digging Sings, Ring Tunes, and Dancing Tunes.* London, 1907. Rpt. New York: Dover, 1966.

Jones, Edward A. *Voices of Négritude: The Expression of Black Experience in the Poetry of Senghor, Césaire, Damas.* Valley Forge, Pa.: Judson Press, 1971.

Kemoli, Arthur. *Caribbean Anansi Stories.* London: Commonwealth Institute, 1976.

Kent, George E. "A Conversation with George Lamming." *Black World,* 22, (March 1973), 4–14, 88–97.

Kesteloot, Lilyan. *Aimé Césaire, l'homme et l'oeuvre.* Paris: Présence Africaine, 1973.

——. *Black Writers in French: A Literary History of Négritude.* Trans. Ellen Conroy Kennedy. Philadelphia: Temple University Press, 1974.

Kierkegaard, Søren. *Concluding Unscientific Postscript.* Trans. David F. Swenson and Walter Lowrie. Princeton: Princeton University Press, 1968.

——. *Fear and Trembling.* In *"Fear and Trembling" and "The Sickness unto Death,"* trans. Walter Lowrie. Princeton: Princeton University Press, 1968.

——. *Philosophical Fragments or a Fragment of Philosophy.* Trans. David F. Swenson and Howard V. Hong. Princeton: Princeton University Press, 1967.

King, Bruce, ed. *Literatures of the World in English.* Boston: Routledge & Kegan Paul, 1974.

——. *West Indian Literature.* London: Macmillan, 1979.

Klein, Norman. "On Revolutionary Violence." *Studies on the Left,* 6 (May–June 1966), 62–83.

Knight, Franklin. *The Caribbean: The Genesis of a Fragmented Nationalism.* New York: Oxford University Press, 1978.

Kojève, Alexandre. *Introduction to the Reading of Hegel: Lectures on the "Phenomenology of Spirit."* Ed. Allan Bloom. Trans. James H. Nichols, Jr. Ithaca: Cornell University Press, 1969.

Kom, Ambroise. *"In the Castle of My Skin*: George Lamming and the Colonial Caribbean." *World Literature Written in English*, 18 (November 1979), 406–420.

Labelle, Micheline. *Idéologie de couleur et classes sociales en Haiti.* Montreal: Les Presses de l'Université de Montréal, 1978.

Laguerre, Michel S. "Voodoo as Religious and Revolutionary Ideology." *Freeing the Spirit*, 3, no. 1 (1974), 23–28.

———. *Voodoo Heritage.* Sage Library of Social Science, vol. 98. Beverly Hills: Sage Publications, 1980.

Lamming, George. "Caribbean Literature: The Black Rock of Africa." *African Forum*, 1 (Spring 1966), 32–52.

———. *In the Castle of My Skin.* New York: Collier-Macmillan, 1970.

———. Introduction to *In the Castle of My Skin.* New York: Schocken, 1983.

———. "The Negro Writer and His World." *Présence Africaine*, n.s., nos. 8–10 (June-November 1956), 318–25.

———. *The Pleasures of Exile.* London: Michael Joseph, 1960.

———. *Season of Adventure.* London: Michael Joseph, 1960.

———. "The West Indian People." *New World Quarterly*, no. 2 (Crop Time 1966), 63–74.

Lanternari, Vittorio. *The Religions of the Oppressed: A Study of Modern Messianic Cults.* Trans. Lisa Sergio. Toronto: Mentor-New American Library of Canada, 1965.

Laroche, Maximilien. *L'Image comme écho: Essais sur la littérature et la culture haïtiennes.* Montreal: Nouvelle Optique, 1978.

———. "The Myth of the Zombi." In *Exile and Tradition: Studies in African and Caribbean Literature*, ed. Rowland Smith, pp. 44–61. Dalhousie African Studies Series. London: Longman and Dalhousie University Press, 1976.

Larson, Charles R. *The Novel in the Third World.* Washington, D.C.: Inscape Publishers, 1976.

Levine, Lawrence, W. *Black Culture and Black Consciousness: Afro-American Folk Thought from Slavery to Freedom.* New York: Oxford University Press, 1977.

Lévi-Strauss, Claude. *Structural Anthropology*, [1]. Trans. Claire Jacobson and Brooke Grundfest Schoepf. New York: Basic Books, 1963.

———. *Structural Anthropology*, 2. Trans. Monique Layton. New York: Basic Books, 1976.

———. *Tristes Tropiques.* Trans. John Russell. New York: Atheneum, 1971.

Lucas, Philippe. *Sociologie de Frantz Fanon: Contribution à une anthropologie de la libération.* Algiers: Société nationale d'édition et de diffusion, 1971.

Lukács, Georg. *History and Class Consciousness: Studies in Marxist Dialectics.* Trans. Rodney Livingstone. Cambridge: The MIT Press, 1971.

Lyn, Diana. "The Concept of the Mulatto in Some Works of Derek Walcott." *Caribbean Quarterly*, 26 (March–June 1980), 49–67.

Macouba, Auguste. *Eia! Man-Maille là!* Paris: Pierre Jean Oswald, 1968.

Mannoni, O. *Prospero and Caliban: The Psychology of Colonization.* Trans. Pamela Powesland. New York: Praeger, 1964.

Martinez, Gil. "Vodou et politique." *Nouvelle Optique*, nos. 6–7 (April–September 1972), 197–200.

Marx, Karl, and Frederick Engels. *The Holy Family, or Critique of Critical Criticism: Against Bruno Bauer and Company*. Trans. Richard Dixon and Clemens Dutt. Moscow: Progress Publishers, 1975.

——— *The Marx-Engels Reader*. Ed. Robert C. Tucker. New York: Norton, 1972.

Mbiti, John S. *African Religions and Philosophy*. London: Heinemann, 1969.

Memmi, Albert. *The Colonizer and the Colonized*. Trans. Howard Greenfeld. Boston: Beacon Press, 1965.

Mennesson-Rigaud, Odette. "Le Rôle du vaudou dans l'indépendance d'Haïti." *Présence Africaine*, nos. 17–18 (February–May 1958), 43–67.

Métraux, Alfred. *Voodoo in Haiti*. Trans. Hugo Charteris. New York: Schocken, 1972.

Mintz, Sidney. "The Caribbean Region." In *Slavery, Colonialism, and Racism*, ed. Sidney Mintz, pp. 45–71. New York: Norton, 1974.

Mintz, Sidney W., and Richard Price. *An Anthropological Approach to the Afro-American Past: A Caribbean Perspective*. ISHI Occasional Papers in Social Change, no. 2. Philadelphia: Institute for the Study of Human Issues, 1976.

Montilus, Guérin. "Mythes, écologie, acculturation en Haïti: Essai sur la réinterprétation des mythes du Golfe de Guinée dans le vaudou haïtien sous l'influence des Fon du Bas-Dahomey. Ph.D. diss., University of Zurich, 1973.

Moreau de Saint-Méry, Louis-Elie. *Description topographique, physique, civile politique et historique de la partie française de l'île Saint-Domingue*. 1797. Rpt. 2 vols. Paris: Société de l'Histoire des Colonies Françaises et Librairie Larose, 1958.

Munro, Ian H. "The Theme of Exile in George Lamming's *In the Castle of My Skin*." *World Literature Written in English*, 20 (November 1971), 51–60.

Munro, Ian, and Reinhard Sander, eds. *Kas-Kas: Interviews with Three Caribbean Writers in Texas: George Lamming, C. L. R. James, Wilson Harris*. Austin: African and Afro-American Research Institute, University of Texas, 1972.

Nettleford, Rex. *Cultural Action and Social Change: The Case of Jamaica; An Essay in Caribbean Cultural Identity*. Ottawa: International Development Research Centre, 1979; Kingston: Institute of Jamaica, 1978.

Ngal, M. a M. *Aimé Césaire: Un homme à la recherche d'une patrie*. Dakar: Nouvelles Editions Africaines, 1975.

Ngugi, Wa Thiong'O. *Homecoming: Essays on African and Caribbean Literature, Culture, and Politics*. New York: Lawrence Hill, 1973.

Nicholls, David. *From Dessalines to Duvalier: Race, Colour, and National Independence in Haiti*. Cambridge: Cambridge University Press, 1979.

Nietzsche, Friedrich. *The Birth of Tragedy and the Genealogy of Morals*. Trans. Francis Golffing. New York: Anchor-Doubleday, 1956.

———. *Joyful Wisdom*. Trans. Thomas Common. New York: Ungar, 1960.

———. *Thus Spoke Zarathustra: A Book for Everyone and No One*. Trans. R. J. Hollingdale. Harmondsworth: Penguin, 1969.

———. *The Will to Power*. Trans. Walter Kaufmann and R. J. Hollingdale. Ed. Walter Kaufmann. New York: Vintage–Random House, 1968.

Obichere, Boniface I. "Black Power and Black Magic in Haitian Politics: Dr. François Duvalier, 1957–1971." *Pan African Journal*, 6 (Summer 1973), 109–25.

Ormerod, Beverley. "Beyond Négritude: Some Aspects of the Work of Edouard Glissant." *Savacou*, nos. 11–12 (September 1975), 39–45.

Oster, Harry. "Negro Humour: John and Old Marsta." In *Mother Wit from the Laughing Barrel: Readings in the Interpretation of Afro-American Folklore*. ed. Alan Dundes, pp. 549–60. Englewood Cliffs, N. J.: Prentice-Hall, 1973.

Owens, Joseph. *Dread: The Rastafarians of Jamaica*. London: Heinemann, 1979.

Paquet, Sandra Pouchet. *The Novels of George Lamming*. London: Heinemann, 1982.

Parsons, Elsie Clews. *Folk-lore of the Antilles, French and English*. 1943. Rpt. New York: Kraus Reprint, 1969.

Patterson, Orlando. *Die the Long Day*. New York: Morrow, 1972.

——. *The Sociology of Slavery: An Analysis of the Origins, Development, and Structure of Negro Slave Society in Jamaica*. London, 1967. Rpt. Kingston, Jamaica: Sangster's Book Stores, 1973.

Paul, Emmanuel C. *Panorama du folklore haïtien*. 1962. Rpt. Port-au-Prince: Fardin, 1978.

Paulme, Denise. "The Impossible Imitation in African Trickster Tales." In *Forms of Folklore in Africa: Narrative, Poetic, Gnomic, Dramatic*, ed. Bernth Lindfors, pp. 65–103. Austin: University of Texas Press, 1977.

Pelton, Robert D. *The Trickster in West Africa: A Study of Mythic Irony and Sacred Delight*. Berkeley and Los Angeles: University of California Press, 1980.

Perinbam, Marie. "Fanon and the Revolutionary Peasantry: The Algerian Case." *Journal of Modern African Studies*, 11, no. 3, (1973), 440–42.

——. *Holy Violence: The Revolutionary Thought of Frantz Fanon*. Washington, D.C.: Three Continents Press, 1982.

Pestre de Almeida, Lillian. "Les Versions successives du *Cahier d'un retour au pays natal*." In *Césaire 70*, ed. M. a M. Ngal and Martin Steins, pp. 35–90. Paris: Editions Silex, 1984.

Postel, J. "Frantz Fanon à cinquante ans." *L'Information Psychiatrique*, 51 (December 1975), 1049–50.

Postel, J., and C. Razanjao. "La Vie et l'oeuvre psychiatrique de Frantz Fanon." *L' Information Psychiatrique*, 51 (December 1975), 1053–72.

Pradel, Jacques, and Jean-Yves Casgha. *Haïti, la république des morts vivants*. Monaco: Editions du Rocher, 1983.

Price-Mars, Jean. *Ainsi parla l'oncle*. Ottawa: Lemeac, 1973.

Radin, Paul. *African Folktales*. Princeton: Princeton University Press, 1970.

——. *The Trickster: A Study in American Indian Mythology*. New York: Schocken, 1972.

Ramchand, Kenneth. *An Introduction to the Study of West Indian Literature*. Sunbury-on-Thames, Middlesex: Thomas Nelson, 1976.

——. *The West Indian Novel and Its Background*. London: Faber & Faber, 1970.

——. "The West Indies." In *Literature of the World in English*, ed. Bruce King, pp. 192–211. Boston: Routledge & Kegan Paul, 1974.

Rattray, R. S. *Akan-Ashanti Folk-Tales*. Oxford: Clarendon, 1930.

——. *Hausa Folk-lore, Customs, Proverbs, etc*. 2 vols. Oxford: Clarendon, 1913.

Rhone, Trevor. *Old Story Time and Other Plays*. Harlow, Essex: Longman, 1981.

Ricoeur, Paul. "Explanation and Understanding: On Some Remarkable Connections among the Theory of the Text, Theory of Action, and Theory of History." In *The Philosophy of Paul Ricoeur: An Anthology of His Work*, ed. Charles E. Reagan and David Stewart, pp. 149–66. Boston: Beacon Press, 1978.

———. "The Narrative Function." In *Semeia*, 13: *The Poetics of Faith*, pp. 177–99. Society of Biblical Literature, 1981.

———. "Narrative Time." In *On Narrative*. ed. W. J. T. Mitchell, pp. 165–86. Chicago: University of Chicago Press, 1981.

Ridouh, Bachir, Lucette Jarosz, and Edouard Cadour. "Approche épidémiologique psychiatrique de la criminalité algérienne." *Revue Pratique de Psychologie de la Vie Sociale et d'Hygiène Mentale*, no. 3 (1969), 135–70.

Rodman, Selden. "Derek Walcott." In *Tongues of Fallen Angels*, pp. 232–59. New York: New Directions, 1974.

Rohlehr, Gordon. "Man's Spiritual Search in the Caribbean through Literature." In *Troubling of the Waters*, ed. Idris Hamid, pp. 187–205. San Fernando, Trinidad: Rahaman Printery, 1973.

Rotberg, Robert I. "Vodun and the Politics of Haiti." In *The African Diaspora: Interpretive Essays*, ed. Martin L. Kilson and Robert I. Rotberg, pp. 342–65. Cambridge: Harvard University Press, 1976.

Roumain, Jacques. *Ebony Wood / Bois D'Ebène*. Trans. Sidney Shapiro, biling. ed. New York: Interworld Press, 1972.

———. *Masters of the Dew*. Trans. Langston Hughes and Mercer Cook. Caribbean Writers Series, 12. London: Heinemann, 1978.

St. John, Bruce, ed. *Caribean Anthology I: Celebrating Lovers, Family, Community*. Bridgetown, Barbados: Cedar Press, 1981.

Salkey, Andrew. *Anancy's Score*. London: Bogle-L'Ouverture Publications, 1973.

Sartre, Jean-Paul. *Anti-Semite and Jew*. Trans. George J. Becker. New York: Schocken, 1965.

———. *Being and Nothingness: A Phenomenological Essay on Ontology*. Trans. Hazel E. Barnes. New York: Washington Square Press, 1966.

———. *Between Existentialism and Marxism*. Trans. John Mathews. New York: Morrow, 1976.

———. *Black Orpheus*. Trans. S. W. Allen. Paris: Présence Africaine, 1976. Also trans. Arthur Gillette, *Strand*, 5, no. 4 [1960], 2–12, and 6, no. 1 [1960], 7–20. ("Orphée noir," introduction to *Anthologie de la nouvelle poésie nègre et malgache*, by L. S. Senghor [Paris: Presses Universitaires de France, 1948]. Also in *Situations*, 3 [Paris: Gallimard, 1949].)

———. *Critique of Dialectical Reason*. Trans. Alan Sheridan-Smith. Ed. Jonathan Rée. London: New Left Books, 1976.

———. *Literary and Philosophical Essays*. Trans. Annette Michelson. New York: Collier Books, 1962.

———. Preface to *The Wretched of the Earth* by Frantz Fanon. New York: Grove Press, 1968.

———. *Search for a Method*. Trans. Hazel E. Barnes. New York: Vintage–Random House, 1968.

———. *What Is Literature?* Trans. Bernard Frechtman. New York: Harper & Row, 1965. (*Situations*, 2 [Paris: Gallimard, 1948])

Schuler, Monica. "Afro-American Slave Culture." In *Roots and Branches: Current Directions in Slave Studies*, ed. Michael Craton, pp. 121–55. Historical Reflections, Directions, no. 1. Toronto: Pergamon Press, 1979.

Sekyi-Otu, Ato. "Form and Metaphor in Fanon's Critique of Racial and Colonial Domination." In *Domination*, ed. Alkis Kontos, pp. 133–61. Toronto: University of Toronto Press, 1975.

———. "Frantz Fanon's Critique of the Colonial Experience." Ph.D. diss., University of Toronto, 1977.

Sellin, Eric. "*Négritude*: Status or Dynamics." *L'Esprit Créateur*, 10 (Fall 1970), 163–81.

Senghor, Leopold Sédar. *Liberté I: Négritude et humanisme*. Paris: Seuil, 1964.

Simpson, George Eaton. *Religious Cults of the Caribbean: Trinidad, Jamaica and Haiti*. Caribbean Monograph Series, no. 15. 3d ed. enl. Rio Piedras, Puerto Rico: Institute of Caribbean Studies, 1980.

Singham, A. W. *The Hero and the Crowd in a Colonial Polity*. New Haven: Yale University Press, 1968.

Sontag, Raymond J. *A Broken World: 1919–1939*. New York: Harper Torchbooks, 1972.

Soyinka, Wole. "And after the Narcissist?" *African Forum*, 1 (Spring 1970), 53–64.

———. "Drama and the Revolutionary Ideal." In *In Person: Achebe, Awoonor, and Soyinka*, ed. Karen L. Morell, pp. 72–128. Washington, D.C.: University of Washington Institute for Comparative and Foreign Area Studies, 1976.

———. *Myth, Literature, and the African World*. Cambridge: Cambridge University Press, 1976.

Tanna, Laura. "Anansi—Jamaica's Trickster Hero." *Jamaica Journal*, 16 (May 1983), 20–30.

Taussig, Michael T. *The Devil and Commodity Fetishism in South America*. Chapel Hill: University of North Carolina Press, 1980.

Thelwell, Michael. *The Harder They Come*. New York: Grove Press, 1980.

Thoby-Marcelin, Philippe, and Pierre Marcelin. *The Beast of the Haitian Hills*. Trans. Peter C. Rhodes. London: Victor Gollancz, 1951.

Tosquelles, François. "Frantz Fanon à Saint-Alban." *L'Information Psychiatrique*, 51 (December 1975), 1073–78.

Towa, Marcien. *Poésie de la négritude: Approche structuraliste*. Sherbrooke, Quebec: Naaman, 1983.

Trotman, David. "The Yoruba and Orisha Worship in Trinidad and British Guiana: 1838–1870." *African Studies Review*, 19 (September 1976), 1–17.

Turner, Mary. *Slaves and Missionaries: The Disintegration of Jamaican Slave Society, 1787–1834*. Chicago: University of Chicago Press, 1982.

Turner, Victor. "Social Dramas and Stories about Them." In *On Narrative*, ed. W. J. T. Mitchell, pp. 137–64. Chicago: University of Chicago Press, 1981.

Verger, Pierre. *Notes sur le culte des orisa et vodun à Bahia, la Baie de tous les saints, au Brésil, et à l'ancienne Côte des Esclaves en Afrique*. Mémoires de l'Institut Français d'Afrique Noire, no. 51. Dakar, 1957.

Walcott, Derek. "The Caribbean: Culture or Mimicry?" *Journal of Interamerican Studies and World Affairs*, 16 (February 1974), 3–13.

——. *The Castaway and Other Poems*. London: Jonathan Cape, 1969.

——. *Dream on Monkey Mountain and Other Plays*. New York: Farrar, Straus & Giroux, 1970.

——. *The Fortunate Traveller*. London: Faber & Faber, 1982.

——. *"The Joker of Seville" and "O Babylon!"* New York: Farrar, Straus & Giroux, 1978.

——. "Meanings." *Savacou*, no. 2 (September 1970), 45–51.

——. "The Muse of History: An Essay." In *Is Massa Day Dead? Black Moods in the Caribbean*, ed. Orde Coombs, pp. 1–28. New York: Anchor-Doubleday, 1974.

——. *Remembrance and Pantomime: Two Plays*. New York: Farrar, Straus & Giroux, 1980.

——. "What the Twilight Says: An Overture." In *Dream on Monkey Mountain and Other Plays*, pp. 3–40. New York: Farrar, Straus & Giroux, 1970

Wolfe, Bernard. "Uncle Remus and the Malevolent Rabbit." In *Mother Wit from the Laughing Barrel*, ed. Alan Dundes, pp. 70–84. Englewood Cliffs, N.J.: Prentice-Hall, 1973.

Yarde, Gloria. "George Lamming: The Historical Imagination." *Literary Half-Yearly*, 11 (July 1970), 35–45.

Zahar, Renate. *Frantz Fanon: Colonialism and Alienation*. Trans. Willfried F. Fenser. New York: Monthly Review, 1974.

Zaourou, Bernard Zadi. *Césaire entre deux cultures*. Dakar: Nouvelles Editions Africaines, 1978.

Zolberg, Aristide. "Frantz Fanon." In *The New Left: Six Critical Essays*, ed. Maurice Cranston, pp. 119–36. London: Bodley Head, 1970.

Index

Library of Congress Cataloging-in-Publication Data

Taylor, Patrick, 1953–
   The narrative of liberation : perspectives on Afro-Caribbean
literature, popular culture, and politics / Patrick Taylor.
     p. cm.
   Bibliography: p.
   Includes index.
   ISBN 0-8014-2193-4 (alk. paper)
    1. West Indies—Civilization.   2. West Indian literature—History
and criticism.   3. West Indies—Politics and government.
4. Politics and literature—West Indies—History—20th century.
5. Black nationalism—West Indies—History—20th century.
6. Blacks—West Indies—Race identity.   7. West Indies—Popular
culture—History—20th century.   I. Title.
F1609.5.T39 1989
972.9—dc19
                                      88-19005